Drug-Trip Abroad

Walter R. Cuskey, Ph. D.
Department of Community Medicine
School of Medicine/University of Pennsylvania

Arnold William Klein, M. D.
Cedars-Sinai Medical Center
Los Angeles, California

William Krasner
Department of Community Medicine
School of Medicine/University of Pennsylvania

With a Foreword by
William L. Kissick, M. D.
Department of Community Medicine
School of Medicine/University of Pennsylvania

University of Pennsylvania Press
Philadelphia

Drug-Trip Abroad:

American Drug-Refugees in Amsterdam and London

Foreword

William L. Kissick, M.D.
Department of Community Medicine, University of Pennsylvania

To refer to the "epidemiology" of opiate-addiction is not a figure of speech or a rationalization for the use of special techniques but a reflection of a literal, burgeoning reality: opiate-addiction and other forms of severe drug-abuse constitute an epidemic, a scourge, and even, in the slums of our big cities, a plague.

Precise and overly nice definitions do not always help reveal truth. Sometimes they help obscure it. It does not help much to argue about whether drug abuse is "really" or "primarily" a legal or moral or medical or social problem. A phenomenon that cripples and kills so many people, has such deleterious effects on society, involves so much suffering, expense, and social and criminal pathology, is, without question, a scourge that has reached epidemic proportions.

How does one treat a plague? Not solely by standard medical consultations during office hours; not by exhortation; nor by isolating the victims in jails in the hope that the contagion will die with them (having first decided of course, that they are unclean, criminal, and expendable). Not only by crying "Bring out your dead!" and burying them quickly; nor even by going among them like the plague-doctors of old, with a pole, a long robe, and a false nose full of aromatics to prevent close contact, infection, and unpleasantness. Not even by pure, but uncoordinated and uninformed, idealism and self-sacrifice.

A total community problem must be met with a total community approach. I do not mean that self-flagellatory "We-are-all-guilty" type of rhetoric that often passes for community involvement, causes widespread concern, but seldom leads to effective community action. I mean what we have come to call Community Medicine—that interdisciplinary mobilization and coordination of knowledge, resources, analysis, and techniques that can diagnose a public-health problem, decide what forms of ameliorative and control techniques will work best, and bring them to bear. Before drug-addiction and abuse can be brought under control, pharmacological research, law-enforcement, medical treatment, psychiatric and psychological care and research, sociological insights and appropriate manpower will have to be organized, coordinated, administered, and applied.

To start with, we need better and more complete information, free from parochialisms and dogmatisms. We need to know what is going on in other nations—how they are handling their different, but in some respects similar, drug-abuse problems, whether they can teach us anything, or vice versa. We need to know all this from varied perspectives and various approaches, statistical, medical, legal, historical; we need to know the life-stories and experiences of the abusers and addicts themselves, as well as of those who treat and observe them. One of the difficulties with present treatment techniques is that the addicts and abusers usually stubbornly refuse to do what we know is good for them; and perhaps they themselves can help to tell us why.

This remarkable book provides us, I think, with some of these valuable but seldom available perspectives. It is written for the informed and concerned, but not necessarily expert, layman. It includes history, general background, first-person observation and experience, and it gathers together relevant research. While some of the background material is not new, it is woven into the fabric of the book in a way that makes the pictures of the drug-scenes in Britain and Holland—and to some extent the U.S. and Canada—sharp and vivid, allowing for deeper insights and broader understanding. It is up to date. Its case histories, almost entirely in the words of the abusers themselves, are enlightening and chilling, and as dramatic as good fiction. We have had much description of the meaning of drug-addiction in statistical terms, and in the rhetoric of law-enforcement and treatment officials. We have even had comparisons drawn between different systems of treatment and control—for instance the British and the American—but seldom before have we received these comparisons through the accounts of persons who have felt both the needle and the boot on their own skins. Throughout, the authors make cogent comments on what they have seen and heard; and in the last chapter they draw sharp, if brief, conclusions. The final test of the efficacy of a system of drug-control and treatment may not so much depend on its exact form as on its ability to remain flexible, to evaluate and incorporate new information and techniques. Rigidity and punitiveness will not work; they may well be alienating and driving away salvageable people, including our own children.

Authors' Note

This book is intended to be impressionistic. It uses solid documentation and background, but the primary intent is to show the current drug-scenes in London and Amsterdam—and, by extension, North America—through the perceptions, feelings, insights, and experiences of those who have lived them. Informed observers and specialists look and comment; the drug-takers and abusers describe their lives.

The material is organized by the logic of a documentary account rather than of a socio-medical study. The soft-drug scene in Amsterdam, the lighter and shorter section, comes first; the hard-drug scene and the addicts who have fled from North America to London come after. The progress is interlaced with visualized scenes and first-person accounts. Most of the more weighty material—background, documentation, conclusions—gravitates toward the end of the section or the book.

This book is concerned with fact. It is also concerned with the broader truths that emerge when real human experience is presented and understood.

W. R. C.
A. W. K.
W. K.

Acknowledgments

So many people gave so generously of their time and wisdom in providing the material and help that led to the preparation of this book that it could almost be called a cooperative effort.

For the British material, we are particularly indebted to Dr. Thomas Bewley of Tooting-Bec Hospital, who gave permission and facilities to interview his patients; to Dr. J. H. Willis of the St. Giles Clinic, who gave so generously of his time and knowledge to act as guide and instructor about how the British clinic system works; and we wish to thank Dr. P. H. Connell for his help in setting up visits for interviews and observation of patients and staff at the Maudsley Treatment Center.

For the Dutch portion of the book we are grateful for the time, information and instruction tendered by Mr. H. R. Krauweel, Director of the Consultative Bureau for Alcoholism, and for the company, guidance and advice of his associate Reverend Hall.

Back home, we wish to thank the Department of Community Medicine of the University of Pennsylvania and its personnel who helped provide so much of the means and help that made this book possible. Our particular thanks to Dr. William L. Kissick, who has written the foreword.

We are indebted to Dr. Helen Davies, who sparked the project by bringing two of the authors together, and to Dr. Carole Hornick and Mrs. Lois Sigel, who read the manuscript and gave good criticism and insight.

More immediately, we owe a large day-to-day debt to Miss Dede H. Fowler, Miss Regina E. Holmes and Mr. Thondiyil Premkumar who suffered long hours in the preparation of the manuscript. We also wish to thank Mrs. Melinda C. Covelli for her infinite patience and invaluable contribution to the production of this book.

Finally, we owe the largest debt to the addicts and drug-abusers both in the United States and abroad, whose stumblings, stupidities, weaknesses and agonies make books on drugs inevitable. And we wish with all our hearts it were not so.

Contents

The WHO Definitions 1

The Drug-Scene in Amsterdam 3

    The Speed- and Opium-Freak 5

    The Speed-Freak at Home 9

    The Very Young Hashish-Abuser 12

    The Light-Show Man 14

    The Top Narc: Conversation with a Chief Inspector ... 18

Making the Scene 22

Visit to *Kosmos* 30

In Paradiso: *A Conversation with the Staff Coordinator* 38

    Excerpts from Paradiso Information Fact Sheet Number 1 42

    Excerpts from Dr. Klein's notes 45

The Drug-Scene in London 51

    Who Wants to Get Busted in the Teeth? 56

    Heroin is Worse than Being Pregnant 60

    Isaac the Gambler 65

    Giuseppe the One-Time Shoplifter 74

    Secret Tunnels Open in the Walls: Claude the Architect 77

The Boys of St. Giles' 86

    Barbiturates in the Air-Force Beer: Ralph Williams ... 91

    Harold the Unwelcome 99

    Hall the Bootlegger 109

    The Jazz Man 116

    At Home with the Jazz Man 122

London and North America 125

    Barbiturates 132

    Amphetamines 134

    Cannabis, LSD, and Other Psychedelics 137

The Treatment-Clinics   141
   The Bethlem Royal and the Maudsley Hospital   153
   St. Giles and Dr. Willis   159
   Tooting-Bec Hospital   163
   Adjustment at Tooting-Bec   163
The Background   169
   Physical and Psychological Dependence   171
   The Interpretation of the Laws   174
   The Changing Scene   176
   The Clinics   182
Looking Back on the Trip   192
References   204

Drug-Trip Abroad

The WHO Definitions

In October, 1968, the World Health Organization's Expert Committee on Drug Dependence adopted the following definitions:

Drug: Any substance that, when taken into the living organism, may modify one or more of its functions.

Drug-Abuse: Persistent or sporadic excessive drug use inconsistent with or unrelated to acceptable medical practice.

Drug-Dependence: A state, psychic, but sometimes also physical, resulting from the interaction between a living organism and a drug, characterized by behavioral and other responses that always include a compulsion to take the drug on a continuous or periodic basis in order to experience its psychic effects, and sometimes to avoid the discomfort of its absence. Tolerance may or may not be present. A person may be dependent on more than one drug.

The Drug-Scene
in Amsterdam

I can be free here, no paranoia about it.
You don't feel that you are doing anything
wrong when you turn on. In America I
feel freer walking down the street. But
here I feel freer with drugs.
   Here, most people put down hard drugs.
A small group do them. Much more hard
drugs—speed, morphine, heroin—in
America. More people using drugs there
per square foot. I got tired of going to
jail in the States. I have only been there
for short times, but they were too much.

*—The "Light-Show Man," 21-year-old
New Englander in Amsterdam*

Amsterdam has become mecca for the turned-on young, for
those who seek joy and revelation—some sort of New Kingdom—
through drugs. From all over the world they have heard its call and
are trooping toward it, to the consternation of the more conservative
Dutch. The people do not especially want them, and Holland has
strong laws against drugs. But there are strong laws and disapproval
everywhere: what really counts is the way the laws are interpreted
and enforced, and, in a very real way, the atmosphere. Amsterdam
does not hate the turned-on crowd. It may wish that they would go
somewhere else, but it offers them more friendly tolerance and
acceptance than perhaps any other city. The laws are not rigidly
enforced for the minor offender. The police usually do not consider
an offender a "dealer" unless he is carrying hashish worth somewhat
more than $300; then they crack down. The flower children are
given more freedom, including semi-official and semi-sanctioned places
to smoke marijuana; tolerant and easily available agencies offer help
with all their problems, not merely drugs. They are not given
encouragement or sanction to take the harder drugs, especially the
injectable opiates, and there seems to be very little of the hard addic-

tion evident in America or England. The official Dutch attitude toward hard drugs may deserve less credit than simple economics, but the heroin addict who fixes is a rare animal, and the public fixer is practically unknown.

If it is possible for a city to serve as a large living laboratory in which we can find out the consequences, good and evil, of widespread use and acceptance of the perception-altering drugs, particularly cannabis and the psychedelics, Amsterdam may be that place. Must permissiveness toward cannabis inevitably lead to opiate addiction? Will hashish and the psychedelics open to us that heaven of love, feeling, communication, and good will of which the prophet Timothy Leary preached? Or must it start us down the inevitable swift slide toward addiction, degradation, crime, and hell of the prophet Anslinger? Or do the flower children, with relatively little fanfare, usually get off at some way-station in between?

If this experiment—the proliferation of pot-houses working closely and intimately with official and semi-underground centers to provide help and treatment for the problems of the young—can be said to have a rationale, it is the attempt to keep the drug sub-culture from being forced out of sight, from becoming what Haight-Ashbury and parts of Greenwich Village and Village East have become. The relatively few flower people who have stayed in these places are in imminent peril. If a hippie neighborhood is classified as a kind of cancerous growth which must be isolated so that it does not infect the total body, then it becomes a magnet for hard-core addicts and vicious predators for whom the flower people, especially the young girls, are easy and attractive prey. The American police have a poor record for protecting ghetto residents. Rape, robbery, and physical attacks are seldom punished inside ghettos; it is different when they spill over into the neighborhoods of the hard-working. If young hippies are considered not quite human by the authorities, they become easy pickings for delinquents, motorcycle bullies, and the like. If the flower children are forced to stay in such environments because no others are open to them, they too must slide into degradation, malnutrition, illness, addiction, and alienation. They do not need active support in their drug habits. But they do need to be considered part of society, entitled to tolerance, understanding, and help. In effect, this is the kind of experiment that is being attempted in Amsterdam —without being called an experiment.

But let us turn to the scene visited on our trip abroad. Listen to some of the voices.

The Speed- and Opium-Freak

Gus is 22, male, white, and a non-practicing but baptized Lutheran. He was born in the west and reared in the mountains.

His mother, a registered nurse, is the director of a convalescent hospital. His father has been less successful: a newsman on a family paper during the depression, he was thrown out of "a few" colleges, and tried various enterprises. He opened a store, lost money for five years, and then sold out and got a job with the city.

"He is," Gus says, "a very authoritarian person."

> When I was seventeen my father had me put in jail and gave me a record. I got stopped one night. I was in a car with a girl at four minutes after twelve. My driver's license had been suspended. It was her birthday, and she had a driver's license, but she couldn't drive a stick shift. They told me I could sign for the girl and take her home, but my father wouldn't sign for me, so they took me to jail the next day. He said that if I promised not ever to lie to him again, and always do what he said, he would sign for me, and I said sure.

But it didn't stick, and he was "thrown out." After that he earned his living and his college expenses primarily by playing cards. "Sometimes my mother would give me money, but not much. The rest I paid. In my state they have card clubs, and I would play there regularly, and for money."

He had only one other brush with the law in the United States.

> There is a warrant out for my arrest for tax evasion for state tax. Eight dollars. When I was fourteen I made $1200 and wrote it down. The law says that you have to pay state tax for whatever you earn above $1000. I paid $250 federal tax, and that left only $950, but they didn't see it that way. So I said, "Fuck you, I won't pay it." That warrant's been following me around since I was fourteen. I got a couple of letters saying it is now $32. Maybe it's $100 by now.

He was not part of any particular drug-scene in the States.

I don't know. I wasn't in the scene. My roommate was a graduate psychologist and we took acid together. And the other guy that we took acid with was a butcher in the shop next door, and the other guy down the hall was a Black Muslim and the guy downstairs was a Mexican who lived in France for seven years, this old hustler who was living with some girl. We taught her how to cook spaghetti. . . . There was no idea of a scene. I really didn't know any drug scene until I got to London.

Nevertheless, he did take alcohol, marijuana, hashish, LSD, and amphetamines in America.

Right after I left my family, when I was seventeen, I graduated from high school. I didn't go to college right away. I worked in a factory for a year, and I was going to be a factory man. I was drinking about a gallon and a half of red wine a day. . . . I quit because I got sick of red wine.

He tried other intoxicants: "I turned on the gas one day, but that didn't do anything." He started smoking cannabis "when I was working for the Navy. I was 17 or 18 and I got stoned every time." He took LSD "once in a while."

When it first came around, I used it. Like if my friend is going to come over and we are going to have a jam session. He brings his amplifiers into my apartment, which is big, the whole end of a house. It was a good scene. Everybody knew that it wasn't going to last. I had my own credit at the grocery store. The man who owned the store owned the house. I didn't have to have any money. I owed him $1000 once in rent, groceries, and money I'd taken out of the cash register. He gave me that much credit. And he couldn't have collected, since I was under 21.

He did, however, pay his landlord back.

He then started taking amphetamines. "I just swallowed pills, not even pure amphetamines. I met some guys who were giving them away. I was 18."

His last residence in the States was at a western college where he finished two years of liberal-arts studies, doing well enough to make the Dean's honor list.

Why had he come to Europe? "The last semester of those two years was spent in Yugoslavia. And it is beautiful—the mountains. Remember, I was raised in the mountains."

After deciding to stay in Yugoslavia, he had trouble earning a living at first.

> During the summer I supported myself by playing saxophone with groups in little tourist villages all along the coast. I stayed in Yugoslavia and tried to do my best. I got engaged to—I was living with this girl, the daughter of an important city official. I was promised a job playing saxophone. That was in September.
>
> But I got thrown out after the Czechoslovakian invasion. Police followed me around every day, they beat up my friends, and every Yugoslav person who would help me, give me food or a place to sleep, they took their jobs away. After the invasion they were very suspicious of foreigners. They wouldn't give me a permit to stay.

After more of the same, and a bureaucratic run-around concerning permission for him to stay as an immigrant student at the conservatory of music, he finally left Yugoslavia, went to Vienna, and stopped in Italy to take his physical examination for the United States draft. When he had first come to Yugoslavia he had sent the draft board his new address, but had not asked for permission to leave the country. Eventually, after considerable trouble, he got a student deferment.

He went to England.

> I met very good people in England. I lived with a guy and when I got completely broke, this group who works with *Amnesty* gave me a phone number and they said, okay, you can stay with us, and I went out there. I had about ten dollars. I sold my suitcase, a very good one, and I lived on that money with this guy, this writer, while I looked for a job.

He injected heroin once in England. "It's good, but I don't really like to live that way."

How does London compare with Amsterdam?

> London is a different city. You can't walk across it. People have to learn to put up with one another when they get stuck in one room—and at 11 o'clock, when the trains quit, they have to stay there, they have to learn to talk to one another. But they do it in London in a very strange way. When I don't want to talk to somebody, I just want to be able to say, "Fuck you." So I freaked out very often.

When his permit ran out, the British would not give him a new one, and he had to leave.

His career in Amsterdam has been erratic. "I've been arrested three times here in Amsterdam for sleeping in the street because I didn't have enough money. One time I was arrested because I was working." His sex-life is equally erratic. "Not at the moment, nothing. Last summer I was living with six girls at once, and I got so sick of it I couldn't do anything."

He had started taking opium about eight months earlier—Chinese opium, made for smoking. He speaks vaguely of getting a pipe to smoke it in, but then states abruptly that he has had no opium in two months. His real love is amphetamines. He started dropping pills a year earlier. Now,

> I discovered that when you can taste it on your tongue, before you shoot it, you have hallucinations, depending on the quantity you take. I just discovered it last week. That's when I first started doing speed. Now I've been up for the last six days, and I want to go buy some more tonight. I'm going to spend all the money I've got on it. About six hundred dollars.

Where had he suddenly gotten so much money? "I just spent two months building this guy's apartment. I didn't spend any of that money."

Presumably because he is high on speed, his conversation wanders, he seems to confuse time and place, and he contradicts himself. He was off of opium for two months; he is now being treated for opium; and so on. "It is the first time I've taken opium. That's why I never got into the drug-scene before." The girl he was with last night started him on opium. On the other hand,

> She blew her mind on speed. She didn't know what to do. She took the shot and she said, "It's too much for me." It's not. When you take so much, it's not like speed any more, it's more relaxing. The rush lasts for about three hours, and the colors are beautiful.

His statements, in fact, are often like the rushes he describes:

> The reason I started taking opium involved a lot of things. I had flashes just everywhere, and it was funny. I took acid and I don't know what I'm doing. I know that it's raining and I'm walking and I don't

have any shoes and I'd go to the market in the morning and pick up some socks. There was this guy that I knew from college and he was Yugoslavian, and he and I were the two competitors for the chief head of the program. Who was going to be the big head? I was a year older than all the other people, but all the other people came from my class which is really bourgeois, and his father was a general or something. I turned on most of the people who were in the program to smoking hash, because they were just coming from bourgeois high schools in California in 1966. . . . I just flipped out.

Does he think that it is better to be in Amsterdam than in America?

Yes, because I don't like the looks on the faces of the people I see coming over from there. I like them less and less each year for the last three years. . . . I like the people, but their faces are getting sillier and sillier. They look like they are all slippery inside. That's why I left.

Like the time they got the riot squad on our campus. It was before all the big campus happenings. I can't stand that frustration. I would just have to kill them, if I see them.

I've met a couple of Americans who have come here to get off the stuff. They've come here because American . . . well, I met one guy who was taking heroin for years, and he got so sick of it that he just got on a plane one day. Those guys got a lot of money, and when they live in Europe, they find out that the money system is quite a bit different. That's when they start living in Europe. I can make my own money in Europe. I can get a job in Amsterdam, I can go get a job and earn 250 guilders a week, easily, in an easy job. If I want to work hard, I can make a hundred dollars a week, and I can go drive a truck for this guy. . . .

What does he want to do with the rest of his life?
"I don't want to think about it. I don't know what I want to do."

The Speed-Freak at Home

After the interview, Dr. Klein asked Gus if he could accompany him for the rest of the evening. First, he wanted to observe him outside the relatively formal interview situation—to see the speed-freak in his own milieu, so to speak; second, since Gus, however blissfully, was suffering distortions of perception and even delusions, Klein felt some responsibility to see that he got home safely.

The perfect courteous companion, Gus agreed, adding casually that he was driving. Before Dr. Klein had quite recovered from the realization that he was to be driven by a man freaking out from speed, he discovered that Gus was driving a small motorbike rather than a car. Klein was expected to ride behind him, holding the tape recorder.

Taking the recorder in one hand, and his life in the other, Dr. Klein climbed on behind. Before they started, Gus stared fixedly at the sidewalk and announced that he saw pearls, many and many of them, of all sizes and qualities, in the cracks in the pavement, and that he had to pick them up. He crouched down and began to scratch vigorously in the cracks, gouging out the dirt and exclaiming over the pearls. Klein began to wonder if this would continue the rest of the night.

Finally Gus announced that they would proceed to his apartment, but not directly; he had to make a score first. They proceeded, popping and bouncing, to the X Bar in the Rembrandtsplatz. Many of the amphetamines and even harder drugs come to the Amsterdam market through American soldiers on leave, who take them from medical stores or get them by prescriptions on their bases and trade them for hashish. The X is a dingy and dark bar, popular with the drug set. There Gus scored 50 grams of amphetamine from a boy named Michèle, who sold the drugs despite his knowledge that Dr. Klein was there.

They started out once more, presumably for the apartment, but like Odysseus Dr. Klein still had a stop or two to make before he could reach safe harbor. Gus announced that he had to make one more score, and they went to another dingy bar in the same general area, made their score, and then stopped to pick up a steak. Thus fortified, Gus went home.

They climbed to a third-floor attic, and Gus prepared the steak. At the Maudsley Treatment Center cafeteria in London, Dr. Klein had been unable to eat a steak because there were no knives; here there were knives, but no forks. They ate it anyway, washed down with some old soda-pop that was lying around, and supplemented with some stale and slightly moldy bread.

They talked about Gus's life, his goals and ambitions, and the fact that speed was an essential part of it this week. Gus said he was earning much of his living by painting pipes, but that the only time he liked to paint pipes was when he had injected speed and was flying. He sold the methadone he got to buy speed. Although it was obvious that little of what he said could be trusted, Dr. Klein concluded that, on the evidence, he was probably not really addicted to opium.

In the course of the conversation Gus brought out a box full of old jewelry that he swore he got by going through the cracks in Amsterdam's sidewalks.

He talked freely, philosophically, and at length about his life in both America and Amsterdam. Life in Holland, he said, was far superior. It was the free life—going his own way, doing just what he wanted to do—and drugs were an essential part of the kaleidoscope of experiences. This week it was speed; next week it could well be another drug scene. He showed Dr. Klein some of his equipment; apparatus useful for preparing drugs can apparently be bought easily and cheaply in Amsterdam. He had a whole bottle of sterile water, and an assortment of syringes and needles.

In his own way, and for his own purposes, Gus shows many and varied talents, and considerable flexibility and imagination. He is remodeling the apartment of his young landlord, who lives below him. The landlord, the son of an American doctor, keeps large amounts of barbiturates in his apartment, and Gus can get as much as he wants. But perhaps his most original and exotic source of income is his method of shipping hashish to America for sale. He takes photographs, front and back, of pieces of sculpture; between the two prints he slips in a whole sheet of hashish, then laminates and seals the package tightly in heavy plastic. The hashish, hidden from view, cannot be detected unless the plastic is ripped apart. He then sends the laminated photographs to the United States by first-class mail; he claims he has sent about 20 ounces this way. When Dr. Klein expressed doubt, Gus whipped out a pile of photographs of sculpture.

This enterprise has led to a great deal of business in LSD, which Gus says he often receives instead of cash in exchange for the hashish.

He takes the LSD to Michèle, and either sells it for money or swaps it for more amphetamines. He said that he had on hand about 800 guilders, and that he didn't really have to work much because the remodeling paid for his rent.

As Gus becomes more and more proficient in his various enterprises, he also becomes a more accomplished dealer in addicting and harmful drugs. Through people like him, and such other sources as the American soldiers and the American doctor's son, drugs are slipping into the Amsterdam market, perhaps in quantities and under circumstances beyond the ability of the authorities to control. Gus's cheery improvisations create an increasingly ominous situation.

The Very Young Hashish-Abuser

The American drug-abusers interviewed in Holland were generally quite young, were seldom hooked on heroin, and did not have extensive criminal or hospital records.

One major category consisted of 18-to-20-year-old hashish users who were at an early crossroads of their lives: ready to enter college, or perhaps in their sophomore years. They were uncertain about themselves, wanted to stay in Amsterdam, and insisted that neither their voices nor their names be recorded or reproduced. They were almost paranoid about the tape recorder, although it would seem that they had a good deal less to fear than the addicts in England who, despite their long police records, were so breezy with their confidences—their histories of unrecorded crimes, drug-abuse, and dealing that they must have known would fascinate police and employers alike.

The youngsters in Amsterdam seem to be particularly uncertain about their future. Unlike the depression generation, few of them face poverty or the lack of hope or roots should they choose to return. Although they resemble the frustrated and embittered bohemians of the Lost Generation that gravitated to Paris's Left Bank after World War I, they are for the most part unsophisticated and apolitical. Having had their fling in Europe, they should be ready to go back to their junior colleges or state universities, yet they talk vaguely, and often circuitously, of staying on in Amsterdam. The future, and its ultimate choices, have fuzzy outlines, and seem to recede as they look at them.

They cannot easily be labeled and dismissed. Although some of them are long in hair, beard, and intervals between baths, they are not hippies, even by Spiro Agnew's definition. In fact, most seem to be small-town and small-neighborhood kids, relatively uncorrupted, unexposed to the Babylons of the eastern seaboard, who are now finding it as difficult to stay down on the farm (or mill, or college) after they see Amsterdam as their grandfathers did after they saw Paree.

America should take warning that these young people also represent a badly formulated, confused, but nevertheless quite real rejection of much of American society and its values by a segment of youth that has seldom questioned these values before. The freedom they think they see in Amsterdam may be as dim and hallucinating as hashish smoke. To believe in it and reject America may be to sentence oneself to waste and disillusion. But even if they go back to the "farm" they are not going to pitch hay quietly and believe what they are told.

This hashish-abuser, like many others, will not give his name or allow the interview to be recorded. He is 18, an American addict, formerly a student at a community college. Very large for his age, with long hair, he looks as if he had just walked through the sooty gates at the steel mill at the end of his shift—past some barrier of time and space—into freedom. He has come to one of the Amsterdam agencies for help because he says he wants to stay. Amsterdam has a severe housing problem, and jobs for foreigners are not easily procured. But he does not want to go back. Why? He replies earnestly that he has come to "understand people" more fully in Amsterdam; it is very neccessary to develop a deeper understanding of others; and he wants to continue that developing process of insight and empathy. He will not return to the United States or to school.

Under questioning, he admitted that he felt guilty that he had lately increased his use of LSD and cannabis. He was urged by the counselors to reconsider. They pointed out that it was not his vague desire to gain insight and understanding that made him want to stay, but that this was an easy way out of going back and facing his responsibilities and the anxieties of the future. He was lazy. He didn't want to go to college. With that prop kicked out from under him, he was undecided. He said that if Amsterdam was not the place for him, he would go to Denmark. After more discussion and argument, he left, half convinced that he could stay a while longer and think about it—and *then* go back to the United States, perhaps a wiser man.

The Light-Show Man

Donald was born in New England, 21 years before the interview, and his last residence in America was there. He is white. Formally a Congregationalist, he is not religious, and he is similarly quick to reject most of the other things his parents represent. Although he flunked out of both high school and a private school, he managed to get into a midwestern university. He comes from a background that would seem to offer many material, educational, and social advantages. His father is a professional writer, his mother self-educated; although they have plenty of money now, old experiences, or neuroses, make her keep scrimping, saving, and worrying about money still.

After Donald quit school, he worked for some time as a short-order cook, living away from home. His parents tried to get him to come home. Then he was arrested for sniffing glue. "It was an intoxication charge. I was arraigned and sent to jail. It was all treated like a big drug-case."

His alienation from his family intensified. "My parents left me there for about a week. Really nice people."

He got probation,

and somehow, I don't know what happened, I was sent to Daytop Village. It was a big hassle. I didn't belong there—the only thing I had done was just pills and smoked grass and sniffed glue. I left there one night, and hitchhiked back to town, and went back to my house. But my parents were in Europe, and my aunt was living there—and she wouldn't let me in. I couldn't get in. . . .

So I went into the city and got a job driving an oil truck. But the police were telephoned and picked me up almost as soon as I got back

there. I hadn't broken any laws. I had some insane doctor that wanted
to send me back to Daytop Village. But they couldn't do anything to me.

Donald continued as an oil truck driver, and went seriously into
"getting high."

I was living with another guy, and we were just getting high. When
we could get chicks and highs we would get chicks and highs. We
overdid the scene a little bit. Too much drugs and we got ourselves
busted. We were using pills and grass—anything that would get you
high. Phenobarbital, dexedrine. Just popping.

He was not addicted to narcotics. But they were arrested for

possession of narcotics, violating the narcotics act. We also violated the
Dangerous Drug Act for all the pills. I had left the house two days
before because I was just too freaked out. The police called my house
and said I better come to the house. I went, and there was a bust.
They didn't have a search-warrant, but the bust was still on because they
had fast and speedy search to avoid loss of evidence.

Donald went to the state penitentiary again. After about ten days
he was released with the proviso that he go to the state hospital.
"I was there for a month and a half with five other people on drugs,
and all alcoholics."

After he got out, when his case was due to come shortly to court,
his parents informed him that they were going to Europe, and gave
him the choice: come with us or go to jail. Although he didn't want
to do either, he finally chose Europe and went to Germany.

That was three years ago. Finally I decided that I had to get away
from my parents because the whole thing is bad, and so I went down to
Munich and I lived there. I had a friend down there, and we had dealt
drugs together.

He had started fixing speed in the United States. By the time he
went to Munich he was dependent on it. He was taking about 15 fixes
a day, 15 to 30 milligrams per fix. He does not know exactly what
this cost.

I was supporting it with my dealing, and I was getting a lot of it by
somebody bringing me dexies, pills, which is methedrine, methamphetamine. You can buy it in Istanbul, Turkey.

How long did this last?

About four or five months. I got busted. I was put in jail, and was there for about two weeks. But I knew they were coming the night before, and so I cleaned house, and when they came in all they found was one vial with one fix of speed and one syringe and two needles. So they couldn't pin anything on me. They had witnesses who said they had seen me smoke, but nobody could say they had seen me sell.

I was lucky. But I was lucky before, too. My other case has been thrown out of court and stricken from the records. Now I can go back to America because I am free there.

Donald was being treated by a doctor in Germany, but after continuing the treatment for a while he finally decided to go to Amsterdam. "I don't want to do speed any more. I don't want to fix drugs."

Despite his bitterness toward his parents, he accepts considerable money from them. He gets 100 guilders a week to put on the light-show at the *Paradiso*.

I put about 200 guilders a week into the light-show. My parents are helping me out, investing in the light-show, and then as soon as I have the money for it, I write them a check back. Right now I need a lot of money—about $7000—for the light-show. I have an idea for a new type of thing in light-shows. But I'm not going to deal for it.

He claims that although he was arrested five times in the United States for "drug-related causes" (including some arrests for traffic violations "because I was high") he has never been jailed in the United States for pushing. He insists he does not push.

I got arrested here too. They found 24 kilos in the house—hash. What happened was that it was some people I knew. It wasn't my house. It belonged to a friend of mine and somehow he said that they could keep their stuff there. And the police came in when I woke up and I was taken to jail. . . . I was in jail for as long as they could hold me, and I made my statement that I didn't know that the hash was there, and that I didn't know the people and I didn't know anything about it. They let me go. That was about a week ago.

Donald has thus been arrested once in Amsterdam, once in Munich, and five times in the United States. But "I was only convicted once. In one more year, if I don't do anything wrong, then I get my record expunged."

He has used tranquilizers, but does not know what kinds. "I liked them and they got me high. I got them at my parents'. My father was always taking pills. I took a lot of his pills. I was 15 or 16." He first used marijuana when 13, "but didn't get high on it." He used alcohol at 14, barbiturates at 15 or 16, and anti-depressants. His first arrest was for sniffing glue.

I liked it a lot, but people told me not to do it, but I did it anyway. I was really rebellious. The more people who told me not to, the more I did it. I tripped when everybody told me not to.

When I was 15 I went to New York with another kid and we met this guy who was the night-watchman at the Ritz, and he was a speed-freak and so my friend got way up on speed, and we met this chick there and we all did speed and we had a really good night together.

Donald takes enough speed to hallucinate "almost every time after a day or so of speed." He can usually taste it on the tip of his tongue. "The only thing in my blood is water and speed." He gets speed from "connections, and from hospitals, doctors and things like that." He takes speed because "speed made me feel . . . everything that I felt wrong in me feel right." He has not used LSD, on the other hand, although its effects are "fantastic," because "I tripped so many times before that I know what it does, I know what's happening and it doesn't mean so much. I just feed back the same problems and I have to work them out first." He has also used morphine. "It was a good high, but it didn't lead to anywhere, I didn't like the state it left me in." He took as many as four fixes a day for "a few weeks" and then quit, addiction or no. "I got sick when I stopped." He got the morphine free, from friends.

Why did he really leave the States?

Because I didn't want to go to jail. And the hospital was worse than the jail. The doctors let us out a few weeks before I left because they saw that it was useless to keep us there, they couldn't do anything with us. And they didn't have the time anyway.

My parents said that I could stay with them or they would put me in jail, because they would rather put me there while I was still alive than see me dead.

The Top Narc: Conversation with a Chief Inspector

Inspector: The Dutch use all kinds of drugs, what you call soft drugs and hard drugs. Hard drugs are forbidden. We try only to prosecute the dealers. It seems as though we do nothing about the use of drugs, but that is only because we lack the personnel. To serve Amsterdam and Rotterdam, there are only eight men who work with drugs. Only eight.

Klein: What do you do if you just pick up someone for playing rock-and-roll guitar in the street, and he has a cigarette of hash?

Inspector: He is charged for the drug. If we pick someone up for another crime and they have drugs with them, they are prosecuted for possessing the drug. We give him a warning, and send him along to the prosecutor, who can do what he wants. Usually the person is fined.

Yes, every person picked up and found with hash can be prosecuted. The question is—is he only a user, with just one cigarette? Such a person is usually not prosecuted at all. Or he can get a very small fine. But if he should have ten grams, then he is put on trial, and the judge gives him a penalty of from one hundred guilders to prison, or probation. The rumor that you can get up to nine years in Holland for possession of one cigarette of marijuana is not true. Who told you that? It is impossible. The heaviest dealer in any drugs—LSD, heroin, morphine—can only get the maximum penalty of four years. That is the maximum —and it is never given in Holland at all. We caught an American dealing in LSD—250,000 pills he imported, that's a big dealer, I think—and he only got two and a half years. That is about the heaviest penalty we give in Amsterdam.

Five years ago, if we found on one man this one cigarette, he got perhaps a week or two in prison. But these things are changing. The ideas about the use of drugs—soft drugs—the judge now gives a penalty of about ten guilders for something like that. No one gets put in jail for using any more.

Klein: How do you decide who is a dealer and who isn't? Do you set an arbitrary amount as the criterion? I have been told by people in *Paradiso* that your amount is 20 grams.

Inspector: Yes. We have set a limit. You can't say that the 20 pounds you have are for your personal use only. Generally, we know our people who use, and we know the dealers, though I don't know the exact number. I don't know all the dealers. But I certainly know the large ones.

Klein: What about amphetamines?

Inspector: To use amphetamines here you have to go to your doctor and get a prescription and get it filled. But you can only get them from a doctor legally. So we know if they are illegal, and can trace them.

Klein: So why don't you arrest the big opium dealers? For instance, Michèle is only dealing amphetamines, but I know that he is dealing. A patient I know buys from him. He took me to the X Bar, and if I know about the X Bar you certainly must, but you don't arrest them. Why aren't these big dealers arrested?

Inspector: Because I have to prove that they have something in their houses or with them. When I pick up a dealer in opium I know that. They must have something in their possession. They can hide it easily, and it would be very hard to prove anything. This year we arrested four hundred men. That's quite a lot. About half of them were dealers.

Americans get the same treatment as Dutchmen. When one is arrested for possession of drugs we don't do anything. A case in point: a boy was found two weeks ago with 27 pounds of hash—an American who was sleeping there. He disappeared, but he would have gotten the same treatment as any Dutchman. Perhaps the judge would give him two and a half years.

Klein: If you found an American on the streets with hashish, you would deport him?

Inspector: Yes, he can't stay in Holland. In the last two months we have deported about 50. I don't know the exact figure. We don't just pick them up for drugs. They have to be doing something against the law, and then we find the drugs on them, and send them home. Sometimes we have to pay for the voyage home, and that is the question that is very difficult.

We don't have the hard-drug usage here that you have in America. I have been in this job for six years now, and I never met a heroin-user here.

Klein: You have opium-users here though.

Inspector: Five hundred, yes.

Klein: What would you do if you saw heroin and barbiturates, the two worst drugs, in this country?

Inspector: What can I do? I don't have the men, but I do my best. As it is, we work about 16 hours a day; we can do no more.

Klein: Why haven't you seen heroin? I don't understand.

Inspector: It is very strange. In England, the use of heroin has come, it is very normal. The only thing we find is that LSD, opium, and morphine are the only heavy drugs.

Klein: How many Americans were arrested last year?

Inspector: Of the 500 arrested, about half were not Dutch. About 62 were Americans. A little more than one in ten.

Klein: Have you had any deaths from drug-related causes?

Inspector: Between four and six. Overdose from a mixture, the mixture of opium and amphetamines. Or when they use LSD they say they can fly and they fly out of buildings. I have had two cases like that. Here there is so much drug-use among the youth. A report from one of the professors in the high schools says that 11 percent of the Dutch youth use some drugs.

Klein: The figures from America are certainly much worse than that. For instance, a study of a well-to-do suburban high school outside Philadelphia, a long way from the slums, revealed that as many as a third of the upper-graders had used marijuana or some other drugs, and close to 40 percent had used, or at least experimented with, marijuana. You would think that medical students, at least, would know enough not to use drugs, but I surveyed my medical school and found that in the first-year class alone 85 percent used marijuana, 16 percent LSD. The comparison is even worse—if your figures are accurate—because we have such a terrible problem with heroin.

Inspector: Until now heroin has not appeared here, but I am sure that in one or two years it will.

Klein: I understand that if an opium-user is convicted, the judge can sentence him to a clinic instead of a jail. I think this is great if true. Is it true?

Inspector: Yes, but we cannot force that man to go to the clinic. The law can't say you must go to the clinic and have a treatment. They can only go voluntarily. But they do have that choice. Unfortunately, we now have only one clinic in all of Holland and it has existed for less than a year. It is only the beginning. I think in a few years we will have more clinics.

Klein: What do you think of rock festivals? And places like *Paradiso?*

Inspector: They are a crazy business. At the rock festivals, they have drug teams; that is, in a way, a form of legalizing the use of drugs.

One big problem is that the police are of two minds: some want to prosecute everyone, and some want to prosecute only dealers and leave users alone. We find it almost impossible to control places like the *Paradiso* to stop people from selling hard drugs. The only thing we can do is close it, and the community does not want that. We talk to the people who run the places, but they don't want to follow our ideas, because they want to use drugs themselves. It is very difficult. The staffs of the *Paradiso* and *Fantasia* and the rest are elected by the community, and we can't control that. It doesn't really increase the drug problem, but it does increase the problem of control. For me it is much easier with addict houses than with these houses. I could do something about the people in charge; but in the clubs I can't. For instance, I can tell the proprietors of a bar that sells drugs that I can take away the music license if they don't do something. But I can't stop the *Paradiso.*

Klein: What about the X Bar? It is a center for dealing in hard drugs. Right in front of the bar, on the street, and in the bar itself.

Inspector: We can't do anything about that either. You get an offer in the X Bar, but the drugs are never in the bar, because that man looks out for everything. He doesn't allow the drugs inside. If they deal on the street that is not his business.

Klein: Also, it seems to me that there are a lot of hard drugs being dealt in the street in front of *Fantasia.* When I was there there were people injecting in the club.

Inspector: There are some hard drugs. But we have never found morphine or heroin at the *Fantasia.* Some opium, but only a little. They do inject, but that is mostly amphetamines.

Yes, we try to control things, but we could use 20 people.

Amsterdam will remain the drug-center for young Americans, the home away from what was never really home. Not only Americans but many Italians and French, some Swiss and Germans, and long-haired representatives from many other countries, flock there. There seem to be thousands upon thousands living in the street, the open places, the squares, or the youth hostels. The city has even provided special housing for the visitors. Walk down any major thoroughfare and you can see them panhandling, trying to get money for drugs or for living. The atmosphere is extraordinarily receptive, the people remarkably friendly. If they exert any judgment at all, the abusers can smoke their marijuana, or take their other soft drugs, without fear of molestation from police. Representatives of the flower children have been elected to public office.

A favorite gathering-place is the square called the "Dam," a memorial to the dead of World War II. In the summer the visitors lounge on the steps, and many of them apparently also sleep there. Hashish and marijuana and the psychedelic drugs (LSD, psilocybin, mescaline) are the most common. Opium is smoked or drunk with other materials. Many carry their bedrolls with them, and when not sleeping on the Dam they may be found almost anywhere.

Unfortunately, drug-abusers are seldom responsible people, and it is not in the natures of some of them to restrain themselves from pushing a good thing too far. *Together,* a little newspaper printed in four languages to welcome newcomers, has found it necessary to issue polite warnings, reminding the youths of the official policy about the misuse of national monuments such as the Dam. After all, some of the square Dutch citizens might take their World-War-II experiences and monuments seriously:

Last year Amsterdam was a popular meeting place for thousands of European and overseas youngsters. Some of them stayed in youth hostels, which are abundant in Amsterdam, or in low priced youth hotels. But others, tempted by the fine weather, preferred to stay the nights out in the open. This happened mainly in Dam Square near the national monument which was erected to commemorate the victims of World War II. Due to those sleepers in Dam Square last year, the monument was nicknamed the 'international mattress.' This was greatly resented by part of the Netherlands population. At present the use of the monument as a place for meeting others or for sleeping is subjected to certain rules. You are not allowed to lean against the monument, to sit or lie on it, or to place objects on it. This does not apply to the steps leading to the monument. As to sleeping on the steps of the monument or on Dam Square itself, you better refrain from it because it might lead to situations which could result in prohibitive measures on short notice.

Many did not heed the warning, with the result that at the end of the summer of 1970 a confrontation took place between the police and the youths; the police won, and the Dam Square was cleared, at least for the time being. Of course, young people cannot for long be forbidden the use of a public square entirely, and the pattern may repeat itself annually, or until an adjustment and understanding takes place.

The letter of the law does not determine its practical application. All laws depend for their effect on interpretation, selective enforcement, the personalities of the policemen, and the time, place, and surrounding atmosphere. *Together* warns the young abuser that the possession and use of both hard and soft drugs are illegal in Holland; the police do enforce those laws for purposes that they consider meaningful. Generally, however, they are not after the user seeking his own pleasure and fulfillment. Legally any hashish found on a person can result in his arrest, followed by trial if he is a Dutch subject or deportation if he is a foreigner. In practice, the police will not bother you unless they find enough to make it seem clear that you are a dealer; then enforcement will be swift and sure. But the police, like the populace, are not Calvinists seeking out original sin in order to punish the sinner, for the sake of their souls and his. "Even if you have long hair and dress in outlandish clothes," Klein says, "the people of Amsterdam are very friendly. They are much more willing to accept you than any other people in the world, it seems to me."

Amsterdam, as the blue plates in old-fashioned restaurants remind us, is a city built around canals. Along the banks American youth sit, on bright days, smoking hashish—much more potent and purer than American marijuana—which can be purchased for pennies. "It's a sin to be in Amsterdam and not get stoned every night of the week," one of them said. There are many inexpensive restaurants, many cheap or free places to sleep, many convenient places to gather. And if a visitor has trouble finding any of them, there are people and publications to guide him. At midnight a visitor to one of the automats will find not only food available, but young people sleeping on the floor. If you happen across a guilder you can buy a drink, or a sandwich and potato chips, and sit down on the street to eat. An Amsterdam delicacy is a cone filled with french-fries covered with mayonnaise, a convenient dish for the curbstone trade. Herring carts, which sell fish as American carts might sell hot dogs, line the canals, with kids alongside munching. The famous Heineken brewery, which dispenses not only beer but the equivalent of a free lunch, is very popular. Drug-users often line up and wait for hours for the brewery to open so that they can enjoy the free beer, cheese, and crackers along with the pot they bring with them. Many pitch tents in the little park nearby. One can live in Amsterdam for 60 or 70 cents a day; around the Heineken brewery it may be possible to live for even less.

Drug-abusers have always been skilled moochers; but even the most incompetent and innocent can find his way around in Amsterdam. Besides *Together* there are a number of other printed materials designed to help the sincere seeker after the free and the cheap. One of the most interesting little guidebooks is a pocket-sized, clearly and concisely printed little book called *Freeway,* put out by one of the pothouses. *Freeway* is worth dipping into not only for the information but for the philosophy and spirit it dispenses with a minimum of waste time. Its cover symbol is a naked and potbellied little man with a crabby expression, plunked down in the middle of the freeway, who carries a sign saying, "NOT FOR $ALE." The "free" theme is continued inside, where the first three sections are headed "Free You" (everything is free because you are free), "Free Mind" (Za Zen course), and "Free Consciousness" (the only standards by which judgments can be made are happiness and health; if it's here, it's everywhere, if it's not here, it's nowhere).

Having thus disposed of the bourgeois work-ethic, the book goes on to listings and advice. "Dope (DRUGS)" is followed by lists of the best places to score, prices, quality considerations, and then practical "ADVICES": "BEWARE of cowshit and pieces of licorice, etc. Good dealers will let you check the hash first. Smoke some." "If you never took pills before, don't even start. . . . Plan your time: take a whole day. . . . Plan your trip: Go to a place where you are close to where you came from: Mother Nature . . . NEVER CARRY MORE THAN YOU CAN EAT . . . If you want to sleep in the open air: . . . no dope on you, you are an easy prey for the cops that way." Listings that follow include public agencies that can give assistance, as well as clinics; working hours of psychiatrists and other physicians for VD, abortions, etc., are noted. Two pages list cheap "crashpads" with locations and prices, parks that are "the most beautiful for tripping, etc.," communes, "Livingspace: Contact Orange Freestate Housing Department," "cheap restaurants, cheap cafés," and the like. Throughout are bits of practical advice, mostly on how to get by without paying anything or with an absolute minimum of expense.

In all student hotels, second and third helpings. You can also take a dirty plate from someone and get it free; don't do it too often, otherwise they will get hip to this and stop doing it.
Almost all Chinese Restaurants are cheap and you get big quantities.

You can order for one person, which most of the time is enough for two persons, if you ask for some extra rice.

Order a big meal in an expensive restaurant, and then find a bug or a worm (which you took with you) in it and then walk away furious. . . .

Cheap meat for people and dogs at certain days at the slaughterhouse.

Free bathing: Every neighborhood in Amsterdam has public baths.
. . . Student flats have communal bathrooms. Just go up to any floor and take a bath.

Free Transport in Amsterdam. Most trams are automatic now, so you don't have to pay anymore. Walk to the front—after entering the tram at the back—and talk to the driver and look at every stop if a ticket-inspector is waiting (he is always dressed in a grey uniform). If one is waiting, you'd better get off for he might give you a fine. . . .

Of the service facilities available to the young people perhaps the most important is *Release,* which is loosely affiliated with the English *Release* organizations. *Together* describes its nature and function in relatively sober terms:

Release offers direct assistance in the fields of legal aid, employment, housing, military service, medical and psychological aid including drugs and abortion, and help to foreigners.

Freeway, characteristically, cuts to the heart of the matter:

Release. A subversive organization meant as an assistance for people, who are in trouble with the relatively tolerant, but still quite oppressive Dutch establishment. In case of being wanted by the police or being busted. Also if black-mailed by the Dutch intelligence service.

Release will lend you assistance if you are deserted and they will for instance try to get you to Sweden. . . . Apart from that, juridical aid, abortion, busts, drugs, possession, no money, violation of our national "liberation" monument, sleeping where not allowed, etc. . . . Help with hospitals in case of flipping or other medical problems, doctors, psychiatrists, etc. . . . Release is for and run by the underground. No names, no paying, though gifts are welcomed.

The Young People's Advisory Center, called popularly the JAC, which opened on January 10, 1970, is subsidized by the Ministry of Culture, Recreation and Social Work in the Municipality of Amsterdam. Despite its connection with the establishment, even *Freeway* has nothing bad to say about it, recommends it particularly for "people with problems in this domain (*re* dope, etc.)." It is a strictly independent and professional foundation. Youngsters between 15 and 25 may come, on their own initiative, for information, advice, and immediate help, without having to wait for prior screening, testing, or recommendations from professionals. The client can, if he desires, remain anonymous—this provision is part of the legal regulations governing JAC. Help is free and is given directly, in a non-authoritarian manner; in principle it is independent of control or pressure by parents or other establishment figures and institutions, but these persons and resources are brought into the process if the person seeking help requests it.

Generally, JAC does not attempt extended counselling or treatment in depth. The problems are discussed and ventilated, in the hope that the client will be able to see them more objectively and completely, and thus gain the insight and perspective to be able to cope with them. If this is not enough, he is referred to other sources that can give him the specialized and professional services he may need. If referral does not work out, JAC will take the client back, and resume direct responsibility.

JAC works with groups as well as individuals—with cultural organizations, schools, working and independent young people, and unorganized groups that come together for any purpose. Its basic tactic, and one of its major functions, is to highlight and call attention to the problems of youngsters within the society, so that a gap between the young and the establishment cannot arise from a lack of knowledge and communication that hardens attitudes through ignorance and stereotyping. Calling attention to and analyzing the problems, JAC then tries to create activities that might lead to solutions. It seeks to be a coordinating agency between the youths in Amsterdam and the staffs of the organizations and institutions that might be able to help. It goes to a good deal of trouble to make sure that the young should feel no hesitation about contacting its offices; its hours run from 7 o'clock each morning to 3 the following morning, with a full staff night and day. Even *Freeway* recommends it, establishment ties or no.

What accounts for the rise of drug-abuse, and its widespread tolerance, in Amsterdam? The most common explanation is that it came about in large part because the hippies joined the establishment and worked, like common politicians, to shape it to their own image. If hippies become part of the establishment, and help pass the laws, what is left of that fine primitive anarchism that assumes that the establishment by its nature must be and do evil, and that to join it is to cop out? What is left of the hippie ethos if all you need to do to obtain redress of grievances is to write to your hippie city councilman? In any case, whether the election of flower people to the city council was a cause of the change in atmosphere or simply a reflection of it, during the 1960's a prominent Provost in Amsterdam was far to the Left, and during that time a party arose, called the *Gnomes,* composed of what could be called political hippies. The *Gnomes* had complained that nothing was being done for the street people, that if they did not receive consideration and respect a polarization would occur and there would be trouble in the streets. Finally, full of zeal to promote the cause of the drug people, they organized to do something about it. They ran a slate of candidates and, probably to their own astonishment, elected five members to the Amsterdam City Council.

What to do now? How can hippies in a position of power and responsibility remain true hippies? But the *Gnomes,* elected on a platform of help for their confreres in the streets, were under the obligation to deliver. There was potential, if not actual, trouble in the streets. Drugs were coming into wider use. Adolescence, always a troublesome period, is triply so in these parlous, drug- and sex-soaked times. Something had to be done. As a result, the City Council set aside some 200,000 guilders (about $54,000) to give the young people a meeting-place. The meeting-places that resulted allow the use of cannabis—primarily hashish—on the premises, while generally drawing the line at other drugs.

Some of the often-mentioned pot-houses are:

Fantasia, open Mondays through Fridays from 10 A.M. to midnight or 1 A.M. The programs start at 8 P.M. and include records, light shows, pop groups, movies, and dances. *Fantasia* also has sleeping accommodations for young people. Membership costs two and a half guilders a year, and the admission fee is one guilder.

Paradiso is described by *Freeway* as "the best place for scoring dope," but the caution is added that dealing is prohibited, and that the sign above the entrance reads, "Dealers will be thrown out." *Paradiso* is an experimental youth center. Its attractively made-up publication in English, *Paradiso Fox,* certainly one of the most remarkable journals anywhere, describes the establishment this way: "*Paradiso,* a funky red, white and blue Victorian building (church) in Amsterdam, Holland, whose inhabitants may do anything they desire, except prevent fellow inhabitants from doing anything they desire. A blended chaos. . . ." The journal then goes on to describe, sometimes in scatological or pornographic terms, something of what does go on there and by whom, concluding that it is "all under safe supervision." One thing you cannot do there, however, is sleep overnight, as in *Fantasia.* It is large, with room for 1500 persons during the shows. Membership fee is one guilder a year, and entrance fee is two guilders. (*Paradiso Fox* advertises, however, that "you can make enuff bread in a day to live for a week" if you sell their journal.) Open Tuesday through Saturday, 8 P.M. to 2 A.M.

Kosmos. Open Mondays, Wednesdays, Thursdays, and Fridays, 6 P.M. to midnight. Their specialty is a cheap restaurant which emphasizes health food, open from 6 P.M. to 9:30 P.M. Programs tend to be educational: Yoga, ypassana meditations, astrology, experiments in communication, musical improvisation, chamber music, and community singing. Entrance fee is a guilder and a half, membership is five guilders for three months, and 12 for a year.

The *Milk Factory,* or *Milkyway.* Open from 7 P.M. to 1 A.M. Psychedelic programs, movies, experimental electronic music, and a bar. Entrance two guilders for the evening, membership fee a guilder and a half.

There are a number of others, including *Akhnaton, Famous, Studio-7,* and *H-88.* The services tend to vary, some catering to students. *H-88,* for instance, has long hours, from noon to 4 A.M., and provides such entertainment as music and pop groups, and good inexpensive meals.

Kosmos, one of the major youth-clubs, looks like an old mansion. The entrance fee, without drinks, is a guilder and a half (about 41 cents); the visitor usually pays three and a half guilders at the entrance, which covers not only the admission price but a ticket for soft drinks.

The décor is Eastern. As you enter through the line, to your right is a large room of several successive levels, each carpeted, like an off-Broadway theater set. To the right is a snack-bar. The room is partly divided by oriental-style wall sections, but the portions are accessible to one another. In one is a large bookstand. Down the center of the large room are two large oriental-style walls with round holes in the center through which you can spy on the other half of the room.

Soft music in the background; heavy sweet odor of hashish. Everyone seems to be either smoking cannabis or dealing in it. Some are sitting around, talking and eating. Food consists mainly of pastries, soft drinks, tomato juice, milk, cookies, cheese and crackers.

Klein circulated among the visitors, meeting people from home like any other tourist. One group consisted of two couples, all college

students from New York. Perhaps they were not, in the old-fashioned
sense, "couples," since they all lived in the same apartment and the
pairings may not have been formal and permanent. In any case, they
had come to Amsterdam some six months earlier, and were apparently
living off the checks sent by the wealthy father of one of them.

In the main hallway, the lights are blue. The floor is completely
carpeted with Astroturf. Once more there are different levels on
which people can sit and talk without a lot of tables and chairs.
To the left, there is an enormous steel statue, of undetermined
significance, with three candles burning underneath. Again marijuana
and hashish are being smoked and passed around openly, consumed
alongside the most ordinary and innocent kinds of teen-age food
and drink.

In the hallway, Klein encountered a boy he had known at an
Eastern university. The boy had an excellent academic record; he
was very intelligent, a consistent A-student who had been graduated
with honors the preceding spring. At 23, he had been in the drug-
scene for two years. He said he had been traveling all over Europe
that summer—"been everywhere." He carried hashish bought in
Morocco and took out some while they talked. During the two
weeks past he had used LSD twice, and he said enthusiastically that
he was getting into a beautiful "drug thing." He was dressed as
though poverty-stricken, and during the conversation, apparently
presuming on their earlier acquaintance, asked Klein if he happened
to have an extra pair of shoes he could let him have for a while.
Klein, surprised, since he knew that the boy's family had plenty
of money, said that he had only brought one extra pair with him.
"Okay," he replied, "I'll borrow that."

The poverty-role, learning how to make do with little and how to
mooch that, is a popular exercise for Americans in Europe today.
Only very occasionally is this the expression of hard necessity. There
are, of course, young drug-people in Europe who have few resources
and wouldn't want to miss the scene just because they are broke.
But others could manage to get money somehow, if only from their
square parents. Pride is seldom involved; many, like the two couples,
do get what they can from somebody's well-to-do and loving parents,

if not their own. But traveling broke has its own mystique, dividends, rewards, and purpose. For one thing, you meet so many other interesting flower people. Tourists, insulated by travelers' checks, can pass through Europe without touching or being touched; but that is not for one intent on new experiences and feelings. Traveling and living on practically nothing is "freedom"; life among the simple and unaffected is life close to the bone, and to the nerve-endings.

Here are some more hot money-saving tips from what must be a major clearing-house for such information, *Freeway*:

Free Post
Send your letters wrapped in a newspaper, as printed matter.
When two people write each other often—use the envelope addressed to you, with your own letter in it, to send back. Write "return to sender" on envelope.

Furniture
In popular neighborhoods you can find lots of furniture on the streets on the eve of collecting rubbish.

Liberated Money
Accept a job and start—after a day or two, scratch strikingly! Tell them that you are so in trouble with lice and . . . fleas. A week's salary you will nearly always get.
Collect at night, the empty bottles and change them. You can take full ones, if you like milk.
Give a tap to every tram-ticket automatic machine. The chance is great that a guilder will drop out.
To hurt institutions like the empire—the municipality—the bank—the insurance—almost cannot be called criminal.
PROPERTY IS ROBBERY.

The student and Dr. Klein were joined by an American girl named Beth, a Phi Beta Kappa and third-year medical student. They discussed how to get through Europe most cheaply. Beth had ridden through the Pyrenees on a motorcycle, sleeping in the open. She too smoked hashish, had been in and out of the drug-scene, experimenting —tasting the sweets offered, but trying to remain loose and uncommitted. She had taken mescaline once or twice, psilocybin a few times, LSD perhaps ten times. She used marijuana and hash infrequently,

but this was a special event—*Kosmos,* and people from home—so she
started up. She loved *Kosmos.* What a great place. What a great
idea to have such a great place.

Upstairs they found more Americans, college students. The plywood
floor swept around in wide futuristic waves, circling a huge hole
where the patrons could sit. A rock-band played. Wonderful, the
Americans repeated, as had the other Americans on the main floor.
Isn't it a great idea? Isn't it a beautiful place?

Dr. Klein kept feeling that the atmosphere was a good deal like
what Haight-Ashbury must have been in the early 1960's, in the first
flush and enthusiasm of the hippie phenomenon. Hard-drug addicts
were not visible anywhere, nor hard-drug usage—unless one considers
LSD a hard drug. A beautiful world of beautiful turned-on people,
many out, doing it openly. And the ugliness off in the blind future,
if anywhere—perhaps nowhere, man, a dirty unreal shadow alongside
the luminescent present.

Downstairs again. A place for each mood, for each feeling, for
each form of reaching toward one another. A series of meditation
rooms. In one, an Indian man quietly playing a sitar, accompanied
by a man on drums. The patrons speaking quietly, listening, letting
the music ride over their voices. The message perhaps is universal,
the music is Indian, but the majority of voices are speaking English.
Talking to the various people he met all through *Kosmos,* Dr. Klein
found that at least a quarter of them were Americans. Many were
sleeping by the monument in Dam Square, some were bedding down
at warehouses, and many were living in the gigantic youth hostels,
in which there are large dormitory rooms with as many as ten beds
in each. The barges and houseboats moored by the canals—bring your
own bedroll—were also popular. The boy told Klein that the majority
of young people at his hostel were not Americans but Germans;
there were also other nationalities, but they usually looked like they
were playing on the same team, wearing similar long hair and sloppy,
slept-in jeans. Using several languages and a kind of pidgin, they
shared tips on how to get by without buying anything, including
drugs, enjoying enthusiastic citizenship in the disreputable nation of
the happy turned-on.

It would seem logical that in such a gathering no one's marijuana would be safe; that much of the liberation that took place would consist of liberating from one another drugs that were not closely guarded, as well as other valuables and necessities. If property is robbery, what's so bad about robbery? This was not, however, what actually occurred. The pipes went from hand to hand, and whoever wanted a drag had only to ask, or wait. Peace and contentment everywhere, brother—and forever.

Dr. Klein encountered another medical student, a graduate of an Ivy-League school, who said that although he had been Phi Beta Kappa on graduation he had not then known where his head was at. Now he knew. He loved the life and his adventures, loved Europe, loved the drugs. He had used many drugs—LSD, mescaline, peyote, psilocybin—but his main choice was marijuana, or hashish, which he smoked two to three times a week. He loved it all, and all he possessed was two dollars in cash, which would have to last him for the month remaining until he caught his plane for America. What did he eat? Well, he reported faithfully, as many others did, to the Heineken Brewery at 9 A.M., and waited about two hours for his free cheese and crackers. This was not only a physical necessity but a social enjoyment; you met almost all your American friends there. Another American nearby, a member of an especially happy group, chimed in to say that he felt as though he had died and awakened in heaven.

In the offices upstairs Klein spoke to Paké, who might be called the head of *Kosmos,* and is one of the organizational leaders. He is a Hawaiian, educated in the States at various California universities, and holds a master's degree in social work. He said that it was a group of the drug kids themselves who had had the greatest direct responsibility for the organization of *Kosmos, Paradiso, Fantasia,* and *Milky Way.* The rise of the party of the *Gnomes,* and the election of five of their members to the city council, had been important perhaps, but incidental. In 1968, Paké said, some of the young people had joined together and decided that what Amsterdam needed was a series of coffee and soft-drink parlors organized for, and in large part operated by, the young people themselves. Then they decided to allow the kids inside to use soft drugs; at this point any superficial parallel with American teen-clubs collapses. When the places were opened, the police were much opposed and made some passes at interference. But too many had flocked to the pot-houses. The police could not arrest them all without consequences that they did not want to face. Finally, after conferences with the groups of social-workers (including Paké), who backed up the kids and were in favor of allowing soft-drug use, the police reluctantly agreed to let the houses continue as long as they remained peaceful and the soft drugs did not lead to anything worse. The organizers themselves felt that they were actually preventing, through the pot-houses, developments that could have been a good deal worse. The clubs continued without active interference by police; and they had grown.

There were, Paké emphasized, two sides to this apparent permissiveness toward drugs. They come down hard against the introduction and use of hard drugs, and are very watchful. If someone is caught selling hard drugs, or even with them on him, he is immediately ordered out and told not to come back. There are large signs on the walls, warning users and pushers. Known addicts and hard-drug users—and after a while all the regulars become known—are also quickly shown the door, whether or not they are selling, or using, drugs at the time.

Some conclusions can be drawn from even a superficial and subjective view of a place like *Kosmos*. It seems to have accomplished at least some of the purposes for which it was founded. The young people want it, enjoy it, use it. To keep it open, most are motivated to avoid abuse. They take their cannabis openly, but do not seem to go on much beyond that. At least in *Kosmos* they are not driven to loud argument, violence, or crime. Many seem so stoned by the time they leave that it is difficult to believe that they can do very much on the way home. In fact, they seem to behave a good deal more sedately than any equivalent group of people turned-on by alcohol in an American bar. "Last night," says Klein, "was very, very quiet, and people were mostly grooving to the music or anesthetized by the drugs." They are off the streets, disturbing—and being disturbed by—nobody outside. There is a hippie variey of Adam Smith's laissez-

faire philosophy, which assumes that if the young are left alone, free
to experiment with whatever takes their fancy, free of the outside
restraints of material possessions and the work ethic, then an unseen
hand will reward them, and perhaps all of us, with love, peace, fulfillment, and transcendental truth. On a good night, with the hashish
smoke filling the air, many of those on the floor at *Kosmos* believe it
to be a demonstrated fact.

Paké himself is very active in the Amsterdam area, being one of
the ruling group at the youth advisory council. Naturally, he also
has historical and sociological theories about the need for, and the
success of, places like *Kosmos*. He believes that with the breakdown
of the kinship relations that provided structure, satisfactions, and
purpose in life to earlier generations, new forms and substitute structures have become necessary to prevent alienation and loneliness. The
extended family is gone, and even the nuclear family is breaking down.
In a complex, mobile, and depersonalized society in which the young
put off the responsibilities of adulthood longer and longer but break
away from home early, mother and father back in their apartment are
no longer enough. Enter the new structures, organizations, persons,
and compensations such as *Kosmos*. *Kosmos* has come to provide
recreation, food, enjoyment, and even something of home and religion,
if not of home and mother, to some of its patrons. It is, in short, a
good deal more than just a fun place to spend an evening.

For all its solemn grandiosity, such a rationale circles around some
basic truths. A city that tries to understand changes in needs and
behavior, and to provide facilities to meet them—even if it inevitably
guesses wrong sometimes—must be commended. Certainly this approach is superior to neglect, fear, and scolding.

But the problem that faces *Kosmos,* and the places like it, is a
good deal more specific. Will it stop or deflect the drift toward hard
drugs by its permissiveness toward soft drugs? Will it perhaps
aggravate the situation? The young people like *Kosmos*. It looks
good to them and feels good; they compare it to heaven. But it is
difficult for anyone not overwhelmed by drugs or enthusiasm to
believe that the hard-drug users won't try, with some success, to come
in, and bring their fixes with them. Later interviews with some

habituées indicate that this has to some extent happened in other pot-houses. The directors of *Kosmos,* and those of their clientèle who are content with a soft-drug heaven and don't want it spoiled, are alert. But crusading fervor in organizations, particularly those run by or catering to flower children, does not last long. If heroin can be smuggled into the prisons and guarded drug hospitals of the United States, it is not going to be kept out of *Kosmos.*

The relaxation of fervor in the good cause is to some extent illustrated by the recent history of the *Gnomes* themselves. An older member of the city council told Dr. Klein that once the five *Gnome* councilmen had been elected, and the fine fury of resolve had ended in success, they began to flounder. They get interested in things, he said, but they don't carry them through. The day-to-day routine of committee meetings, discussions, and parliamentary procedures is not really for them; much of what they accomplish therefore tends to be marginal or superficial, without real importance.

It should also be noted that many of the hippies who turn up in Amsterdam are really only part-time or phony hippies. They are college-educated, bright, healthy; and they are going to leave the hippie life and go back to their universities and careers. Perhaps good will come of it. Perhaps their values, and life styles, will have become altered for the better. But they will be gone, and only the hard-core will be left. What then? How far away, really, is Amsterdam 1970 from Haight-Ashbury 1970?

38

Klein: How did you start the *Paradiso,* and how did you get the city's permission?

Coordinator: The city nearly started it itself.

Klein: How long ago?

Coordinator: In early 1968. It was the idea of the Provo Movement— which itself is really just an image.

Klein: Is that like the Orange Party?

Coordinator: Not really, but you can say that the Orange Party is an institutionalized version of the Provo Movement. Orange has always been the color of this kind of movement. Provo had orange organizations too. Orange is the color of our royal house.

But the Provo Movement doesn't exist anymore. They just decided that they didn't want to exist, so they had a big meeting in the park, and said that they didn't exist any more. And then all the people went over to the Orange Free State [Party]. They dissolved in 1967. . . . Some of them—one of them actually—is in the City Council now. There were a lot of leaders, and the one in City Council was one. He was the one who worked out the theories behind the White plans. These are plans to emphasize the effects of air pollution—the white-bicycle plan, white-chimneys plan, and so on. Thy paint them white. People in Holland didn't really know anything about air pollution. It's a big problem. But now they are starting new policies.

Klein: And the Orange Party came out of that?

Coordinator: Yes, really, you could say that the roots go back to 1960.

Klein: How did the Orange Party figure in establishing places like *Paradiso, Fantasia?* Places that the kids could come in to smoke marijuana and not get arrested?

Coordinator: The Orange Party was not really involved. And it didn't start as a marijuana house. It was for art. But the kind of people who had the idea to open art houses like this all smoked marijuana. . . . They tried to open a house as a student center in 1967 or 1968. It operated a few months and then closed. Then a house like that was opened here; the idea was to have a house for young people where crafts could be displayed that couldn't find a place in any other part of town or in the country.

Klein: Did you tell the city before you opened that you planned to let kids do things here that they wouldn't be allowed to do outside?

Coordinator: Oh, no. But it was a natural part of the behavior of the people who came here that they would smoke. They didn't come for that, but they did it just as you might smoke tobacco. The whole thing was going on here. Now, true, it was forbidden. But after *Paradiso* had been in existence for a few months, the authorities only had two choices. The police would have to be here all the time, or they could close it. If the police had to be here every day, they might as well close it. But it was an important project for the Department of Art and Culture in Holland, and they wouldn't close it.

Klein: Who gave you the money originally?

Coordinator: At first we had a subsidy from the local government. Then we got a subsidy from a foundation that had some equipment.

Klein: Didn't you have a bust here a few years ago? The police came in and arrested someone?

Coordinator: In the beginning they did that. At that time when some-one was arrested, he went to jail. Now if someone has just a small piece of hash with him or is smoking marijuana, he just has to pay a small fine.

Klein: A lot of people suspect that hard drugs are dealt here. I've seen a lot of Amsterdam, and I feel that most hard drugs are dealt over at Rembrandtsplaz and the small bars over there. What do you do here to control hard drugs?

Coordinator: We can see if people try to inject. Or we hear about it from others.

Klein: What about pushing marijuana?

Coordinator: If we see someone with a big piece of stuff, and he is obviously a dealer, we remove him. If it is someone giving some to a friend—"Here, smoke this in the corner of the house"—then we leave them alone. Sometimes we find people on the steps saying, "Do you want to buy hash? Do you want to buy hash?" Every night we remove three or four of those.

Klein: Do kids ever come here who need help with drugs?

Coordinator: Not any more. I think that addicts don't come here often now. They used to. A year ago we were open in the daytime too, and there was little control. People could play chess, or sit and talk, and it was a nice place for addicts—a place to go during the day. We learned our lesson. . . . Anyway, I don't think this atmosphere, now, is inter-esting to addicts. Addicts are solitarians. They want to stay in the small rooms, have their own connections.
   A year ago we had to close down for a month. There were special drug problems. We were becoming a classic drug-house. But when it closed down it hurt a lot of people. People were upset, and there were a lot of protests to reopen. So the city knows what is going on here, and they tolerate it because they know that there are important things going on here for art.

Klein: Do you produce art here?

Coordinator: Yes. Not for a while now, but we do. But we also get a lot of tourists here. About 70 percent of those who come here are tourists. It's like the leaning tower of Pisa; if you go to Europe, you must see it, you must be able to tell the people at home that you were at *Paradiso*.

Klein: Do you think marijuana should be legal?

Coordinator: Did you read the report of the Canadian Commission? Then why should I answer? . . . I have read that and other reports. After it came out a lot of the prosecutors in Rotterdam came together. They knew that a lot of people were using marijuana. They said, "Should we do anything about it? We know it has no bad effects, and in a few years the law will be gone." Now the law itself hasn't changed at all. You can get a maximum of three or four years for having marijuana with you, and the law makes no distinction between dealers and users. In practice, of course, they do make differences. The head prosecutor said that they don't do anything against users normally, but did prosecute dealers, especially big dealers . . . big dealers in marijuana. The police figure that, legally, they can pick up nearly every student in Amsterdam if they want to.

Klein: What do you charge?

Coordinator: We charge a guilder and a half for membership, and two guilders at the door for entrance. But that is only on Wednesday, Friday, and Saturday. The rest of the time is free with membership. We are a non-profit organization. The money we take in at the door is for our programs. The more we make at the door, the better our programs. But the city pays the salaries of the staff. It pays about 250,000 guilders a year for building and staff.

Klein: Is there anything you would like to say about the *Paradiso* that has not been said or printed before? Some of the articles that have been printed make this place look like an opium den.

Coordinator: That's our constant problem, to keep from becoming a place where people come only to smoke, or where tourists come to watch smokers. We try to hire people to run our programs, we try to raise the level of our programs. And it is hard to do with so many tourists.

Klein: Where do you get the staff?

Coordinator: The people that founded *Paradiso,* as I said, wanted a place where people could meet one another and there was art. They wanted youth-workers, art-committee people, and others like that. They knew this building was empty and wanted to use it, so they placed advertisements for staff members.

Klein: How can you afford to pay the musicians?

Coordinator: We can't. But they enjoy playing here. We have really good jazz and other groups.
The maximum number of kids we can handle is 1500, and there are always about 1100. When we get 1000 or 1100 in, we try to stop.

Klein: And what do you do with kids who have problems with drugs here?

Coordinator: As I mentioned, we keep the hard drug cases out. But about once a week a kid will flip out on LSD, and if we can, we take care of him. Sometimes they will ask for librium, but we can't write prescriptions for it. And if, finally, we can't help, we send them to *Release.*

Excerpts from *Paradiso* Information Fact Sheet Number 1.
(Printed in *Paradiso Fox No. 2.* Errors as in the original.)

Yeah, Paradiso, I see your spiraling dayglow eyes
Caught in the sinking glamour of a fading rock star
Yet ignited by the spit-fire of youth unchained,
You heave the heavy sigh of non-chalance,
And time, too often remembered.

It tires. It Quickens.
It spreads. It sickens.
And time, too often remembered.

So hold me on your knee, Dear Auntie the Dealer,
And tell me the saga of the *Paradiso;*
Speak not of the exaggerated tales constructed so slickly
by the bourgeois press and their villainous cohorts,
But the real beginning of strange change,
The starting gun of another long race:

Some young citizens of Amsterdam convinced the city council that there should be a place for young people where they could be them selves. At the time, the city council also felt this because of the provo movement. The church was empty then, and not in use anymore. The youngsters had already occupied the building several times. So the city council agreed to subsidize together with the cultural recreation center. They subsidized the building and the staff's salary, and the rest earned by ourselves or at the door with entrance fees. They founded a council called the "Stitchting Vrijetidscentra Amsterdam" (free young centre). Their first project is *Paradiso*. The board of the foundation installed a staff which works as a team, consisting of a co-ordinator, a financial manager, two program leaders and a secretary-hostess. On the 31st of March, 1968, *Paradiso* was opened.

A project for youngsters.
And the creaking first crack
Of your grillwork oak door,
Soon were drowned in the clatters of eager stoned feet.
Produced by that one shackle smashing sentence—
"You can smoke and you won't get busted."

They did not escape that contagious kindness and togetherness
That kindles and glows when paranoia takes its leave,
And their eyes always sparkle
Yet, hardly ever about the same thing—

He: There is no escape from reality.

She: The only escape is within yourself.

He: I don't want to stop the use of drugs, just keep them under control.

She: We try to be a bridge.

He: If they want to sit on their ass, its up to them, but we will try to educate them.

She: We are elastic enough to cope with most situations. Maybe we are more idealistic.

Drum Shatter. Pulsation.
From the catacombs that are your bowels,
Energy electric and an avalanche of deafness.
Individual communication has evaporated
And sound floods every nook and cranny and goose and granny;
Annihilating all cerebration. . . .

Our programs are centered around fine new pop music, avant-garde jazz, Theatre in which the audience can participate (total theatre), non-drug turn-on programs, and underground & comic movies. We are working on an information center about sex, drugs, medical aid and other cheap thrills. We assist young people in realizing their alternatives for this late capitalistic consumption society. Nearly started is the alternative clothing house. There are 500 inexpensive beds for young travellers. Not to mention the experimental research groups arts starting now.

I am overcome with the experience of experience.

And this, Lady Paradise, was your program for today.
But, let no one sit in judgement of the real and the dream,
For what transpires within your rickety wooden womb,
No one could really say,
Save the occasional wizard,
Gingerly picking his way back to freedom highway.
He has learned how fruitless it is
To chase this rainbow illusive,
Will lead the very clever wizard
To the hand of a fiend to touch.

And lo, the faithful pilgrims at your steps;
They are the innocent life force
Who nourish and sustain your evasive, illusory mystique,
And never question why you are.
Coming to you with open mind and heart, they will not suspect
You are just a building—
Crumbling—
Who's only real magic is nothing more than
Youthful love profusely given
But, that's real magic. . . .

And very soon another trip:

The Experimental Group Alternative Academy

Paradiso will be starting a kind of total alternative academy. It means all sorts of creative activities in which everyone can participate. Schooling, degrees, education in whatever field is not at all necessary. No methods of artistic teaching, just technical advice, if you want it. Some activities are: Film, photography, painting, sculpture, graphic arts, weaving, total and technical theatre, joy groups, politics, etc. If you would like to participate in one of these things, or if you know of something else, make yourself known to *Paradiso.*

Excerpts from Dr. Klein's notes, August 6, 1970

At about 7:30 Reverend Hall, an ex-alcoholic now working at a bureau for alcoholics in Amsterdam, picked me up and we went together to *Paradiso.* As befitted the evening, I had on a brightly tinted shirt and a pair of old blue-jeans. But Reverend Hall looked very straight, like a man of the cloth working with the unfortunates.

Appropriately, *Paradiso* is housed in an old church. But it was hardly recognizable as a church any longer. It is located on the edge of Reitzeplane, one of the central honky-tonk districts of Amsterdam. It is very brightly painted on the outside, in sweeping, psychedelic bands and patches. Although it was not due to open until 8 P.M., there was already a huge group of kids, about 200 in all, filling the steps and milling around. For them the evening had already started. As we walked around we could see the kids openly handing joints from one to the other. Pipes were also conspicuous, being lit, being passed around. Probably there was some dealing going on; it was hard to tell. But there was no major selling; mostly kids were just giving each other hashish, helping each other out.

On Thursday night there is no admission charge because there is no band music, although the membership fee of one and a half guilders is still collected. When the doors opened at 8 P.M., we went in. We passed through turnstiles, as if entering a theatre, and immediately found ourselves in a very large room decorated with metal pipes across the ceiling—not for sewage or water, but laid out in a futuristic pattern as part of a deliberate design. Varicolored lights played on the ceiling and along the walls.

Despite our age and appearance—particularly the Reverend Hall's sober dress and demeanor—we were immediately accosted by a young American who wanted to know if we would like to buy any hashish. Moderately flabbergasted, I said no, but the young man was not going to miss such obvious tourists who were probably looking for a story to bring back to Des Moines. Well, how about some speed? Good stuff. We thanked him kindly but refused.

Reverend Hall must have recognized the various parts of the old church, and had some feelings about their present use. We were in a high-ceilinged room perhaps two stories high, which had probably been part of the original auditorium, with mostly blue lighting all around. The pulpit must have been in the back or along the side. The kids filtered in, sitting down together in small groups. They proceeded to light up and settled down to the evening's serious business of getting stoned. Before me a woman held a baby whom she was nursing. Although this was the night without the band, the music was deafening. Despite the lights I saw everywhere, the light-show was not being given; it took place only on band nights. This was, apparently, the quiet and dim night.

We went upstairs, to a sort of midway platform. Here were the refreshment stands: marijuana and hashish pipes, inexpensive ice cream, soft-drinks, and beer. Clothing was available.

We climbed again, to the top level. We found ourselves in a low-ceilinged room in which kids were sitting around, passing the pipe and talking. Soft-drinks were for sale here too. Because of the lower ceiling the smoke stayed lower, and the electronic music was ear-splitting. People spoke to one another, but unless mouth was close to ear they seemed to be part of an old silent movie. Perhaps the most unusual feature of the floor was a small balcony, something like the upper balcony in a theater, from which visitors could look down on the third floor.

On the way out, we passed through a long corridor on the upper floor that was lined on both sides with kids. This, we found, might be called the native quarter, since the kids were almost entirely from Amsterdam. We stopped and talked to them, politely declining the ever-pressing and ever-passing pipe of peace. Everyone feels free and welcome. As we left the floor we were stopped by another youth, who put in my hand the largest piece of hashish that I had ever seen, and told me that it could be mine for only 50 guilders. At the standard rate of exchange, that was about $13.50; in actual purchasing-power or on the black-market it was probably less. A piece that size in the United States would sell for at least $100. Despite the get-rich-quick temptation, we again declined.

It was now about 9:30 P.M. The place had filled up rapidly, although this was supposed to be an off-night, and there were already about 1000 persons. Many were lying around stoned by the drugs. But the music, at all levels, was loud enough to knock out anyone who was not already anesthetized. We noticed a number of children there, with indulgent mothers. To allow youths to experiment, in a place set aside for them, with cannabis and the newer forms of psychedelic, sensory, musical, artistic (and pseudo-artistic) expression, and a certain amount of easy-going sexuality, it seems to me, is one thing. To allow even a small audience of very immature children to observe and inevitably to some extent participate in all this, under the casual control of mothers with no more sense of responsibility than to bring them in the first place, is something else.

Before we left the Reverend and I decided to go look for Frau Bax, one of the directors, a social-worker who happens to speak excellent English. We wanted to ask her how they handled their various problems and prevented abuses, particularly the overriding problem of keeping hard drugs and addicts out or under control. We found her walking around the place, and asked her about it. She said they did all they could to keep dealing down: she walks around continually, observing, and when she finds dealers they are thrown out. She realized that she could not eliminate the problem; but perhaps she could keep it under control.

We asked if there were any heroin addicts, particularly American ones, that we could interview, and get their opinions on the situation in Amsterdam. She introduced us to the boy who runs the light-show, a former heroin- and amphetamine-abuser who has taken treatment in centers on both the east and west coasts. He told us that his present addiction was to his light-show, which he gave every time he got the chance. We spoke to other officials and workers, including a social-worker who was once a teacher of art at an Eastern university. Many were involved in trying to police *Paradiso* without acting like policemen. They do try to enforce certain rules: 1) little children are not allowed; 2) no drugs are sold on the premises. We had observed that they were not succeeding entirely in enforcing either rule. But they were aware of the problems, and were trying, at least, to keep them under control.

By 10 P.M. the crowd was so dense in the main room that it was hardly possible to move about. Standing in the main rooms of places like *Kosmos* and *Paradiso* has a dismaying resemblance to standing on a corner of Times Square; sooner or later the faces from home swim by. We were joined by a student from a New York university who informed us brightly that he had just sent a postcard to his mother telling her that he had been to the *Paradiso* and was stoned. He obviously was; perhaps that was why he did not tell us how she was likely to receive the information.

Paradiso would be open until 3 or 4 A.M., but I was having trouble forcing myself to stay a few more hours. I was given a copy of the *Paradiso Fox,* which has something of the same relationship to the *Paradiso* as a good university newspaper would have to the university. It is even further-out (in other words, pretty far out), conducting a love-hate relationship with the establishment it represents, representing it and part of it, and yet scolding it for not going far enough and demanding that it go still further. The excerpts above give a good idea of its contents. It is remarkably well designed and printed in several colors, with many illustrations, on very heavy glossy paper of the kind that might have been designed to be cemented into somebody's corner stone, instead of being intended for the NOW generation. Its contents are uneven. The first page gives information about what to do and where to go "if you are in amsterdam" (lower case). The second contains a long, very mystical poem, with mixed and confused symbolism, presumably about the nature of God. Page four has an official-looking document described as "a proclamation by the Orange Free State in declaring its indepence [sic]", surrounded by drawings of Disney dwarfs; this faces the American Declaration of Independence, surrounded by drawings of colonial soldiers. The next page contains a long, scatological poem of the kind that high-school boys pass around in the lavatories. Other pages have psychedelic drawings and prose to match, politics, astrology, the Information Fact Sheet, and an appeal for free travel between nations.

Over and over we were told that *Paradiso* should not be regarded as a drug- and/or orgy-house, whatever the media might say, but a place where each free person can do his own free thing. The employees and officials were emphatic about this. Primarily, *Paradiso* was meant to be a meeting-place for young people, a kind of YMCA of the psychedelic age, offering classes, current events discussions, Zen groups, and art.

By 11 P.M. it seemed to me that things were winding up. Everyone seemed to be getting very tired; a number were zonked out, stretched out on the floor in all directions. An energetic few were making mad, passionate love in the corners; and the others were still grooving to the shattering music. The night seemed, for all practical purposes, about over, and I was amazed to find that there was still an enormous line at the door waiting to get in. When 1000 to 1200 people are inside, enough to cover the floor from wall to wall, newcomers are held up at the door. Although the next shift was waiting to take over, the first shift would not go home.

Paradiso and *Kosmos* cannot really be compared. Perhaps the difference is a matter of emphasis or degree, but it seems to have become a matter of kind. *Paradiso* seems much more drugged-out, and to attract a more drugged-out set. *Kosmos* provides more time, room, and atmosphere to think; *Paradiso* seems very fast and loud by comparison. People jump up, dance frantically by themselves or in small groups, put on entertainments for one another. Everyone, even the people who run it, seem to be under the influence of some drug, at least marijuana. Or perhaps one comes to act that way after several hours of battering by that music.

How many young people who simply want to be part of the scene are introduced to marijuana in this place because it is the major part of what is happening? There is little doubt that the officials are perfectly sincere in their desire and efforts to control the institution and to guide the young people, without coercion, into constructive channels. They may be succeeding to some extent. But *Paradiso* is itself an extremely attractive and potent drug that must be handled with great care.

I had come to Amsterdam, and to the pot-houses, with the idea that they were primarily involved with soft-drug use, but I came away with the idea that about half of the problem is, or will be, hard-drug use. There are a number of reasons. *Paradiso,* which embodies many of them, may constitute the worst example.

The fact is that in *Paradiso* anyone can procure almost any drug he wants. The officials deny this. They say that they can stop the sale of most drugs on the premises. In fact, they do not and probably cannot. Hashish, which is sold freely, is probably not as important as LSD, injectable amphetamines, and opium; these are hard, dangerous drugs, even if they are not in the same class with heroin.

To anyone familiar with the professional dealers and pushers who operate in the United States, places like *Paradiso* look like pushovers—Paradise itself to the weary, harassed, unscrupulous, and greedy. The market is waiting, and it seems to have great potential. Persons with enough determination, organization, system, and financial backing should not have much trouble selling hard drugs in *Paradiso*. What will stop them? The anxious and earnest efforts by people like Frau Bax to police the place by walking up and down and peering into corners? If the dealers felt no inhibition in trying to sell hashish to Reverend Hall, it is hard to see what will inhibit them.

The people who run *Paradiso* live in their own high atmosphere. They have good intentions, but they are as blind to the dangers and realities of their own position as the conservatives of the United States are to theirs. They say that marijuana is harmless. Although it is not a hard drug, and should not be treated as such, its complete harmlessness has not been proven and its use cannot fail to be encouraged by the *Paradiso* atmosphere. If the directors are wrong, some young people will pay for the mistake.

Worst of all, perhaps, they are not really honest with themselves. A case in point: I was told by the directors and the boy who gives the light-show that the boy was drug-free, that he had been kept from drug-use by being there and giving his light-show, which had become his only "addiction." Not long after this reassurance, I learned that he had been caught with 27 pounds of hashish.

Paradiso is undoubtedly the worst of the pot-houses and bars I saw in Amsterdam for drug-abuse.

The Drug-Scene
in London

Well, there is Graf. The Mounted
Police knocked his teeth out. All his
front teeth. And he had them replaced;
but it wasn't a very good job.

Is he a good, working citizen, would
you say?

Yes. Very good. He washes cars all night
long, and he sleeps during the day, and
weekends he goes with a girl—a
Canadian girl—that he went with while
in Canada.

And is he happy over here?

Oh, yes. Who wants to get busted in the
teeth?

—Interview with Hall, a Canadian addict

When Klein, who collected most of the first-hand and interview material used in this book, arrived in London in the summer of
1970, he quickly followed the path of most drug-dependents (and
tourists) to Piccadilly Circus. "Circus is a circle, a center of inter-
meshing—and often clashing—traffic, a coming-together of roads and
ways of life."
But Piccadilly is more. It is

sort of London's equivalent of Times Square, very honky-tonk, a lot
of kids.
    And there smack in the middle of Piccadilly, across from the statue of
Ares, stood a bunch of kids with straggly long hair who would take any
handout you were willing to offer, and sure enough, among the group
were the toothless addicts—you know, in the sweltering time of the
summer (it does swelter in England)—wearing long-sleeved shirts.
Their eyes are miotic, very small, a few of them standing there looking
for handouts, for anything they could use to keep going. This is the
area where the addicts hang out in London, the equivalent of the New
York drug-area—though they do not spend most of their energy and

time looking out for policemen or pushers. Nor does all, or even most, of their scrounged, begged, and perhaps occasionally stolen (though far less frequently stolen than in America) money go directly into drugs. At times they all seemed to cluster about one particular fish-stand, getting their fish and chips, talking to one another. When time came for them to get their prescriptions filled, for the various drugs that they were entitled to, great lines would form and stretch out in front of Booth's Pharmacy, the drug store right across the way.

Despite the great notoriety of Soho as the center of the drug-scene, both in America and in London itself, Klein did not find much visible evidence of addiction at first view.

Various ethnic groups inhabit the area along with a lot of Hari Krishna people in their long flowing peach robes, and probably a few psychedelic people. But the drug people, the addicts, seemed to concentrate and cluster around Piccadilly. . . . Of course, a lot of kids hung out at Cumberland Green area, around the St. Giles Center, but Piccadilly was where you scored. That was where, when you ran out of a little bit of heroin, you had friends who would oblige you with more stuff; and when your turn came, you returned the favor. . . . It was a together place.

Klein later got to know Soho, and its significance in the drug-scene, better. He went to the all-night clubs, where habituées would stay up around the clock, exchanging and taking their concoctions, moving from one club to another. But his original impression that Piccadilly Circus was the drug center for all London, all England, did not change.

Through therapy in the various centers, I came to know some of the addicts. One boy, one of the toothless addicts on both barbiturates and heroin, seemed to be in Piccadilly whenever I came by, day or night. He was very much at home there, friendly with all, greeting me when he saw me. I also saw him a few times at St. Giles Center, where he came for therapy. Those two places—and especially Piccadilly—were apparently the two centers of his life.

Like Klein, those who want to know about or be part of the drug-scene in Britain, especially addicts from the United States and Canada, usually go to Piccadilly with few detours. The tourists go too.

But this is not, as the American tourist would have you believe, the entire addict population. It is more or less the most delinquent portion—

the non-working members, those most resistant to treatment, the hippie types, the lowest individuals on the drug totem pole.

In the clinics other addicts also appear for treatment—businessmen, professionals, a cross-section of the staid middle-class. They wear business suits and put makeup on their hands and arms to cover their injection marks. For the most part, they stay away from the drug-culture gathering-places like Piccadilly, and keep up standard routines of life and work as far as they are able; it is impossible for their neighbors or the visiting tourists to know that they are addicts. They are carefully maintained on their drugs, under supervision.

What is seen and noticed—with the impact of a bad LSD trip—is the other end of the spectrum of respectability, the addicts of the 'Dilly, seated on the corners, lined up before the Booth Drug Store, milling around the record shops, congregating or sprawled in the alleys on Jerrem Street just off Piccadilly. All around are the many clubs frequented by addicts, where people inject openly; and there are the all-night clubs preferred by the "speed-freaks." The prostitute addicts solicit freely. The 'Dilly addicts are the most hopeless ones, the ones most apt to die from overdose or suicide—and deaths occur there frequently.

It is a horror, an open sore. Nevertheless, says Klein,

> nowhere in Britain do I think they have anything that could have matched the drug population of the *Electric Factory* in Philadelphia, while it was still open. And nowhere in England did I see anything that could really match the East Village—St. Mark's Place—for sheer concentration of addicts per block.

But these are areas that most Americans tend to avoid, out-of-the-way places that are carefully circumvented. People who live in the major cities of the United States need never know the streets and alley-ways of Harlem, the hippie hangouts, or any of the other drug-centers in the big cities. In fact, the concentration of drug addiction in the slums of America, and its careful screening when it appears in the suburbs, practically guarantees that most people will not see it. If they try hard enough, they can ignore its existence, but everyone in London, sooner or later, goes down to see the 'Dilly.

What about the black-market, and the drug underworld? How easy is it to buy drugs in the 'Dilly? Klein was a stranger, rather obviously a foreigner, without contacts or friends when he first came there. He did conform to the local décor—he did not wear a suit, or shave, and he let his hair grow long and was careful not to comb it—but he had no other recommendations, and could have been a narcotics agent as far as the general run of addicts were concerned. Standing at a fish-and-chips stand, trying to look like someone who knew how to eat them in a British manner, he accosted a known addict named Philip. He broke the law—and was liable for arrest— with his first question: "Do you have any stuff?"

Since the British do not use the expression "stuff" to mean heroin, Philip should have been suspicious from the first. "What do you mean?"

"Do you have any H—horse?"

"Oh, sure. What do you want?"

"Oh, I need a few tabs."

"I haven't seen you here before."

"I haven't been here before."

"How many do you need?"

"I need three tabs."

"You know, I really can't sell it—I don't have that much extra. But, I'll show you someone who could give it to you."

They walked down the street, across from a cinema, and there Philip, without further checking or questioning, introduced him to someone who could meet Klein's needs. Heroin was available; in addition, he would sell tuinals for two bob apiece. He also had some mandrax, or "mandies,"—methaqualone, a much-abused barbiturate-type drug that is combined with dyphethydravene-hydrochloride, and is a sedative. He also had some amphetamine, though not much. He was willing to sell any of them, right in the open on the street corner, to a total stranger.

The question of availability was answered: the drugs were easily available to anyone who wanted to buy. Any child could have come up and bought those drugs. What was more, the prices were low; practically anyone could afford them.

Does this necessarily mean that their use and sale is spreading throughout London? Apparently not. It is Klein's opinion, based on interviews with addicts and from other sources, that the availability of drugs has drastically decreased since the clinics have been opened. After he told Philip that he really didn't want the drugs, that he simply wanted to see what was available and how easy they were to buy—and after Philip had recovered from the fright induced by that revelation—they talked, and Philip reminisced. It used to be, he said, that when you went into Booth's for drugs people would fight over who would sell them to you, trying to underbid one another. But that was no longer the situation. The sellers were beginning to become cautious. They generally did not want to sell to outsiders, preferring to deal with people they knew, in the drug sub-culture, who needed extra drugs. The fact that Klein had come over to Philip, who was known to the salesman, might have made that particular transaction different.

In any case, the illicit market in Britain has a good deal of an amateur let's-help-a-friend-out flavor—perhaps a manifestation of what Louria calls the "needle-sharing camaraderie." There seems to be little of the American hard-sell, organized for profit. Klein has the impression that drugs are a good deal more available in the United States, and are being pushed more vigorously. The English underworld is not an underworld in the American sense of a criminal operation out after money, but rather closer to what is usually called a sub-culture: a group isolated from society, to some extent outside the law—at least not accepting the law as a legitimate curb on their drug activity—with a basic common interest and to some extent a similar way of life; apart from society and content to stay that way.

For deeper insight into the life of the drug-user, let us listen to what he has to say about himself. The addicts from Canada and the United States whom Klein interviewed were for the most part male, close to middle age, of working-class background. It is hard to generalize since there are always exceptions, the sample is small, and much depends on interpretation; their lives have not been ordinary or normal, and some of them seem to have been lifted directly from a picaresque novel or from a nightmare. They lived on the fringe, they saw prisons and hospitals, they committed crimes and follies, and their family lives in North America were unstable. It could be said that they were weak and irresponsible. But some have shown remarkable stability in their later years in England, although that could be due to maturity as well as to the English system, and the same information that seems to show an inability to settle down and a weakness of character could also be cited to show an occasionally amazing adaptability, resourcefulness, and endurance. The interviews in this chapter record conversations with patients at Maudsley.

Who Wants to Get Busted in the Teeth?

At the time of interview in the summer of 1970, Graf, a native of Western Canada, was 45. He had not been home since January 1962. He is conscious of no particular ethnic or religious affiliation: one parent was Roman Catholic, the other Protestant, but both left their churches at marriage, and did not try to direct him toward any faith or denomination. "I've been to a few churches but I didn't take much interest in it." His father was a mechanic, self-taught.

Was it a broken or loveless home? Did he suffer great hardship of any kind?

> No. No. My parents were—I came from a family of five children. I am the only one that ever became an addict. One is a bank manager. Another of the boys is a pilot. And of the girls, one is happily married. And one died in childbirth, during a Caesarean section, from entirely physical causes.

Graf dropped out of high-school in his first year.

> It was war time and I went to work. Everybody was making good money. . . . You wanted to make good money also. I went to work in the shipyards during the war, building ships. And the first job I had I maintained it for about 19 months, and then I started drinking heavily and missing work.

It did not take him long to get into trouble.

> Finally, I left that job and when I was broke I went to another shipyard and I only lasted there about six months until I had accumulated a little more money and started drinking, and one New Year's Eve three of us,

we got to drinking and stole an automobile, and I ended up in prison for six months.

Klein: Do you still drink at all?

Graf: Yes, occasionally a beer, I enjoy it on a hot day.

Klein: Did you ever get off the liquor?

Graf: I very rarely use it now.

In itself the story seems ordinary enough for wartime—the quite young boy who left an unexciting home-life for freedom, good money, life with older companions and temptations, and relatively few controls away from his parents.

How did he start on drugs?

In 1943 when I was drinking and—oh, after I had been in prison for six months for stealing the automobile, I came into contact with numerous addicts and what-not, and the price of heroin when it was available during the war was $20 a grain over there and I was always getting into trouble drinking so I figured, well if it's worth the $20 a grain, and I wanted to experiment and through the jailhouse contacts me and the friend that I went to prison with we went down. . . . We were unable to get heroin the first time so we got some morphine. He knew how to inject it.

Klein: You injected it into your vein the first time?

Graf: Yes.

He got his buzz, and then got sick. But he found that

I was able to maintain myself more normally [than with drink]. Under the influence of drugs I was able to control all my actions and then, whenever I had the money, I'd hunt up a black-market pusher and obtain some.

He did not know when he became addicted. "I thought it was just in a person's mind, that I had the will-power to stop if I wanted." He discovered, in jail that he was addicted.

I was stealing to buy the drugs and I was picked up and lodged in the city prison for investigation of a crime, and while I was in there I thought I had the flu or something coming on. I started to feel chills and my nose and eyes were running and cramps and. . . .

Then he finally realized that he was having withdrawal symptoms. It was about three months after his first injection. "It was whatever money I could come up with and whatever drugs were available at the time. By that time I was using heroin, opium, morphine." It cost him about $20 to $30 a day to maintain his habit.

Once he became addicted he could no longer work steadily enough to maintain his habit, and had to steal.

It was a continuous rat-race. In and out of prison, beating, being beaten up by policemen in search of drugs, and stealing, and every way possible maintaining or accumulating the money to buy the drugs off the black-market.

Was he ever treated or imprisoned in Canada for drug-use?

On numerous occasions. Voluntarily, at least five times I committed myself. I got a doctor and went into sanitariums and tried cold turkey, tried hyacinth cure, tried gradual withdrawal. When it got down too low and I would feel pangs of addiction, the craving would return and I would throw up all attempts to come off, and I would check myself out. . . . So the only time since 1942 that I was off drugs for any length of time was in prison.

What of the authorities? Did they try to treat him, or merely throw him in jail? "Just throw you in prison."

Altogether he had undergone withdrawal ten times or more. "About five times under medical supervision, on my own, and about five in prison." But it hadn't worked. He had always gone back, never finally kicked the habit. Now, on maintenance in Britain, he no longer wanted to. "I'm quite content."

Did tolerance manifest itself? Did his habit increase in Canada? "Sometimes I was sick, or money was hard to get. . . . But if I had the money my habit would increase, yes." The drug-scene in Canada, when he left in 1962, was

only heroin, or mostly heroin in the west of Canada. In Canada the opium comes in a paper, the kind of paper butter is wrapped up in, grease-proof paper, and the heroin used to come in capsules in a powdered form, the illicit heroin.

He had come to England because

I had a friend and his wife that had come over and after they had been here a month they wrote to me and told me the conditions. And they said the conditions here are far superior to Canada. And so I applied for a passport and I followed them over. When I arrived here the friend that I had corresponded with introduced me to his doctor, a Lady Franco, and after an interview and taking my case history, she pre-scribed my heroin.

How did you come to this clinic?

Oh, well, when the drug-laws changed here and were taken out of the hands of the private practitioners, all the doctors recommended a clinic.

Does he like it? "I'm quite satisfied."

He has been stabilized on heroin now in Britain for eight and one-half years. He takes some barbiturates with his heroin, and the clinic maintains him on both (12 grains of heroin and eight and one-half grains of seconal daily—considerably more than he took in Canada). Marijuana made no impression on him, and after experimenting he stopped. He has taken no amphetamines or methadone. Anything else?

When I first arrived in this country I was on cocaine, but I gave it up on my own, more or less. I saw what it was doing to me, my appetite. And I was starting to get hallucinations, I believe, and I saw I couldn't continue to work or sleep properly, and so my doctor and I worked out a schedule to wean myself off of it. The last bit I had I think I one day just flushed down the toilet.

He has taken LSD only once—as part of some experimental work conducted by a physician in 1962, when it was still relatively new, just after he had emerged from a prison.

I had the impression while under the influence of LSD that this life, this world, was nothing. . . . There was a religious connotation during it. . . . At the time I would say I enjoyed it and thought I understood myself better. But afterwards I was very depressed and to this day would advise anyone against it.

Had he stolen to support his habit in Canada? What means of support did he have now?

> I've been working ever since I arrived in this country. I've been working at the same job for eight and a half years now. I work in a taxi garage.

What about his sex-life? He was single and remained single.

"I have a girl friend who is an addict. We spend our weekends together, but our sex life is nil."

So far as sex is concerned, his life on maintenance cannot be quite normal. What about his life otherwise?

> I feel here that I'm able to live like a human being. I am not in fear of being in prison for my illness or because of my addiction. . . . I am able to work and have as close to a normal life as I believe I possibly can with this personality defect, I'll call it. And I believe that under this clinic system in England, other than my sexual life, I now have a perfectly normal existence.

Heroin Is Worse than Being Pregnant

Hightower was born in Central Canada, some 45 years ago. In the latter years of World War II, his family moved west. He came to England in 1962. He is white, Protestant. His mother was religious, but neither his father nor he is. He can't remember the last time he went to church.

His father was a prison guard, and his mother, fresh from the farm, lived with him at the prison. During World War II the father joined the army and traveled around. The parents did not get along.

> She was scared to death of him. He used to beat her and scare her and everything else. I've even seen her run and hide in the bush when she knew he was coming home on the weekends.

Just before the war her parents died and left her a farm. "This time he was at some place out west, and she had an auction sale and sold everything and moved out."

Hightower has been married and divorced. "I was 18 years old when I got married, and my wife was eight months pregnant. And I joined the army ten days later. I was in the army for two, two and a half years."

His wife had a baby girl. He came home occasionally, and she got pregnant again. She was living with his mother.

My mother and her didn't get along very well and after I got discharged—they were all living at my mother's place—my mother didn't like the idea of her staying there, so she sent her back to her own parents. And in the meantime I was supposed to be taking an accounting course, or something.

Three or four years later, when he was finally settled, with a job and a house which his mother bought, he called his wife. But she refused to return. She had found somebody else; and she was at home where she was brought up, where she knew everybody. There were no arguments. They were divorced in 1946.

He worked in Canada on railroads, logging camps, mines, construction jobs. "At just about everything."

He is unclear about when he started on tranquilizers and amphetamines, but it must have been about 1948, "just before I started using heroin in 1949." He tried tranquilizers, "but I didn't like them. I lost all my teeth. I fell down the stairs and didn't know anything about it." He used Nembutal and "this stuff [Benzedrine] that in war-time they gave pilots to keep them awake." He has never since taken marijuana, LSD, "purple hearts" or any other drug but heroin. "No desire. 'H' is too much for me."

His initiation to heroin "just happened."

We were just fooling around like youngsters do, and there was an older chap around and apparently he had had an experience with drugs before and. . . . It was downtown. You know, just looking for action. Anyway, I took a [skin] "pop". . . and just laid across a bed there and I thought I was in heaven or something, you know.

He realized he was addicted about a month later ". . . and I caught a cold and I went home and I just couldn't understand why I couldn't get over this cold. Couldn't get to feeling proper, you know. And a little later I realized that it was the heroin."

He was still only skin-popping, and only once a day. He never used very much in Canada. When he left in 1962 he was mainlining, but only three caps a day, about thirty milligrams, of adulterated heroin.

> It's a funny business. See, they all cut it down. They got middlemen—they got this man and that man and street pushers and all this—and they all put in a little bit of milk sugar, and so on, and try to make more capsules out of it. Everybody trying to make a living on it, except the poor users.

He has never tried to push drugs, or earn the cost of his habit through crime.

> I even went to work while using drugs, and what a bloody. . . . I was sick as a dog half the time trying to get my job done. It was on a railroad—a switchman—climbing and jumping off of these cars and. . . .

He was arrested, convicted, and imprisoned three times for using, not selling, drugs.

> And the fourth time could have been for life. Any time you have three convictions that have a minimum sentence of five years, you can be locked up for life.

They never attempted to cure him. "The only cure is total isolation. I mean you're locked up and that's it." He was, once, in a

> medical pilot scheme they started up. They built a nice little house all by itself and they gave everybody their freedom . . . but no drugs. And we had meetings and discussions and all this.

He stayed off drugs for a while, and he went

> way up north and I worked there for about six, seven months. And then they shut the whole thing down. All the building part of it which I was involved in. Building those steel power lines.

He was off drugs for about a year. "But the minute I got back I was looking."

Facing life imprisonment if he got caught again, he came to England. This was but "part of the reasons" for coming; the rest was a girl. She was not on drugs. "She wouldn't even think of it. Thank God. But it was rather hard on her—we couldn't have a proper life, you know, sex-wise or otherwise."

He had heard something about the British system: "A few people had heard, and we had money, or could get it." His girl had originally been from England.

> She went to Canada with a soldier she'd married over here during the last war. And they split up and she tagged on to me, and I actually couldn't get rid of her til we got over here. Her mother lives on the coast, has a big house there where she rents rooms for the summer.

They split up, primarily because of drugs, and he hasn't seen her since. "Things weren't right with us."

Like others, he went to the doctor called **Lady Franco**. He heard about her from "the chaps I met over here." Like the other addicts she impressed him greatly, and her death affected him. "Bless her dear old soul." All went well at first, "and then she seemed to be in pain, or something, I don't know what it was." She had tried to be good to the addicts. He didn't think, in spite of the Brain Report, that she had overprescribed. "The addicts asked for the world, you know. You know what I mean." He went to another doctor, and worked to increase his dosage. "I kept going up until I got to ten grains a day." Ten grains is 60 pills, 600 milligrams, of pure heroin, as compared to the 30 milligrams, adulterated and cut, he used in Canada.

It was no trouble to register. "We came over here and we went directly to the Home Office, and told them we were drug-addicts. And I don't know whether that constitutes the registration of a drug-addict." He did not fear deportation, although he thought a couple of Canadians had been deported. "I think most of it involves theft, things they didn't need to do."

When the clinic system was set up he came to Maudsley, at the suggestion of his physician. He did not plan to seek withdrawal. "I personally don't think it would do any good." He had, however, tried to withdraw some time earlier in England, before the clinics had been established, when he was with a private physician. His habit has not increased since he has been going to the clinic. His attempt at withdrawal occurred

> five or six years ago. Well, I was taking cocaine then, and I started hearing voices and thought people were looking into windows and all

this sort of stuff. I had to quit. I put in a year going in and out of hospitals.

He had been put on methadone, alternating with heroin, during part of this period. Finally, however, it had failed, and he had gone back to drugs.

With his heroin, presently, he takes a drug called Mandrax (really Methaquilone) which he characterizes as "sleeping-pills." Although a non-barbiturate, it is addicting. He uses about

> oh, very luckily only twenty a week. . . . If you haven't got it . . . if you go without it, you know, and you're sitting . . . Jesus, your arm will shoot up . . . and if you're laying in bed you think your bloody neck's broken . . . it jerks so much, you know?

How much did these drugs cost him?

> Counting the Mandrax, one week it's five bob. And they send them in two weeks, so one prescription, including the Mandrax costs five bob, and the next week it's only two and six.

Every week, in short, he paid an average of a little more than three shillings, about the equivalent of 36 American cents.

He has been an addict too long to get much positive buzz or high from his drugs. "I just feel normal with it." When he runs out of Mandrax, he tries another drug called Mogadon, until the next prescription.

> It's much better. It doesn't affect your stomach. You wouldn't sleep, and you might get some withdrawal symptoms, but you can eat. With Mandrax, it just cuts out all the desire for food and you get heartburn all the time and you have to take something to settle your stomach. It's terrible. Every time you bend down you think you're going to burn to death. And of course heroin knocks hell out of your teeth; it's worse than being pregnant.

The usual final question: would he care to compare his experiences and feelings about the drug situation in Canada and England? "In Canada you can't live. You can't work and live a normal life, be a normal person, and here you can work, be normal." Did he feel like a criminal in England? "No." In Canada?

> Christ, yes. If you got jumped on every five minutes. . . . In Canada

you're locking the door and listening for footsteps and searching the house before you attempt to fix. . . . The only way you can do it in Canada is push, or else you're sick half the time, or more than half the time.

Isaac the Gambler

He is white, 50 years old, born in Western Ontario. He came to England in 1960. He is a Jew, though he has had little formal religious training. "My father was an atheist, but my mother was conventional, you know. She went to *schul* twice a year on the high holidays, Passover and Rosh Hashanah. And that's it." He never goes to synagogue; went as a child only because it was expected of him.

His father was an immigrant from Russia, with very little formal education. He had been a cigar-maker and became a pawnbroker. His mother was born in Canada, and had more formal education— perhaps high school, but he wasn't sure when she was graduated or whether she had ever finished. He himself dropped out of high school in his junior year. "I left. I lost interest, and there was a depression at the time, and I left."

He has never held a conventional job, "Not in the sense of nine-to-five." In Canada he supported himself, and eventually his habit, by "gambling and stealing." Living close to the United States, he visited it often, and "spent two years over there at various times." He was arrested there. "Oh, nothing of any consequence. In Detroit I was arrested for larceny from hotels, for illegal entry. . . ." He was never arrested in the United States on a drug charge. All his arrests in Canada, despite his illegal methods of earning a living, were on drug charges. "In the neighborhood of a dozen arrests, I would say."

Unlike most addicts, he uses, and likes, alcohol—almost never, or very seldom, hard liquor.

You know, most addicts don't drink; that's been my experience. Well, about two years before we left Canada, I was at a friend's place, and she said, "I have some nice wine here. Why don't you try a glass of it?" I did. It was a rosé wine, Anjou Rosé. I liked it very much, asked her where she got it, went down and got a dozen bottles. That's 12 years ago, and from that day to this I've been drinking an average of two bottles of it a day.

He does not consider himself an alcoholic.

He has never taken LSD, barbiturates, or amphetamines. He did smoke marijuana

as a kid around Detroit and Windsor, yes. This was the way back when I was 15, 16, 17. It was very common around Detroit. You could get a Prince Albert pipe-tobacco tin of marijuana for about $3 in Detroit. And the kids used to go over from Windsor and bring it back; it cost them a dime on a bus and they'd get $5 for it in Windsor. You could get about six cigarettes for a quarter—and I mean the size of tailor-mades, not like sticks. In Windsor they were a little more, maybe two for a quarter there. And I used to smoke a little. We never heard the word "pot" then, we said "grass" or "tea."

He lived in Ontario then; in the late 'thirties he lived for a year in Los Angeles, and "I smoked a little marijuana around there."

He had an "odd fix" of narcotics when 15, but started to use it more regularly in Canada, at 17. He has used marijuana very seldom since he was 20. The last time it only gave him a headache.

That business of a tie-up between marijuana and heroin, I don't believe in that at all. I don't see the point. I mean if you're gonna use that type of logic then you have to go all the way and say that anybody that's taking a drink, or smokes cigarettes, and so on, you know.

That odd fix of morphine was offered him by an addict shortly after he quit school. Reminded that most kids offered fixes don't take them, he said, "I agree with you. I imagine that people that do take fixes there must be some emotional or psychological lack somewhere. That they're looking for something. . . ."

He knew the addict from a carnival where, as a teen-ager, he used to work the "different wheels and so on, and gambling games on the show." He was not charged for this fix.

His first habit was opium, when he was 17.

They called it "mud." At that time out in Western Canada there was no heroin or morphine on the street. It was all opium, coming from the Chinese; they were getting it from China to smoke, and they would sell it to the hustling girls who in turn would sell it on the street, or their pimps would. And this is what all the addicts in Vancouver used.

They injected it. You cook it up in a spoon. You know what a stick of gum looks like—well, half a stick of gum would look exactly like it. It was in a sort of rice paper that you would put in a spoon, cover with water, and boil, and the opium would dissolve in the spoon, and you'd take the paper out and draw it up through a cotton and inject it. If you missed a vein you stood to get an abscess.

That's what everybody out there used right up until the war. In the rest of Canada, the big cities, Winnipeg and Toronto, they were using heroin. Then the war came and the opium supplies came to an end. For a couple of years there was nothing. The black-market was supplied by doctors in Canada or thefts from big hospitals or big wholesalers and so on. But not much. Then about 1944 heroin started to show on the street—it was coming from Mexico—it was brown 'H.' Then shortly after that other heroin, from I presume Marseilles, or wherever, started to show, and from there on it was all heroin. After the war, opium never did come back.

He became hooked on heroin during the latter part of the war and was rejected for military service as an addict. During the period of his addiction in Canada—from about 1945 until he left in the early 1960's—the cost of his habit varied considerably. "There were times that it cost me maybe $20 a day and there were times that it cost me $60 to $70 a day, you know."

He finds it difficult to measure his dosage by the usual standards.

See, Canada, to the best of my knowledge, always had stronger stuff on the street than they had around New York and Detroit, and so on, much stronger. For the price. And a capsule (these small capsules, they call them Number 5 caps) they should hold roughly about a grain. But this is a grain of pure stuff, not the stuff that's generally cut. In Canada you were getting stuff I would say that averaged anywhere from 20 to 30 percent. Much superior to what was on the street anywhere in the States. And even in Canada it varied—like western cities through the years have generally had much stronger stuff than in the East, though in the East it's generally cheaper, so I guess these things sometimes balance out.

He tried withdrawal in Canada, but never successfully, even for a short time.

I went into a sanitarium in Ontario, but left after a few days. I under-went withdrawal under a couple of different doctors at home . . . [but] . . . I was never off for one day. I was never off for a day voluntarily:

the only time I was ever off was while I was in jail. I went into the sanitarium and nursing home out West once, you know, voluntarily. But I've never stayed off drugs for one day in Canada voluntarily.

He tried methadone. "But I found in my case it was useless. It was of no help."

In 1954 he went to prison with a four-year sentence.

For drugs. Just possession. That's all I had ever had charged. Never trafficking or selling or anything—it was always straight possession there. Canada's got the most severe laws in the world for drugs; more severe than the United States. A lot of people aren't aware of that. Even Canadian addicts aren't aware of it.

Did they try to maintain him on a drug in prison?

In the 'forties and 'fifties, when I went in, it was cold-turkey, nothing but cold-turkey. In the last few years there's been changes—out on the west coast (1 don't think in the east) they do give them a certain amount of withdrawal on methadone or something. But prior to that, it was just cold-turkey, that was it.

He had been married in Canada, and divorced because of drugs.

She wasn't an addict. We were married for about eight years, and I spent about three and a half of those years—perhaps four—in prison. That, and the hardships she had to endure during the year that I was out, made for a bad scene. So she finally got a divorce.

He came to England

because of the fact that drugs are legal here. This was the reason. I had heard for years, you know, that drugs were legal here. But you could never get any accurate information. You'd get conflicting information. But I thought they were legal here. And I discovered that at that time, under the immigration laws, any member of the British Empire, like a Canadian, couldn't be kept out of Britain. Even if he was a murderer, they couldn't keep him out, according to the immigration laws then.

He came over with his friend, fellow-addict, and gambling-partner, Giuseppe.

We came here in 1960 when gambling became legal here. In Canada, it's not legal; it's the same as in the States. And I had worked in different clubs in Canada—illegal clubs, you know—for periods of time.

We took advantage of the fact that it was legal here, and used what skill and knowledge we had of craps, dice, something more or less foreign to this country. This gave us an edge. As a result we have been dealers here, dealing poker and craps since we've been here.

But again, it was not the opportunity to gamble or the legality of gambling but the legality of drugs that brought them over. They sought refuge rather than riches.

Drugs was the only reason we came here. All I could see was me spending the rest of my life in prison in Canada. The Mounted Police there have been charging addicts. You see, in Canada if you've got three previous convictions, they have what they call the Habitual Criminal Act: they can put you in prison for life. And the Mounted Police have been using that for years against addicts. Right now there's two or three hundred addicts—maybe five or six hundred—doing life in Canada. And I could see myself being one of them. So I thought the time had come, in fact been long past, for me to get out. And my only regret is that I didn't come twenty years before I did.

In the English drug-scene they found

a world of difference. Absolutely. There were very few addicts when we came here in 1960, and, oddly enough, the doctors themselves didn't know very much about it, you see? We landed in Liverpool, we drove down to London, and we had a little stuff to last us so we thought we better start inquiring. We went to two or three doctors and they threw up their hands: "Oh, no, I'm not allowed to treat you." So we thought, "What the hell? What's going on?"

We finally went to a lady doctor. She said, "If you're agreeable, I'll call up Scotland Yard and ask them." So we figured, "Well, what the hell, we may as well find out one way or another. Go ahead." She called and said, "I have two Canadian addicts here. What should I do?" They told her to phone the Home-Office drug department, and so on. She asked us again if she should do that and I said all right. She called them, and they told her to go ahead and treat us. "Go ahead, prescribe." She asked how much she should prescribe at a time, and they said, "Give them a week's supply at a time."

She was a National Health doctor, and she wouldn't accept any money. We went to the chemist and we come out of his shop and just sat in the car glassy-eyed. Here we were with bottles of hundreds of tablets they had given us for nothing. And it was perfectly legal, you know . . . and all the years we'd spent in prison fighting to survive and everything, and here. . . .

The doctor referred them to Lady Franco, a consulting psychiatrist who had once treated alcoholics and had started to treat addicts. They stayed with her until her death in 1967.

They had been used to buying black-market heroin by the ounce in Canada because it was much cheaper, costing between $400 and $650, about one-third what it would have cost on the street, by the cap. Because of this difference and the differences in strength, they were not sure what their habits were, as expressed by the milligram or grain of pure British heroin.

> They wanted us to tell them in grains what we were using. So we took a guess, and I said "16" and Giuseppe said "12." It turned out to be too low. So you could say that our habits increased, but they didn't increase really. After a couple of months with Lady Franco jockeying them up and down, we finally leveled off. Me at 20 grains and Giuseppe at 25.

Giuseppe also used cocaine; Isaac did not. "We stayed at that dose all along for years and years, you know, until the clinics opened." The clinics lowered them, gradually, to 14 grains apiece. But they could not get along on that.

> We've had to buy stuff ever since we got down to 18. We've been buying an average of six to eight grains a day. The clinic knows that we are buying outside heroin. Our doctor—our family doctor—has argued with them. We were quite disgusted here because when we came to this clinic we were told by the head doctor at that time that at no time would they ever reduce us involuntarily. They would never forcibly reduce us. And we also had them check with Scotland Yard to prove to their satisfaction that we had never at any time sold any stuff here, all through the years.
> I've written numerous letters about it, to everybody but the Queen. Our argument was that if we'd ever sold any stuff here at any time, even if they didn't have the proof, the Home Office or Scotland Yard would have at least heard some kind of rumor or something. And they never had. Our second argument was that we could have got much more stuff than we were getting if we wanted to, but we didn't because we didn't need it. We leveled off and stayed at that amount, voluntarily, all through the years. We felt that we were stabilized and should have been left that way. Now they promised to do that. That doctor— the Senior Registrar here then—said they would. Then, six months

or so later, he turned around and said, "We've decided to reduce you whether you like it or not." He denied that he had ever made that promise: "I never tell a patient that, and I didn't tell you that." They just went ahead and it got to the point where we had to go and score.

Finally Dr. Connell met us. We had tried to get to see him for two months, but he was too busy. When we finally did see him, he said, "I'll tell you what I'll do. I'll leave it at fourteen" (at that time we were down to fourteen grains each) "and I'll promise you that I won't cut you any further, unless there's a change in government policy or something. Otherwise I'll maintain you at this dosage." And that's been the story since.

They continue getting their supplement of heroin from the black-market. Being men with contacts, proficient at shooting angles, they have not had to buy it in Piccadilly.

Fortunately we were able to contact a couple of people that we've been able to get it off of, and get it a lot cheaper than we would have had to if we were buying at the 'Dilly.

Isaac has not tried to withdraw in England. Generally, he and Giuseppe have deliberately avoided contacts with other addicts. They have retained contact with a few that they knew back in Canada. He mentions Graf. And

there's another chap here that I know, who incidentally has to leave the country soon because he came over here a couple years ago on one of those six-month renewal things, and now they won't renew.

The laws in relation to immigrants from Canada have changed, and toughened; Canadians are treated much as other immigrants, including those from the United States.

How does the English system compare to those he knew in North America? He finds it vastly superior, but is very disturbed about current trends.

It's obviously superior. There's no question about it. Anybody that argues that it isn't is ridiculous. They treat addiction as it should be treated. It's a medical problem, not a police problem. And the only bad things about this system are those they copied from the Americans.

Their attitude up until the changeover to the clinics [1968] was the proper attitude. A private doctor treated a patient as he saw fit. Now they blame the spread of addiction on a half a dozen doctors who were overprescribing, which in my opinion is pure nonsense. I've read the Brain Committee Report numerous times, and it's an hysterical document. It's a vindictive document, and an untrue one. I could point out line by line things that were not only wrong, but deliberately misleading. For example, if a doctor, a scientific man, wants to discuss the amount of drugs that another doctor is prescribing, to start with, the only way he would really describe the amount is in grains, or in milligrams, whatever the case might be. He wouldn't say that the other doctor was prescribing a "hundred pills" because, scientifically, that means nothing. What size are the pills? There are various sizes.

But the Brain Report gives all the figures in numbers of pills. "Such and such a doctor prescribed, in a period of such and such a time, so many thousands of pills." See? Now, why? One good reason could be that since they were sixth-grain pills, this made it sound six times as much as it actually was. In other words, if they had said "one hundred grains" instead of "six hundred pills," a hundred doesn't sound as bad as six hundred. Second place, they didn't even give the figures how many addicts the doctors were treating. So to say that a doctor's prescribing thousands of pills without telling how many patients he's got . . . you follow me? This is completely unscientific and can have only one purpose, to mislead and alarm. And it's served that purpose. The papers here went stark mad. And for a year they screamed and blamed the spread of addiction on these few doctors.

After Lady Franco died, they went to a Dr. Rocher, who was to become notorious for overprescribing. "Oddly enough, the Home Office sent us to him," but "we left Rocher because of all the publicity he was getting."

Since we came here drugs have become a secondary thing in our life, you understand? We wanted to keep it that way. We felt that just like a diabetic, you need insulin. And we wanted to keep it sort of in the background. So when Rocher started getting all this publicity, we didn't even want to be near him. So we finally changed to a private physician who agreed to take care of us until the clinics opened. Everybody knew they were coming in in a few months.

Again, drugs had been for us, for the ten years here, a secondary thing in our life, until this business now with the clinics. Now it's become a hardship again, you see? Because we now have to raise money to get the. . . . And it makes no sense, you know. The clinic's prepared to prescribe 14 grains . . . why not 18? But Dr. Connell has told me twice, "My policy here is never to go up, never to go up; always down."

Fourteen grains, Isaac says, does not even keep him feeling normal. Many other long-time addicts report that the goal for years past has not been to get much of a "buzz" but merely to go on feeling "normal." "Just like a diabetic, you need insulin."

What seems to disturb Isaac most about the greater control over drugs exercised under the clinics since the Brain Report is the trend they indicate, the direction the British system seems to be taking. "And the only bad things about this system are those they copied from the Americans."

I think that the clinics here, the system they have here, even now, is a thousand percent better than there. Naturally. Secondly, I think that the spread of addiction here has nothing to do with the method of disposal, of distribution and so on, of the drugs. It's perhaps a little beyond me, but I think it's a worldwide thing.

Here in London, the responsibility wasn't where the Brain Committee Report put it. I think that the best system of handling addiction was what they had prior to the clinics. Even if some of the doctors did overprescribe, there was nothing to stop the medical association from doing something—even to go as far as to take away his license to prescribe, or even to practice. They claimed that they didn't have that power, but they did, and they finally acknowledged it. Therefore there was never any need to switch to clinics. They claimed that without the clinics they couldn't control the doctors—well, that just wasn't true.

He thinks that the organization of the clinics not only made the rise of a black-market in drugs inevitable but will cause it to grow and become increasingly powerful, moving along the path he dreads, toward the patterns of North America.

Yes, yes. Because the clinics, it seems to me, are more concerned with being able to show that they're putting out less and less heroin than with real treatment. And from the stories I've heard from the other clinics—apparently this applies to all of them, right through—they're not interested in the patient so much as just to be able to show at the end of the year that they cut down on the heroin dosages. They want to be able to say, "We were putting out such and such amount of heroin at the beginning of the year; now we're putting out such and such an amount less. Therefore we have been successful." The fact that their patients may be going out and buying on the black-market, that they may be turning to nembutals and this and that to try to get through the day—that's just ignored, you know. I think the black-market will continue as long as the present attitude continues.

But there's nothing to stop them from changing that attitude. I definitely think they should change. The addicts that they figure they can treat and cure, good. And the ones they can't, they should maintain them. But maintain them. Don't just make a show of it. Don't keep them on a dosage that's not equivalent to what they need.

Giuseppe the One-Time Shoplifter

Part of Giuseppe's story has already been told. He is Isaac's partner in gambling and his companion and friend, and their lives have been intertwined since they met about 30 years ago. They came over to England together, set up in business together, sought and secured drugs together; and the story Isaac told of his vicissitudes in going from doctor to doctor, and then to the clinic, and having his drugs cut, is the story of both.

Giuseppe is 49. He is white, of Italian descent, was born a Roman Catholic in Canada. He was a religious Catholic, he says, until about 18, but is so no longer. "No, no."

He had two years of high school, then, like Isaac, left. "Looking back, I can only blame it on the environment." Both parents were born in Italy. The father operated a poultry business. He was uneducated; but Guiseppe's mother had gone through high school, including some schooling in Canada.

Also like Isaac, he doesn't mention working at any trade except gambling, which he "started at a very young age." Nevertheless, he "developed into a professional gambler and croupier." He met Isaac when 19, and, except "when he was away or I was away," including jail sentences, they have been associated ever since.

He was married in 1944, and separated a year later. He has no children. They were "just not compatible." She was an addict also, and older than he.

He has been jailed, in Canada, seven or eight times. "Always, you know, related to drugs." Whether related to drugs or not, his longest sentence was for "a swindle . . . larceny" for three years. With time off, he served about 28 months and ten days.

He has never been jailed in the United States, and, he says, has never pushed drugs anywhere. He has never lived in the United States, but has "been through it often, working, hopscotching here and there."

While in prison he had to withdraw cold-turkey. The longest he has ever been withdrawn from drugs, since addiction, except in prison, is six weeks.

He drank alcoholic beverages for a while, but here he differs from Isaac, who drinks wine steadily. Giuseppe drank

> for a while, but it was getting out of hand so I just stopped it entirely about a year ago. . . . I could go through two bottles of liquor, whiskey, a day. It was, you know, ridiculous. So I stopped it altogether.

He has never used amphetamines or LSD. He used marijuana "years ago, as a kid. But I don't even remember the effects." He has been using barbiturates for the past seven years in England. They were prescribed by Lady Franco

> because I was using a great amount of drugs at the time, including cocaine, and cocaine has a tendency to, you know, make you very high-strung, and so, as a result, I began taking Nembutals to counteract it. Just orally.

He first began to use narcotics when about 19.

> I was partners with a jockey; we grew up together, and at a very young age we were around the racetrack, you know, every day. And he became a prominently well-known jockey at the time. He began using drugs. And naturally, me being with him, you know, all the time practically, I went along with it.

They started with morphine. Shortly after, he was addicted.

He did not switch to heroin by choice. "It wasn't a case of deciding; it was a case of necessity at the time. It was during World War II. There was no heroin available when I began using." And then suddenly it came on the market, and his addiction switched over to it. At times he spent as much as $100 a day for his habit.

He left with Isaac in 1960. "We thought it would be a good idea to get away from all that pressure back home, and try to live a comparatively normal life."

He knew of no illegal selling of drugs when they came, "because doctors were prescribing, and were prescribing pretty well what the patient asked for and required."

He and Isaac followed the same route of doctors, including leaving Dr. Rocher when they became aware that he "wasn't dependable." Their habits differ somewhat, however. Giuseppe takes barbiturates; he started cocaine about nine years earlier, getting it from Dr. Franco, who also later prescribed the Nembutal to diminish some of the effects of the cocaine. Why cocaine? "Well, I just wasn't satisfied, and I was afraid of drinking; and I thought—well I heard, you know—others were using it too." So he thought he might as well try it.

His habit has decreased since they came to England, not entirely by voluntary means. The 25 grains he received daily through Dr. Franco was, he thinks, about the same he had been taking when he left Canada. He gets heroin from the black-market to supplement the 14 grains the clinic gives him daily. He needs, he feels, a minimum of 18 grains altogether.

He also takes seven grain-and-a-half pills of Nembutal daily. He would like to come off of them "just like I would like to stop using heroin—if somebody could wave a magic wand and say, you know, you're going to be all right."

He has, however, succeeded in withdrawing from cocaine. "I withdrew myself. I asked them here to reduce me, and I gradually came off it."

In England he and Isaac have been arrested only once, about two years after they came, for shoplifting. In Isaac's words: "Well, it was Christmas time, and we were short of money and there was some people we wanted to send some presents back to. Some men's dressing gowns, about four of them." They were let off with a fine, and have not been in trouble of that kind since.

Their average weekly income runs to 80 or 90 pounds, a very respectable wage for addicts.

He shares Isaac's preference for the system before the clinics came in. "I think the system when we first came over here was as good a system as one could hope to find. It may not have been perfect, but it was as close to being perfect as one could hope." He feels it changed his entire life.

I was able to live a normal existence with no pressure on me and not having to worry about the door come crashing in, being arrested for even having a spoon or a trace of drugs in my possession. It was like being in another world.

About the clinics: "Well perhaps I'm a little prejudiced because of the drastic reduction in my heroin. . . . But I preferred it when doctors were able to prescribe."

Secret Tunnels Open in the Walls: Claude the Architect

He was born in Boston. Before coming to England, he lived in the East Village. Although the East Village is a bohemian and hippie center, with a lot of drugs available, and full of drug-addicts, dependents, and experimenters of various kinds, and though he did join in the life sufficiently to take marijuana there, he did not get on to heroin until about five months after he crossed the Atlantic. He came to England in July, 1955, and started to take heroin during a trip to Paris that November.

Despite being an acute observer—and despite a trip back to the United States during which he stayed off drugs—he is not really familiar with the American drug-scene, and has, in particular, no first-hand knowledge of an addict's life there. Unlike almost all the other bi-national addicts interviewed, he did not come to England because of drugs, and his experiences tend to have more in common with the native British dependents than with the addict immigrants, or drug-refugees.

He is white, 46, was born conservative Jewish. He professes little religion now. He entered the army during World War II, at 18, spent four years in the army, was married, went back to college when he came out, and was divorced. "My wife and I didn't see eye-to-eye about very many things."

An educated man, he worked as an architect in the United States. He did not hold any job long "because in the States it's traditional in architecture that young men work for a year or a year and a half in a job and then move on. That's the way they get the experience and clip for the raises, and so on."

He took marijuana in the East Village, enjoyed it, and "I still do when I can get it."

> There was a junk-scene in the Village; there always was. And there was people that I was fairly close to that were on it. But I didn't want to know, and nobody inveigled me in, so that was fine.

Pressed, later on, to explain why he had come to take heroin although he had some knowledge of its effects, he concluded that he must be a self-destructive person. "I knew all about it, I'd known a couple of junkies." In the East Village

> I knew my friends were popping it and that anybody that was on it was in desperate trouble. They were stealing stuff and so on, you know. These people would come and ask me could they stay in my pad, and, you know, I had to look out that they didn't take the furniture, and so on.

He was arrested in the United States only once—for "vehicle homicide." "I was absolutely not culpable, and they had to sling me in because night-court in New York was closed." He was neither drunk nor stoned on marijuana. "Somebody just ran out in front of the car on a rainy night." He was not sentenced. "You know, the police said, 'You poor guy. We have to keep you overnight, but it's not your fault.' "

Some time after his divorce, he married for the second time. "I met a girl and we liked each other and lived together for three years in New York. When it came time for me to come here, we got married, because we wanted to have children. We now have four children."

His first job in Europe was with the American Air Force in England. He was able to hold on to it even after he had become addicted.

> As long as I was with this Air Force business, it was all right; because that was a pipe dream. I mean the whole thing was a pipe dream. Anybody that had any sense at all and had the ability to speak could get on. I was a liaison type between our forces and their ministry.

There are elements in Claude's story that would seem to support the American law-enforcement attitude toward drug-addiction. He did not become addicted in the United States, at least partly because he was afraid—to such an extent that he withdrew and stayed completely off during his trip back. It was only in the more permissive

European atmosphere that he became hooked; and he was led to it, in large part, by his desire for cannabis.

> I got to England in July, 1955, and I went back to Paris for a few days, a little less than a week. And I ran into somebody that I used to know in Paris as a hash connection, and, well, it was through him that I got involved in horse.
>
> I knew an Arab in Paris and he gave me incredibly good deals, and I used to go back there every three or four months to pick up. . . . I don't really know what was in it, of course, because you can't tell what the composition was, but for a four-ounce liquid medicine-bottle stuffed with powder, I'd pay 30 to 40 thousand francs. This used to last about three or four months.

For two years he did not inject; he simply "snorted," or sniffed heroin up his nostrils, and he did not snort daily.

> I was up in Lancashire (the base I was working at was way up north), but I would come to London, and I had a friend with an apartment here who gave me a room. I used to drive down here weekends and use it on the weekends.

Did his wife know about it?

> Well, at the beginning she knew all about it because she used to use it on weekends with me, actually. But she never really went very far on it at all. She didn't like it. She toyed with heroin.

He decided he was addicted during a trip to Paris with another girl, with whom he was having an affair.

> She and I were in about the same boat, but we suddenly came out of it one morning to realize that we'd been there for a week and we hadn't had any days off. We sort of assumed we were [addicted]. We'd been on it for a solid week fairly heavy, and we thought this was probably it. Anyway, we didn't make any experiments to find out. We had stacks of it.

He was still snorting; and, unlike many of those who snorted for long periods, he had had few bad physical effects. His nasal septum has apparently not been damaged to any great extent, and he has had no stomach cramps.

> I had had a drippy nose for a long time. I can't remember whether it

started with that or some time before that. I have a post-nasal drip—"It's a pip," as the old song goes.

He had thought, even after he started to inject, that because he was a foreigner he could not be registered.

And there was another thing: I was working for the Air Force, and the penalties for being on when you're on an Air Force base all the time were incredible. I didn't want any kind of feedback, kickback, or anything else. But when I began to learn my way around and realized that this so-called registration didn't really exist at all, there wasn't any list available to anybody . . .

he was willing to be registered.

He started injecting, as he remembers, about 1958. What happened then? When did he decide that he should do something about his addiction?

Well, I don't know exactly when this happened; it's something I probably arranged for myself, I don't know why. But one morning I finally realized that I had next to nothing left, I didn't have either the money or the opportunity to go back to Paris, and things were going to be pretty tough. So I went all over trying to find some doctor to get registered with and I didn't make out; and I finally made out on the black-market after going half of cold-turkey.

I found someone that would give me two grains a day, steadily, and I used to buy from him. And then he either got arrested or died or disappeared or something, and I was in trouble again. Then I managed to get on a list, as it were, with a doctor who is now deceased also, named Lady Franco. . . .

As close as I can estimate it, that would have been about 1958, something like that. And, well, she was a very funny woman in many ways. And one day that I was complaining that I was not getting enough sleep and I found it hard to stay awake at night and so on, she asked me if she'd given me any cocaine "lately." She had never given me any cocaine, but I only answered the question she'd asked me, so I wound up on both of them.

And that really fixed me up. I was on cocaine from then until 1964, a good solid five years. And it really ruined me; I lost job after job, and I couldn't work, and this and that, and we were on assistance, and, oh, it was great, a great performance. I have a big family. To make things even nicer, I got a case of hepatitis.

Despite his bad experiences with cocaine, he still feels hunger for it.

Oh yeah, I die for it every time I think of it. But it does me absolutely no good, I get terrible hallucinations, I get the horrors something awful, I'll fall asleep over my work, and I'll sweat and all this and that and the other thing. I get as paranoid as you could possibly get, or at least as possible for me to get.

He does not get antagonistic, but "shit-scared."

I see secret tunnels opening in the walls and everything else, you know, and it's really too much. And yet if, by some mischance, they started to give it to me here I wouldn't refuse it. I know I wouldn't. . . . Oh, I would try to rationalize it, I suppose, that I would manage it better this time or something. But I wouldn't.

Except during his experience with cocaine, he has always managed to earn a living for his family. He stayed with the Air Force job until he decided to quit to go into the antiques business. "Five years is enough work at an air base. It was very boring."

The antiques business, however, turned out over the long term to be a disaster.

At one point I put everything into a shipment of stuff in the States . . . no drugs, no junk in any sense. No smuggling involved in it. Unfortunately, we had a dock-strike at that point and everything I owned stayed tied up in the London docks for three or four months. When I finally did get to go, everybody else's shipments got to go at the same time, so there was a big glut in the States—everything showed up at once. And I had a very bad time for a while.

He stayed with the antiques business until it failed, "until I finally went broke on it. Then I played poker for about six months. I stayed alive that way." Earning a living at poker, he considered himself a professional player.

Not that anybody hired me. I just won enough to keep the family going for six or seven months that way. But I began to get swollen ankles from sitting up all night, and it was a bit nerve-racking as well. And there came a time when there seemed to be a little lull in things. As long as there were plenty of expensive tourists and Persian princes and airline pilots around it was okay; but then things got slack and there was nobody around but the sharks. They couldn't feed off each other. So I went to work again. I had had little part-time jobs from time to time. I worked in a bedding-shop part-time for a while, while the antiques business was folding up.

The first job he got after withdrawing from cocaine in May, 1964, he held for two and one-half years.

> Then I went to another office—I won't say I was all that good. I've gotten the push from time to time from some of these places, too . . . usually for not wanting to do things the way they want me to do them.

At the time of the interview, he had been working at his latest job for the better part of a year. Apart from the cocaine, did he feel that drugs affected his ability to work?

"Oh, sure. I used to be a red-hot hotshot. Now I'm a red-hot fake. It's not really very good."

While he was on cocaine, he parted company with Lady Franco.

> I was on National Assistance at the time. . . . And she said that I couldn't afford to be a patient and get private prescriptions and pay, you know, a pound out of two pounds a day for a script. So she said I should get under a National Health doctor somewhere, and therefore cut me off.
>
> I did finally manage to get a National Health Service doctor. It was quite a sweat. I had to go back to Lady Franco and howl and go over and blackmail her into giving me another couple of days, and so forth and so on.

At that time he was on eight grains of heroin and eight grains of cocaine daily. He considers his National Health Service doctor, Dr. Owendorf, to be "about the best there is. . . . He's no self-seeker, that's for sure. I thought he was very, very good. And he did a lot for me in a practical way, too." He stayed with Dr. Owendorf until the clinics opened.

Had he ever attempted withdrawal with any of these doctors?

> Oh, yes. I did it once with Franco before I was on coke. I had to go back to the States for a business trip. I thought I was gonna be gone for four or five weeks, but it turned out to be four or five months. And I just cut down a little at a time and I had the last pill the day before I went. And somebody ran into me the same day and gave me 165 pills. And I thought, well, that would keep me for four or five weeks, that's great. But I chickened out and I flung them down the toilet on the boat train, which is the best thing I ever did, because I wound up there for four or five months, and I just wouldn't have made it. (And the only reason I stayed off was because I was shit-scared, you know.)

While I was in New Orleans somebody got busted for benzedrine and he got four or five years. So you know, I just didn't go ask anybody; I just did without, and that was that.

But he went back to heroin as soon as he returned. "I was on the next day, practically."

He tried again, two or three years later. He found it to be much harder, because this time he was on cocaine. But

I got kind of desperate and I asked Franco to put me in a hospital and she said she was too busy that week and so on and so on. This went on for quite a while, and then one night I busted into a chemist's shop up in Logan Lane and I almost got caught—I got away by the skin of my teeth. And I went to my family's doctor who hated the sight of me. But I finally managed to get a letter from him to a psychiatrist at [a hospital by] Hyde Park Corner on Knightsbridge Road. He was very good about it and got me a bed immediately, which at that time was very hard to do—they were overloaded. They knocked me out with something . . . and I slept for about three or four days, off and on; mostly sort of half-conscious. And I had no particular trouble. No discomfort at all, that I can remember.

I was getting in fights in the hospital, and finally I fixed up through the music therapist to see a consultant that was around there. And he said that he thought the best thing to do was for me to work somewhere and live in the hospital. And I said, "Well, you know, I have a family and all that. How long do you think I have to keep on like that? A year, two years?" And he said, "Well, what's a year, what's two years?"

And I left. I had things fixed up with Franco on the phone before I left.

As soon as he came out he was back on.

This was the last time he tried to get off all drugs. But when he was hospitalized in 1964 for hepatitis he used the opportunity to get off cocaine altogether, and to cut his heroin-habit down. When he went in, his habit was eight grains of heroin and eight of cocaine. When he came out, just before Christmas, he was down to a grain and a quarter of heroin and no cocaine. His heroin-habit is now back up to nine grains, but he is still off cocaine. Like the rest of the addicts, he has been with the clinic since it opened.

The clinic system is a pain in the ass, but you know I should imagine it's containing it a bit more than it was before. Because when any physician could do it there was always a Rocher around or somebody.

A man of considerable native ability, he is making a living, but not a very good one. In the United States, before leaving, he was making $7,800; at the air-base, at the time of his addiction, he earned the equivalent of $13,000; now he gets the equivalent of about $6,000. He feels that drugs are to blame.

A girl he loved, the one he took to Paris and stayed with for some weekends, is dead as the result of an overdose. He believes it was an accident—the doctor who treated them both says it was—but the suspicion of suicide in such situations is always strong.

He has little respect for himself, and is inclined toward depression.

> I have a predilection for doing the wrong thing, you know. Every time I've had an opportunity to do the wrong thing, I've seen the path clearly outlined before me, and gone right ahead. It's something I've done all my life.
>
> I'm depressed because I'm sitting here thinking about my married life, which is a complete fiasco.

Do his children suspect his drug habit?

> The oldest boy must if he's got any sense. He's 14. At his school they have trouble about this sort of thing. I think he's probably caught on by now. He doesn't say anything about it. Which is all to the good, I guess.

Would he consider his sex-life adequate? "Not with my wife it isn't." But he does have sex relations with other women.

He takes no barbiturates. But

> I don't sleep at all, hardly at all. The only sleep I get usually is from about 2:30 in the morning until about 5:00 in the morning. I can't sleep in my own bed, put it that way.

He would, however, fall asleep "standing up, or in a corner, in the kitchen. . . . But once I met this girl, now I get a few hours' sleep at her house, almost every night."

He used amphetamines a little, for awhile, "just for kicks, when I was out, you know, helling around at night. But that's about all. I've tried methedrine and I don't like it at all." But he does use a dexedrine, "only to wake up every morning. I fall asleep too much during the day without them." He gets 60 five-grain tablets a week, but doesn't use them all.

He does not use LSD. He has used mescaline, when back in the States, and "it was a terrific thing. I enjoyed it a lot." If he was content with mescaline, could he have stayed with it and kept away from heroin? He doesn't think so; and speaks again of his "predilection" for accepting the wrong option, if it is presented to him.

Despite the circumstances of his own addiction, he does not think that marijuana leads to heroin.

> That's all bull. It does in the sense that it puts you in contact with people who turn on. In fact, it is through grass that I got on too. I went to get hash for somebody, and when they couldn't pay for it they said, 'Will you take some 'H' instead?' And that was how. . . .
>
> But as far as I can tell, there wasn't anything addictive about grass. I've read any number of stories and books where somebody's always dying for it, for a joint. But this isn't true as far as I know, except in the same psychological sense or whatever it is that people get addicted to cigarettes or alcohol.

And despite his own abstention and withdrawal in America, he believes that the system for containing addiction in Britain is superior to that of America.

> Because there's not as much money to be made in it, and so it doesn't attract the gangsters. I mean, I should think that outside of any reasoning about it—how many addicts are there in the States?

There are perhaps 60,000 in New York alone, and only (at the time of the interviews) about 2,000 in England.

> Okay, if everyone of those was carrying three others on his back—which they're not because they don't get enough—there'd still be only 8,000. I don't think the civilizations are so different that there's more of a reason for it in the States than here.
>
> It cost me a lot to be here, in a sense. But I like it here. The fact I stay here, I believe, doesn't have a lot to do with the fact that I'm on. I really mean it. I couldn't see myself going back to New York to live. Things are very different in the States than they were.

The Boys of
St. Giles'

> And I'm not the one to be a pessimist.
> I'm living the best life I ever lived. The
> only thing I can't get a flat. But Jesus!
> The United States!
>
> I wish you luck, of course; not for
> myself, but all the junkies . . . those poor
> dogs lying up in the Tombs, on the Ninth
> Floor, throwing up over each other. Dying
> —using drugs for what? It stinks.
>
> Let's face it: I'm a drug addict 19 years.
> The odds are I'll never stop. Right? So
> what am I gonna do? Live here or live in
> the United States? I'm gonna stay here.
>
> —*Harold the convict, living in England
> under an alias*

The immigrant addict occasionally has trouble being accepted into the British system. The British, understandably, are becoming increasingly cautious, and occasionally deport individuals who have had trouble with the law. Usually, however, the difficulties are indistinguishable from the red-tape and standardized routines common to any country. For instance, in the last year an American who had just come into the country, an employee of a major computer firm, came to St. Giles to see Dr. Willis, and attempted to be registered and to be maintained on heroin there. But Dr. Willis had his full quota of addicts and referred the man to Maudsley, in the hope that there might be more space there. At the Maudsley Center he was told that he would have to go outside and be maintained by a private physician on methadone (private physicians are still allowed to administer methadone), and that he might then seek in-patient or outpatient maintenance. If the addict can survive this kind of shuttling about and uncertainty about where he is going to get his next fix long enough, he will presumably be accepted and become one of the Maudsley or St. Giles regulars. The law is still lenient enough so that the foreigner who sincerely needs help, and will obey the laws, can ultimately receive maintenance. Obviously, as the problems and abuses grow, difficulties for foreigners will also grow.

Like other center directors, Dr. Willis has given a great deal of thought to the broader aspects of drug addiction and treatment and what may be done about them, and has done considerable research into the mechanisms of addiction, in the hope that the conclusions might lead toward the causes, and eventually to techniques for amelioration. Some of his analyses and conclusions, reflecting the nature of the problems and addicts he deals with daily, are contained in two papers comparing the histories and characteristics of samples of American addicts and British addicts.

Both reports compare similar age-groups in London and New York. In "The Natural History of Drug Dependence" (Willis, in *29;* nos. in italic refer to the list of references, p. 204), all subjects were hospitalized heroin in-patients, all under 25. Those in London (42 males, 16 females) averaged perhaps two years younger than those from the New York hospital (35 male, 15 female). All subjects were identified as addicts, with histories of daily self-injection with heroin for more than six months, and unequivocal evidence of dependence.

Asked who had first introduced them to heroin, they most commonly responded, as might be expected, "a friend"—although that friend on closer examination usually turned out to be some casual acquaintance. Significantly,

the only incidence of introduction to drugs by a "pusher" or professional peddler of drugs was found in U.S. subjects. This reflects the absence of a professional black market. [Often that good friend who introduced the U.K. addict to heroin did it to pick up a little extra money, using a surplus he had perhaps inveigled out of a doctor, and to this extent might be considered a pusher; but he was not part of a professional group trafficking for profit.] Author's note.

Common belief, and common mythology, holds that "elevation of mood"—euphoria—is the most persuasive reason for taking heroin; but fewer than a fourth of the British addicts and an even smaller portion of United States addicts gave it as their motivation. The most common reason was "curiosity about effects"; this reply was overwhelmingly predominant among United States addicts, and about broke even, among U.K. addicts, with the "desire to raise a depressed mood." Of the United States males, three of 35 mentioned interest in overcoming depression: the United States females—five of 15—gave the second lowest number of responses in this category. It is unclear to what extent we can trust the statements about "curiosity," especially since they involve so much hindsight. But it is clear that "kicks" were not the primary motivation: in Willis' words, "they had ill formulated expectations about drug effects," didn't really know, or think clearly about, what they were getting into. The four American males and one of each of the female groups who said they had been "persuaded by others" were found without exception to be "ineffectual individuals of low intelligence who had moved into drug use [for] . . . acceptance."

The differences between the groups reflect the differences that characterize the drug-scenes of the two nations. Consistently, the United States addicts started earlier; 50 percent of them had been exposed to heroin by age 16, over a third by age 15. In the U.K., heroin has only recently been available, and no U.K. addict was found who had taken his first dose before 15. It was not until 1960 that the first heroin addict under 20 became known to the Home Office. Commonly, United States addicts started by "snorting," but the powdered heroin used in snorting is not available in the U.K.

Daily self-injection—the signal by which the onset of addiction is recognized—varied considerably. In general, U.K. addicts seemed to start daily self-injection a little earlier; but this figure is affected by the fact that the largest number of U.K. female addicts started "immediately." Willis finds that the U.K. females "as a group showed a consistently higher level of personal and familial pathology." The modal range of irregular drug use was wide, ranging from one to six months.

The figures also led Willis to an important corollary conclusion:

> The pure English heroin as opposed to its heavily adulterated U.S. equivalent has often been incriminated as a more potent addictive substance, but these figures do not appear to support such a contention.

Once more the familiar question arises: Why? Surely a purer and heavier dosage of heroin must have considerably greater pharmacological and physical effects. The answer must lie in that poorly defined and charted realm of psychological addiction, and in the complex interplay of psychological and psycho-physical factors.

When both groups were questioned about other drug use, the U.K. addicts were far ahead. About 94 percent of U.K. addicts used amphetamines, compared to 28 percent of American addicts. The use of LSD was about 40 percent for the U.K. group, 8 percent for the Americans; the latter spoke of LSD with misgivings, while the U.K. addicts were enthusiastic. A sizeable number of U.K. addicts injected other opiates, particularly morphine, but only one American did. Cocaine is very popular in the U.K.: 33 of 42 males, and all the females, used it, while of the United States group only one male and one female (2 percent) did. Willis's study supported previous findings that alcohol was a frequent precursor of opiate use, occurring among about 40 percent of U.K. and 28 percent of the American dependents. In the latter—particularly among Puerto Ricans—the pattern reported included bouts of wine-drinking among the very young. In all cases, the addicts had stopped alcohol once addicted to heroin.

In his second study, using the same subjects (*31*), Willis found that U.K. addicts experienced greater decline in social class after becoming addicted. This is hardly surprising, since United States addicts come predominantly from lower strata of society. Willis noted a considerably higher percentage of Roman Catholics among the American addicts—again a reflection of slum origins, in this case because of the great numbers of Puerto Ricans studied. Addicts in both nations tended to come from broken or disturbed families: the addicts recorded considerably higher percentages of parental loss through death or separation, and of parental addiction and alcoholism, than among the general populations. He found high rates of addiction among the children of addicts in America, considerably higher than in Britain. This finding may reflect the fact that addiction has been a problem in the United States for a much longer time, and on a much larger scale, than in the U.K. There was a consistently high rate of truancy in childhood among both groups—a critical finding, since truancy is often an important indicator of general delinquent behavior. Truancy among addicted children, of course, is hardly surprising; and America has a greater percentage of very young addicts, or at least experimenters, than Britain has.

One of the most important findings has to do with the job histories of the two groups. The U.K. subjects had better records; they held more jobs longer. Willis suggests that this may be social in origin, apart from the drugs. There are always fewer job-opportunities for dark-skinned slum-dwellers than for the middle-class and working-class groups that make up much of the addict population in Britain. Both from observation and statistics and from the interviews with addicts who have been in both North America and England, and who often reflect this pattern in their own occupational histories, we feel that the British system also gives the addict in Britain greater opportunity to fit into the work force, and hold regular or irregular employment. The addicts who came from the United States and Canada were neither less addicted nor less desirable as employees when they arrived in England than during the years before; yet their work records—according to their own testimony—have been consistently better. An addict in the United States or Canada tends to have only one job, and one major interest—how to get his next fix. He has too much need of money, and too little time, to take and hold a regular job. Most of the immigrant addicts interviewed said that the British system allowed them to reduce the time, money and concentration devoted to their habits, and to devote them to other purposes such as earning a living.

Willis does not find significant differences in the number of arrests and court-appearances for drug-related offenses between his sample groups, but does concede "that thefts, etc., to support a drug habit are less common in this country [Britain]." This too is hardly surprising, both for the reasons we have given and because of the illegality of securing and possessing drugs in the United States. The addicts we interviewed, with few exceptions, stole, gambled, pushed, or otherwise broke the law to buy the heroin they needed in North America. In Britain, most of them worked—including the gamblers, since gambling is also legal in Britain.

Interestingly, some 50 percent of both U.K. and United States addicts showed homosexual inclinations or orientations. There was a high degree of impotence among both groups of males; although this is a common symptom among heroin addicts, it may also reflect the high homosexual component. Homosexuals are not highly sexed, and the confusion of roles, social rejection, and shame tend to complicate the pattern. By no means all of the men interviewed, however, gave the same response. Although most indicated that they had experienced some sexual diminishment, several were equivocal. The man who was impotent with his wife but not with his girl-friend is a case in point.

Willis found high incidence of personality disorders in both groups. He concluded:

> The overall impression, comparing the two groups, was of two series of highly disturbed individuals. In the U.K. series they appeared to have chosen drugs as a form of relief of turbulent feelings against a setting of intra-familial disturbance, with a negligible socio-economic deprivation. In the U.S. serious personal pathology was set clearly against a background of real material deprivation and environmental influences where delinquency and hopelessness seemed omnipresent.

Barbiturates in the Air-Force Beer: Ralph Williams

Willis: Not long after Ralph came, there was a bit of a clamor in the Aliens' Department to get him back to America. I resisted this because, as far as I could make out, he hadn't been misbehaving, he'd found a job—although, strictly speaking, it was not legal to employ him. You know, he was being very cooperative and sensible. . . . And here was this poor unfortunate fellow from the South, you know, who was really sort of doing his best, and they were all trying to get rid of him.

Klein: But he's a very intelligent person. It shocks me that he was sort of railroaded into this addiction therapeutically.

Willis: Also, of course, there was a curious paranoid element in his thinking somebody had put drugs in his beer in the army.

Klein: Worse things have been imagined about the American Army.

Willis: Well, there's a universal belief in the services throughout the world that people put bromide in the tea to suppress sexual activity, and so on, but his was a bit more firmly established than that.

Klein: As I understand it, if you're American or Canadian, and you come over to this country, you can get a work permit. Americans can have them as well as Canadians. And as soon as one comes in with a work permit—if he came over addicted—you can treat him in the clinics, provided he starts paying his stamps immediately.

Willis: I think that's what it amounts to, yes.

Klein: But if they're here just on a visitor's permit, they're treated privately?

Willis: Yes.

Klein: And if one gets a job and starts working, then you can treat him in the clinics?

Willis: Yes.

Klein: But if he commits a crime, then he can be deported. . . . And you can also deport him if he is over here as a visitor and goes off one day for a trip outside the country, and then tries to come back in?

Willis: Yes. I think you'll find that an American can be deported anyway—that they're merely here on sufferance, and the Home Office could withdraw their permission to stay. But they can't do this with Commonwealth citizens . . . unless, of course, they breach the agreement under which they came.

At the time of the interview Williams was 38 years old, a native of the South, where he was living when he came to England. He is white. He is a Methodist; his father was a Baptist, but followed his wife to the Methodist Church. Ralph was, he would say, "average religious," and still is. "I don't attend any church at all now, but I would say I'm fairly religious." He believes in the doctrines of his church.

His mother was a truant officer, "a pupil personnel supervisor now they call it, I think. She's retiring this year." She has a college degree from the same college he attended. His father had only a high-school education, and had been a farmer in Central Canada.

He graduated from high school and went to college for a short time. He got an appointment, through his congressman, to Annapolis, but decided not to take it. Instead, he left college in 1950 to join the Air Force, "which really led me into—I mean it was really the wrong step to take for a lot of reasons."

> I joined the Air Force, I believe, because I wanted to go ahead and get it over with. And I didn't think I wanted to make a career out of the service, which I would have done by going to Annapolis. Although I would also have gotten a good education. I regret turning it down for that reason.
>
> But I was also going steady with a girl that I sort of wanted to get away from. . . . I was unsettled, in other words. I wanted to party awhile, not ready to knuckle down like I knew I would have to at Annapolis.

But when he joined the Air Force,

> I found out that things were really pretty bad there. When I began to have trouble, I began to get sick. I had an attack with my stomach.

In the service he developed an ulcer, which was aggravated by his troubles.

> I went AWOL three times in the service. Two when I had an attack with my stomach. I had these attacks maybe twice a year, maybe just once a year. I had had a couple before I went in, when I was in high school; but there were long periods between, you know. Then the two when I went AWOL—I had them because I couldn't get any treatment in the service. One place I was stationed I went down to Base Complement Squadron and we didn't even have a doctor. They had to fly us to another base to see a doctor, and I was late for the plane, and they let the plane go off without me once . . . and things would happen. . . .

The nightmare deepened for him.

> In the last place I was stationed, there were reports that the beer was drugged, that it had a barbiturate in it. I know that Senator Kefauver came through with an investigating committee at about that time, because there were so many suicides, so many AWOL's—me for one. Gambling was wide-open, too. They said that Kefauver's visit was on account of gambling. But I believe that this beer being drugged had a big part to do with it.

His ulcer ruptured when he left the service in 1952. He was in the hospital for a week, in 1953, for an operation, and was given morphine to relieve the pain. After he left the hospital,

> I knew what it was. I knew it would relieve me. But I had no supply, I mean a place where I could get it. I didn't get it from . . . there weren't any pushers.

He became a heavy drinker. He worked "off and on" and traveled around considerably. Finally, in Florida, in 1959:

> I'd been drinking pretty heavily at the time I had met this particular girl I was going with, and to get off of the drinking I knew—I had had periods before—I knew I could get off of it if I had some medicine to stop pain and to relax the tension. I knew that morphine was what I really wanted because I had had it when I was in the hospital.

He had been to doctors before, and had received shots of morphine to relieve the pain and drinking, but he had not become addicted. Now he was suffering severe pain from kidney-stones.

> I called a doctor and he made a house call. And he gave me a shot. He gave me a shot that night and then left a prescription for 20 cc— morphine sulphate. And when I woke up the next morning the woman I was living with had had the prescription filled, and the vial was sitting on the dresser, with a syringe. So I had it right there. Naturally, I just kept on going to the doctor and he kept prescribing.

So he became addicted. "Really, he kept prescribing for a long time, several months. And nobody ever questioned him or anything. I had all the prescriptions filled at one druggist." Finally, the doctor wanted to quit. "But naturally I pitched a fit, and the woman I was living with, she went down to talk to him and got him to keep on prescribing with the stipulation that I'd go to the hospital." The doctor kept up the prescription until Williams finally went to the federal hospital "just because I promised him."

He went into the hospital in 1959. "I got good medication the first time, pretty good medication. The later treatments the medicine got smaller, and I had harder times kicking it." He stayed only about two weeks. "When I came out I was still sick. I thought I was better, I was over the real rough parts, but I still wasn't sleeping." He went back home.

> Then I had this woman that I was living with to meet me in Chattanooga, and had a fella drive me (I was too weak to drive the car) to Chattanooga. Then she drove my car on back down to Florida with me. I knew in Tennessee I could get paregoric, so I started buying it immediately.

It satisfied him temporarily. "But you have to run so fast. . . . You can only get half an ounce at a place, and it drives you, you have to go continually to get enough to do you."

When they reached Florida he returned to the doctor who had started him on his addiction, but the doctor would have nothing to do with him. "So I went to some other doctors, here, there, and got it." They moved to the large northern city from which the girl had come, and lived together for a while. "She was a real good girl, really. She thought a lot of me, and I did her. But I left her because of the addiction. I was just ruining her life."

He has used barbiturates, but doesn't like them—and reminds the questioner that they were put in his beer in the Air Force without his knowledge. He has also used tranquilizers—like the barbiturates, before his morphine addiction—but they "don't work well on me." He used Miltown "a long time ago," and has taken thorazine, which is used almost entirely in psychotherapy, but points out that "it makes you impotent."

He was given the thorazine in a mental institution to which he went on the recommendation of a Veterans' Administration psychiatrist. He was the only patient who had gone there voluntarily to reduce his drug-habit.

He injected morphine when he could get it, but usually avoided injecting paregoric:

> I have injected it, but I generally drank it. It's too much of a chore to cook all the alcohol out of it, and otherwise it burns your veins up badly.

He has smoked marijuana "a couple of times, and got sick both times." He has never taken LSD, mescaline or cocaine.

He has been using amphetamines since his discharge in 1953, when he first bought them illegally at a truck-stop across from his home. It gave him a buzz, and helped him stay up late to play cards. He does not consider himself addicted, and has not used them regularly, except when he met a druggist in Nashville who would sell them to him. "With the methedrine, I would pick up as much as I wanted. I'd get maybe 50 or 60 of the ampules and use eight or ten a day," injecting them. He was off and on them when he came to England. There he was given amphetamines again.

He has never dealt with the black-market for his opiates, or bought from a pusher. He did, he says, once buy methedrine from a pusher in Nashville; but never morphine or heroin.

He underwent treatment for addiction "a dozen times or more," each time voluntarily, at the federal hospitals at Lexington, Kentucky and Fort Worth, Texas.

> I had hopes the first few times. Then I realized that I was in the same old syndrome and I didn't *want* to quit. I knew it was hopeless, but I kept wanting to find a situation like the first one I had, with the doctor prescribing for me. I got along fine then, you know. I started my own business—even in that period when I was living with this woman—and had no trouble. As long as that doctor was prescribing it. . . .

He was on constant, regulated dosage.

He was arrested several times in America, "but only once on the drug business. I was with a friend; it was his fault that I got arrested." Another time he was arrested for drinking. This arrest involved "a misunderstanding."

> I was living with a girl in her uncle's house, and her uncle had a gun collection and he went on vacation and I got drunk and put the guns in the trunk of the car and was going to hock them.

He got money for drugs sometimes from a woman he was living with, often from his family, and he worked periodically. He knew about the situation in England—"it's common knowledge"—and decided to come as soon as he could get enough money together.

Then, "My father died, and they had a few acres left, and my mother, my sister and I were partners, and sold it. With my part I had enough to get over here."

He came to England in the latter part of 1968.

> I went to a doctor that had prescribed for me years before there, and another one, and I got enough medicine to get over here.

He brought some methadone and morphine. "Just a little." As soon as he came,

> I went to two or three doctors first, who told me about the clinics.
> I didn't know where the clinics were or how to go about it. So I had to move pretty fast. I was pretty lucky too, I guess. I went into St. George's clinic over here and an American doctor . . . he wanted to get in touch with a particular doctor that he had in mind for me.

And it was Dr. Willis that he got in touch with. Dr. Willis maintained him privately at first, then got him on the Health Service. He has been with Dr. Willis ever since. He is maintained on three grains of morphine and ten milligrams of methadone daily, and receives 28 tablets of dexedrine weekly.

Dr. Willis has left it completely up to him whether he will try to withdraw.

> I've been thinking that I will try it, yes. I've been thinking that I will. At first I had no doubt that it was best this way, that I could go ahead and at least help myself and live a legal and fairly useful life if I had the medication and didn't have to spend my time getting it one way or another.

He found that it was not difficult to hold a job while being maintained by the clinic.

> First I went to work for Ross Service, which the Home Office doesn't know anything about, I suppose—maybe they know about it, I don't know . . . but I didn't have a work permit. They were paying me, you know, for working for them, weekly, but they were paying me under the table, so to speak.

He is a self-taught repairman. When Ross found out that he was an addict, he left to take a job doing the same thing for another company, for which he could get a permit. The British, apparently, are not free of prejudice toward addicts. Among other jobs, he has worked as a manager-trainee for a chicken franchise, but says he "got ticks on my hands from some infected chickens, spread them around, then left and never bothered to come back." Most recently, he worked in a hospital as a porter, but left to try again for something in appliance repair.

He says he has a sex-life, but "it's infrequent." However, he has had affairs while he was addicted, and is considering marriage.

> I became engaged when I got here, and we sort of broke up because I haven't gotten off [drugs] yet. When I got engaged I said I would try. But I haven't been to the hospital yet, which is the try she is talking about. So I'm still considering whether to get off, and get married, and maybe plan a little bit for the future.

He still drinks a little, but only occasionally. His drug-habit has not increased. The quantity may even have decreased slightly, but "it has the effect of staying the same, really." He gets no buzz or euphoria now. "I'm past that stage. It is just a task that I have to perform to stay well." He has vague plans to return to North America, perhaps to Canada, but only if he is totally withdrawn from narcotics.

> Well, recently, when it has gotten to the point where the drugs just keep me well, and I don't get any pleasure at all out of them, I thought that I would try to get off of them and see if I could live without them. . . . If I could, then maybe it would be better for me to go to Canada. I could stay off easier, maybe. If I have trouble staying off, then I'm better off in England.

How does he compare the situations, and his experiences in the United States and England? He is unique in that although he was once jailed on a drug charge, he has never had to deal with the underworld for his drugs, nor commit crimes to get them. To the extent that such a thing is possible in the United States, he got the morphine for his habit through legal channels, if not strictly by legal methods.

> There just isn't any comparison, really. People in my situation—they're just in one hell of a situation in the United States. It was hard enough and bad enough. If you can't find one that will prescribe for you—and it's getting harder and harder—you have to keep continually moving or forge prescriptions (which is something I never did). That's bad enough. But the ones that are addicted to heroin and have to buy it from a pusher and have to pay those outrageous prices for it—they just *have* to go to some form of crime to pay for it. You're just in one hell of a situation. You wind up dead or in the penitentiary, one or the other. It's the only two choices you have, in the long run. I've known quite a few that have died, and quite a few that are in the penitentiary.
> Of course the people in my situation have no say-so. And the people

that have to do with making the laws, they evidently are not going to stamp it out, you know. They'd just have to jail everybody.

I mean, you get a helpless feeling in the States. It's quite a bit different here. But it's obvious they can't all come over here. It wouldn't be the right thing for England to have to take care of all the American addicts. What can you say?

Harold the Unwelcome

Willis: At the same time [that Ralph Williams was having trouble with the Aliens' Department] we had another patient, an American who had come here called Harold, who'd been with us for about four or five months. In fact, his name wasn't Harold at all. Anyway, he's got an alias, and when he had previously been in this country he had been deported as an undesirable creep. Well, he got involved in a fight in a pharmacy in London, and he knifed somebody.

Klein: They could really deport him.

Willis: Exactly. They could really deport him. But what happened? They were clamoring to get rid of poor old Ralph Williams. In fact I spoke to the Aliens' Office. I said, here are these two guys. If you want to kick somebody out, you ought to get a shot at this Harold. But Harold had enlisted the sympathy of a group of vicars and people here. So he went into court, and the magistrate practically gave him 15 pounds out of the poor box. . . .

Harold. Thirty-seven. Born Brooklyn, February 2, 1933, at a hospital whose address he can recite. A head for precise details; a great skill at filling out forms full of intimate, yet mechanical questions. His last residence in New York was "a suite at the X Hotel on X Street, between Y and Z Avenues." He was "living off the wealth." He had held few regular jobs in the United States, none in the years just before he left. He had been a professional thief.

At the interview he was accompanied by his English wife. He is, or was, Jewish.

I was Bar Mitzvahed, and that was it. That's the extent of my religious background. I go to synagogue here once in a while, but very seldom. It seems the last time I was in synagogue was in prison . . . unfortunately.

His mother died when he was one. "My father couldn't support me and put me in a Jewish orphanage. I stayed there until I was five," and then was transferred to another children's home

> where I stayed until I was ten. I have no recollection of this one at all. All I can remember is eating cornflakes out of a box dry without any milk because I had to steal it because I was hungry; and I remember being beaten and being locked in a closet all night. . . . A usual happy childhood.

His father, he says, was a very weak man, with no education, although American-born. He collected and bought and sold scrap metal, "old bathtubs, sinks. . . . I think he could have done well but most of the money was pissed away on gambling. This is what I remember."

When he was ten his father remarried. His stepmother had, he thinks, a high-school education. Harold was taken to live with them. "The circumstances were very bad," but he stayed with them until he was 14, in the seventh grade, "when I got into trouble again." He is a little confused about the nature of the trouble. One time he says, "I don't even remember. I think it was for stealing a car." Another time he says, "A group of us broke into a school. I don't think there was any sentence or punishment. The court just decided that it was the best thing on my and my family's behalf" to send him to a place with the rustic name of Maybush Hills:

> a co-ed home for children that have family problems, or no families. . . . I just couldn't cope with my family and they couldn't cope with me very well, I guess, and the probation department decided that the best place was away from this so-called family.

At 16 he came out, went home, and

> from 16 to 17 was the only year in my life I worked consistently. I worked at a cloth company as a knitting-machine repairman. I fixed knitting machines. I worked until 17 and then I joined the U.S. Navy.

He hadn't started drugs yet.

> I was in the Navy two weeks and they discovered I had cancer, malignant carcinoma. They took a biopsy, sent it to pathology, it came back positive—malignant. I was sent to the hospital, they did a left-radical neck dissection. Then they discharged me. I left the hospital. I had nowhere to go. So I flew to California. Finally I got in trouble there.

He forged checks.

I was locked up, given probation, and turned over to the Navy. While there I had nothing to do. I was walking around one day and I saw an ambulance. I went into the ambulance and took out a box of morphine syrettes. I gave myself half a grain of morphine without ever having known a drug-addict or heard of drugs before.

He had, however, smoked marijuana twice when 16, got high from it, but did not particularly like it.

Anyway, I took this fix of morphine. It was too much and I was very sick. The next day I gave myself just a little less. That's how I became addicted. Isn't that weird? No one ever told me about drugs. I never knew an addict.

What happened then? "I was still in the Navy. The morphine ran out, so I just stopped it, just forgot about it." In the same speech he says he was addicted, then denies it. "No, no—I didn't have that much. Anyway, I was sent back to New York, and discharged from the Navy." His discharge was honorable.

That's when I met those people in the neighborhood where I lived. I started hanging out in this candy-store right across the street from where I lived, and I met these friends of mine called Peanuts and Poopie. They were addicts, and they knew heroin, and they turned me on to some heroin and that was it.

How did he work? "I just started stealing—armed robberies." Although he has been in jail, it was "not for armed robberies. Never caught me with a pistol. Thank God!" This went on for a few years.

And I got caught committing burglary. I got caught for robbery— stealing a payroll, I got three years probation. . . . this was my first offense, you could say. Then I got caught for burglary in the third degree. I pleaded not guilty, went to trial. . . .

He claims he was innocent of actually stealing anything.

I walked into a doctor's house. I didn't take anything, there was nothing there. I tried to get drugs—nothing—walked out. Arrested two weeks later for burglary in the third degree and grand larceny.

The larceny charge came from the complaint of the woman who lived there that money was missing.

I was found not guilty of the larceny, guilty of the burglary-3, sentenced to ten years. The lawyer said I should beat it. I went to the Court of Appeals. Forget about it! They affirmed the conviction. The lawyer said, "Do the time. You're gonna have to do the time."

So I ended up taking over the case myself. After four years I got a reversal—myself. Habeas corpus. Got the conviction reversed and thrown out.

No drugs in jail—he had undergone cold-turkey withdrawal. But

I knew I was gonna use drugs again. When I got out I stayed off about five or six months. I got a number of jobs, but every time I got a job . . . I'll give you an example: I got a job as admitting clerk at X Hospital on Y Avenue. And they told me how great a clerk I was, and they'd start training me for the admitting staff, and then after three weeks on the job, they found out I had a record, and they fired me.

After that, as long as he was in the United States, he concentrated on stealing. He speaks with the lingo of a professional to whom imprisonment is a standard occupational hazard.

I was at Upstate twice. The first time they arrested me for stealing this payroll, robbery-2, assault-2, and grand-2. I copped out on the grand-2, and got one to two years and did the two years. The second time I got five to ten years for that burglary-3. I did four years, like I said, and beat the case. And after that it was just every time they arrested me I just beat the case. They never could convict me.

He was arrested several times for

burglary, possession of stolen property, things like that. Never drugs . . . I have a long record, very long record. I mean I had nothing else to do. I had to take care of my habit, so I stole. I was a good thief. And after being in state prison for four years I decided, that's it, I'm not going back to jail. . . . What's the point?

And he never did.

While in jail he had not been so confident. He was married when he went in. His first wife, who did not use drugs, divorced him while he was incarcerated. "I more or less forced her to because I thought I would have to do the ten years. That's over with."

He started using heroin in 1953, cocaine about 1956. He always mixed the two together, and mainlined them. He had also mainlined morphine the first time he used it. "And I didn't like it. It's pins-and-needles, morphine. If I had morphine now I would only use it to keep me from being sick. If I ever get sick over here, which is doubtful."

When he left the United States he was buying about

a half an ounce of heroin every two or three days. It was costing me about $150 a day, something like that. I would buy about four bags of cocaine a day, at $25 a bag.

A $250-a-day habit.

Had he ever been treated in the United States for drug abuse? "Yes, I was in X Hospital, 'M' Building. And they just wanted to admit me to a state hospital, and I wouldn't go for that." There is an irony here. Although Dr. Willis worked at the same state hospital the two did not meet until England. "I checked into Y General Hospital . . ." but nothing worked.

It was always cold-turkey, which I wouldn't put up with. I also went to the federal hospital voluntarily. At one time you could commit yourself, you could check in. I don't know about now—now I understand you can't. Anyway, I checked in there, I wasn't convicted, I wasn't a federal prisoner. I was ten days there, and they had me washing windows. I'm still sick, I'm weak, I don't feel good, I had $250 in the bank, and they want me to wash the kitchen windows? I said, "No good." So I just checked out.

He would not tolerate what he considered neglect or abuse. And the "system" did not intimidate him, nor was it always a match for his resourcefulness.

I checked into X Hospital to kick a habit. Next thing I know, after two weeks they give me a commitment paper. They committed me to a hospital for mentally insane or something. So I just put a habeas corpus to the Supreme Court, and had a hearing, and they discharged me. I wouldn't go for it.

He did, however, once go on his own to the state hospital.

I went to see some social-worker somewhere, and she arranged to get me admitted to the state hospital and I stayed there one day and I told them to rub it on their chests and checked out. They wouldn't give me any medication.

He is unforgiving.

When I was released, I would have been a constructive, helpful, useful, normal citizen had I been able to get the drugs I needed. If I was able to register, get my heroin and cocaine, I would have had my admitting-clerk job and everything would have been fine. But instead of that I wasn't allowed to work. When I got a job they found out I had a record and kicked me out. When I scored drugs I was locked up in the Tombs, in Manhattan, 125th Street; when I stole, if they caught me, I was put in the Tombs.

When a junky is nicked in Manhattan, he is put on the Ninth Floor in the Tombs, given thorazine, and he kicks cold-turkey. I've been on it. I've kicked that way many times. And you lay on the floor, and they throw up on each other, and you're sick as a dog. That's the treatment in America.

What of other, gentler methods in the United States, such as Phoenix House, or Day Top Village, or Synanon? "Not for me, I mean, it's all group therapy." He has never been convicted for any offense "pertaining to drugs," although he has been arrested twice.

I altered a prescription one time. It had a Roman numeral three. I made the first "I" into an "X," and that made the number XII. I was arrested for that, and the grand jury dismissed it. And the only other thing pertaining to drugs, I was arrested for possession of a hypodermic needle in the lobby of the A Hotel on Z Avenue. That's still pending, right now. I'm out on $50 bail. They'll never find me. [Laughter]

He came to England first in 1964. "I made a big score in '64, and I started traveling around. . . ." The "big score" came from "burglaries and a few other things" that he won't specify, "because they could put me in jail."

I lived in Spain for a year when I was using opium, going to Tangiers and getting hash and opium and I came here in '64 meaning to go to the Canary Islands, but when I found out the scene here—that drugs were legal—I just stayed. Until they kicked me out. I was deported from England.

Why was he deported?

For obtaining drugs illegally, for forgery—all kinds of nonsense. I just didn't care about what I did. . . . This happened in X. I was just doing things I shouldn't have been doing. Having too much drugs in my possession. They locked me up for one month at A Prison. Then I was sent to B where they kept me for eight days. Then I was put on a plane and sent to New York.

While in England, before the clinics had opened, he had been registered and had received drugs from private physicians. He seems to have gone, at one time or another, to most of the half-dozen physicians criticized in the Brain Report. Of Lady Franco he says:

She was great. Fabulous. Wonderful woman. Good physician. I mean, she'd check me over, listen to my heart. How many drug addict physicians—I mean how many physicians that prescribe drugs—listen to an addict's heart? She did. She took the trouble to talk to me. She was really good.

When she died, he went to Dr. Rocher, the physician with the bad reputation. But Harold will hear of no criticism of him:

He's a great man, he's a wonderful man! Regardless of his reputation. He was known not to charge addicts down on their luck. He gave me money. This man put 30 quid in my hand. Dr. Marvin Rocher, a wonderful man. His reputation is based mainly, I believe, on envy; they treated him rotten.

Harold's wife put in at this point:

He was made the scapegoat for the whole business. . . . He was in prison the last time we heard.

When Harold went to see Rocher at the hospital, they "said he wasn't there. But I think they were lying; I think they just said that because they didn't want anyone to see him."

He says Dr. Rocher was not an addict, but he did drink "a lot. He gambled a lot. I used to have to go into this horse-racing parlor and pull him out of there."

He denies that he ever pushed heroin, although Rocher used to prescribe "60 grains of heroin and 60 grains of cocaine every other day" for him. "I used it all myself." Reminded that this is a big habit, he laughed.

When he was deported and landed in America, there were no warrants waiting for him; he walked out of the airport into the old life. Before he went back to England, with an illegal passport, he had made up for lost time.

> Oh, God, I've been nicked—God knows. In fact, one judge read off the record—he couldn't believe how many times I was arrested before I left New York. . . . There's four warrants for my arrest right now. Three in the city, and one with the feds. There's that one for possession of that spike [hypodermic needle]; one for burglary in the third degree that they can rub on their chest—they'll never convict me of it; one for possession of stolen property—each charged differently. Then there was a federal warrant for obtaining a passport illegally, which calls for ten years. But I can't see the feds giving me ten years on that. Really it's ridiculous. There's four warrants for me in the States right now.

A few years ago, he "found" a good deal of money, some $40,000, which has since been his major source of support. The exact nature of this windfall, whether legal or not, is unspecified.

When he returned to England, he had to use the passport with the false name for his registration. He thus has an official alias. "The name that was on the passport, Mark Herzberg—a good Irish name."

He registered, went to the clinic, and

> I did everything under that name. I had to. It's on my passport. Until this idiot, Mark Herzberg in the States, went and got a passport under the same name, and they—well, two people, one name, same birth date, same. . . .

They called him into the American embassy and showed him pictures of the real Herzberg and of himself. "They weren't mad. They don't care at the embassy. Why should they get mad? They can't deport you for that."

Shortly after arriving he registered again as an addict. And shortly after that he was arrested. "I was given three months suspended sentence, for that name, for giving false information to an immigration officer." Not long after he got into more serious trouble. "Then I heisted a man here, for going around saying things about my wife." (She was not his wife at the time.) "I just stuck a knife in his throat— very, very mildly. . . . The fine was ten pounds, or one month in jail. But I had to do the three months suspended that I was given for the passport." In prison he was given methadone, and also managed, apparently, to get other drugs illicitly.

Since his return he has lived quietly, mostly on his windfall of $40,000. He has been working off and on, for the past eight months.

"I get a 60-percent disability rating from the Veterans' Administration for my neck, and I make approximately 16 pounds a week, working. Fixing knitting machines, or something."

He has been married for the second time. "We have a very good sex-life. I'm married now since October 4, 1970. We've known each other since August, 1968. We have a wonderful life together."

His present habit?

Every night, 12:00, I go to Bliss's Camera Store, I'm given six and two-third grains of heroin, 40 tablets—and six and two-thirds grains of cocaine. That's my daily dosage, which is beautiful.

Reminded of the large prescription he used to get from Dr. Rocher: "Well, when I came back the laws were different."

He can't stand alcohol. "I think it's horrible." He kids his wife about the port wine with lemon she sometimes takes. He doesn't take tranquilizers. He took amphetamines once, in New York, and "it drove me out of my head. I don't like amphetamines at all, no." Barbiturates?

I take tuinal or seconal to go to sleep once in a while. But there comes a time every so often when I get carried away, and start staggering, which my wife doesn't like. And I can't blame her. It's a pretty disgusting state of affairs.

He has been using them about once every two weeks for the last year. His wife, who takes no drugs herself, comments: "I don't mind the hard drugs, the only thing I don't like are the barbiturates."

He attempted withdrawal once in England. "I checked into Guy's Hospital, Dr. Willis administering to me. And I just couldn't make it. I had to have my fix." He remained there only four days. "They were just giving me methadone, but I wanted my coke and heroin."

Does he have a criminal record in Britain like the one in the States—robberies and the like? "No. I won't do anything here. Why should I?"

He says that he has little to do with other addicts in Britain—a common statement among the North American drug-refugees. "The only drug addicts I come into contact with in England are either at the 'Dilly or at the clinic, where there are groups of them." None of his friends are addicts.

He finds that it is "easier for me to score illegal stuff in the States than it is here." Reminded that for the first time Chinese heroin is coming into the British market, often with poisonous impurities, he says, "I will not touch it. It's garbage." Legal drugs are on the market but very, very expensive in comparison to the price charged through clinic prescriptions and legal chemists.

He does not smoke marijuana, and "the last time I smoked some hash was about five or six months ago."

Would he summarize his opinions of the respective drug scenes?

Over here it's beautiful. Over here I can stand up and walk around and live like a man. Over here I *am* a man. I can walk straight and live decently. I don't have a flat—my own home—now; but when I do find a flat, I know I can have my own home. My wife and I are happy. I don't have to steal, or rob anybody. I don't have to wake up sick and wonder where my next fix is coming from. In other words, I don't need to put a pistol in my hand. I'm sure you don't want me with a pistol in my hand any more than I do.

Would he consider returning to the United States if the situation were to become similar to that in Britain?

I'd have to give that a lot of thought. Because I don't trust the States. It would take a lot for me to put any trust in the U.S.

I can't see a program like this getting on its feet. I think a man like Anslinger and others like him are part of the whole profiteering system one way or another. I mean he was just interested in taking home his large paycheck.

I'd say there's easily six or seven hundred thousand addicts in New York City alone. Eighty-five percent of all arrests in New York are of drug addicts. You know that? I was told this by a detective in the X precinct, on Y Street, between S and T Avenues—85 percent of the arrests in that precinct are addicts.

He believes that narcotics will never be legalized in the United States,

because the people there making the money are the people in the positions. The politicians are making the money. Sure, the medical departments want it legalized, the doctors want to legalize it. But the doctors can't because the doctors don't handle the political system, the legal system there.

Oh, it's a shame. Listen—you know, I lay on this bed and I think of the people I've hurt. I've hurt a lot of people in the States. I've had to. I've been caught in their homes—I had to.

Hey, listen, Dr. Klein, I hate to tell you, but the more I think of it the more I think you're on a losing team. I mean, I hate to knock it, but I know the United States too well. It's a losing game. There's so many people making billions—not millions, billions. You're not gonna get nowhere.

And I'm not the one to be a pessimist. I'm living the best life I ever lived. The only thing I can't get a flat. But Jesus! The United States! I wish you luck, of course; not for myself, but all the junkies. . . those poor dogs lying up in the Tombs, on the Ninth Floor, throwing up over each other. Dying—using drugs for what? It stinks.

Let's face it: I'm a drug addict 19 years. The odds are I'll never stop. Right? So what am I gonna do? Live here or live in the United States? I'm gonna stay here.

Klein: Yeah, but there are different kinds of addicts. You don't look physically run-down for your addiction. Drugs aren't really your life. They're just part of your life. For other people I've interviewed, drugs are practically all their life.

Harold: No, it's not all my. . . . You know, a couple of days ago my wife and I broke up. Not really broke up—just missed each other. I was sick, but before I would go to get my drugs, I went and got my wife. I went looking for my wife. The average addict would go for his drugs. I wouldn't until I knew where she was.

Klein: Anything else you really want to say that you haven't said?

Harold: Yeah, don't take me back.

Hall the Bootlegger

Hall, among the first Canadian addicts to arrive in England, came on a Christmas Eve in the 'fifties. Now 47, he looks younger. "But I'm a good-looking 47."

He was born in central Canada, a Methodist, but quit religion and church altogether at 10. "I was playing hookey from school and doing everything that I shouldn't be doing; if somebody told me to do something, I wouldn't do it."

He received credit for high school while in a penitentiary in California, serving a sentence "for being an alien in possession of firearms and also for being in possession of drugs." At the time he was 28.

His father, although he had little formal education, ran his own trucking firm. Hall and another son bought it in 1942, and it employed 20 persons when Hall left Canada. When he was a child the family lived comfortably on his father's earnings as truck-owner and driver. His mother had little formal education.

> She was a farm-wife, you know? And she was just for my father. They were very, very happy. . . . My mother died at the age of 54, and my father at age 64. Both of diabetes.

He became involved with drugs when 17, while still in high school; a friend much older than he, whom he had met in a café, introduced him to morphine. He had known nothing about drugs before then.

> I and George, who is now dead, were walking home together. And it was rather cool, and so I says, "How about letting me go up to your room and warm up a bit?" He says, "Well, all right, come up." So I went up to his room and I could see there was something wrong with him—his eyes were watering and he was sniffing all the time. And so he says, "I'd just as soon you didn't watch this, because it wouldn't be any good for you."
>
> And so, being naturally inquisitive, I naturally watched him. And I saw him bring out a syringe. And he put a collar on the syringe, you know? And then the collar made the needle fit perfectly to the syringe. . ."

It was morphine. Being "inquisitive," he also tried it, and more than once. "Well, I was one of those guys who thought that I would never become addicted. And it was approximately . . . oh, I'd say about a month before I became addicted."

His early habit was three to four grains a day. How did he get the money?

> There was a Dr. Ham. He is also dead. And there was an army camp, so George and I used to go out there by bus and take food and different types of food-stuffs because he was a very poor man, and he had two children, and he was living in a hovel. He was living from hand to mouth, really. He was only too happy to get this hamper of food, you know. This went on for quite some time—four or five years. He would

give me the drugs, and make it up as if I was a cancer patient on his books.

He did not work during this period, or steal for his habit. "My father always looked after me, you know." He was on morphine for about ten years. Ham was not his only source. "I was able to find other doctors."

Eventually, he

started up a bootlegging joint. I used to sell whiskey for 60 cents a shot. And I also had a girl-friend. We were not married, but we were both satisfied with the conditions. But she never used. I wouldn't let her use.

To get his drugs,

I used to make three-day trips. There were restrictions on liquor. You could only get one 26-ounce bottle a month. So I would get a lot of friends who were non-drinkers and drive them down to the liquor parlor, and give them money for the liquor, Old Parlour Scotch, and oh, you know, a dollar or so for themselves. And as soon as I got what I thought was enough, I made a trip all through the north. I would go to a doctor and would say, "Doctor, do you like a drink now and then?" He would say, "Sure do, but I don't get enough." "Well, I'll make a trade with you. Twenty-four one-quarter grains of morphine sulphate costs 65 cents. Now Old Parlour Scotch costs five dollars. Well, listen, I'll give you a bottle of whiskey if you give me a tube of morphine." And he would be delighted.

"The Chinese owned practically all the cafés in the province. They're the best customers in the world for liquor." He had three bedrooms, and three girls, who were also available for his customers.

And so that went on for ten years. And meanwhile, back at the ranch, things got pretty hot. And the mounted police were going around to all the doctors investigating their books, investigating . . . and it got a little what you could call warmer. So I moved to another city with my girl, and closed down the house. And then was my first experience with heroin. And I thought it was oh, much, much better.

He was paying six dollars for each cap of heroin. He needed new methods of getting money, and stole.

He left Canada in 1953 after he

threw a mounted police out the window and thought I killed him. . . .

I had everything against the door, and four of them hit the wall and the wall came in. And so I grabbed one and threw him toward the window, and the window broke and consequently he went flying. . . . I was under the impression I killed him. I threw him—I grabbed him by the hands and I threw him, and another one I pushed him in his jaw and he went down. I kicked another one—I don't think his wife liked it very much. But I managed to get out of there and go down the stairs.

He escaped, went to see a "good friend" of his, told his story, borrowed money, and bought a ticket out of town. When the bus stopped in a town in the United States,

I told the Greyhound bus conductor that I was feeling ill, and I wished that I could stay overnight. He says, "Why certainly." So I checked into a motel, and got a plane to Hollywood first thing in the morning . . . . From Hollywood I went to San Francisco. And I made a connection in San Francisco—Mexicans.

Again he supported his habit by theft.

I used a piece of celluloid and I used to go to these big flats that looked like they had money. And I used to bring the celluloid down until I hit the lock and then I'd pull the handle toward me, and then I'd kick the door handles from the bottom, and I'd push, and the door would open with no trouble at all. So that's how I earned my living.

He was arrested and sentenced as the result of a complicated series of mischances and stupidities of the kind that although they occur in real life would be rejected by fiction editors as too improbable. "This is a very ridiculous story." He had stolen a mink coat, which he sold to his dealer for $150. The dealer then looked through it, and found, in a small inner pocket, a diamond ring worth $1200 which Hall had not known about.

The dealer was a gangster, and in trying to sell the ring—which had been stolen from Beverly Hills—he was killed. The ring fell into the hands of the police, who were looking for the original thief.

With all this in the air, Hall set out for Tiajuana with a trunk full of guns he hoped to trade for brown Mexican heroin.

And on this day it was very, very warm, and so I was driving with my shoes off and so I had no shirt on, and I had no shoes on, and I was driving like that. And I just happened to beat the light, you know. A police car pushed me against the curb and the copper says, "Do you mind getting out a moment?" Then they saw the condition I was in—no shoes, no shirt. I told them it was terribly hot, and showed them the papers for the car. The copper says, "We've been looking for a car resembling yours. Have you been down to Tiajuana very often?" I said, "No, I've never been there, I was just going for the bull-fight." Then they opened up the boot [trunk] and there were those guns. He says, "Boy! We've got a hot one here!" They made me hold my hands up against the car and stand out, and there was no chance at all of escaping.

So, because he ran the red light, he was charged for the guns, the coat, and the ring, and was sentenced for from one to 15 years.

He was in prison for two years, and on parole two years. While attending school there, he used his time productively, not only to complete his high-school credits. He became friendly with an abortionist, also attending school, who was working in the prison hospital. Hall would get saccharine, which he didn't use, and give it to the doctor, who, out of "the goodness of his heart" gave him morphine in return. No cold-turkey for Hall.

He got out in 1955, and was deported, under a pseudonym, to Canada.

Well, I started up again. A little Pole I knew—he's out of it now—used to go to Marseilles, he would get a girl in England and make a type of pregnancy belt, and put a kilo in the belt. Then he'd take her across to Canada. . . . I was the middle man. And I used to be able to look after my habit—and my girl, you know—and everything went quite nicely.

This went on until he left. Despite old charges and continuing crimes, he was, he claims, not arrested. (Police records contradict this.) But the police did give him their attention, because he was a user.

They used to pull up and say, "Roll up your arms." And I had marks on my arms. They'd say, "Get in." This happened a number of times.

Finally, the mounted police took me out to the woods, and they handcuffed me around this here tree, and they made me black and blue all over my body with an eight-cell flashlight.

And so this copper—a nasty, nasty man—says, "If you want to get back to town, walk back." I couldn't even walk. My legs were so sore. I just slept in the bushes, you know, until I was able to make my way back.

This copper told me, "Hall, if I get you again, I'm gonna kill you; and I'm gonna say that you tried to escape." Now I *knew* that he meant this. . . . So I came over here.

He never tried to be cured in Canada. "I'd rather die."

He was married three times in Canada, and once in England. "Each case I walked out . . . no children. Perhaps, if I were to have had children the condition would have been different."

His record in England is a good deal steadier. He married for the fourth time in 1964, and although he does not live with his wife they are apparently on good terms; his sex-life with her is "perfectly normal."

He has, he says, been arrested only once in England—for forging prescriptions from Lady Franco, his doctor at the time.

I was charged on two occasions and given a conditional discharge on one, and one day on another. This was because they had no record of me, and I was working at that time. Mr. Copperfield of the Home Office—a wonderful man—thought that it was really remarkable that a user should work. You can see the usual type from just looking around here. Also, I got married just after that. And I'm still married.

Despite his steadier life, bizarre incidents still happen to him. He has a burn mark on his neck.

Oh, that's a crazy mark. I put a very unusual knot in my tie once, and couldn't get it off my head. So, I thought, well, I'll burn it off and gradually it'll come through. Silly, very silly.

When he came over in the 'fifties, the drug-scene seemed very calm. If people sold drugs on the streets at all, it escaped his sophisticated observation (an observation that had never failed at making contacts before). He says that none were being sold at the 'Dilly. Drug-abusers concentrated on heroin and cocaine. "When I first came here there was no sensation at all. You never heard about drugs on the radio."

His drug-habit when he left Canada was 15 grains a day. He was taking about 20 pills of barbiturates, mostly Nembutal, and is still taking them, 25 years after he started. He had tried marijuana, in 1951, but did not like it. He has never taken LSD, the other psychedelic drugs, or amphetamines.

He went first to a professor at St. Thomas Hospital, who maintained him on heroin for about three months, then told him, "There's no sense in my carrying you. You can go to any doctor." He then found a physician who told him that he preferred to give him seven grains of heroin daily (about half his Canadian habit) and five grains of cocaine. This started him on cocaine.

He stayed with the doctor about seven months. Then,

> I met two fellows that came over here because they knew I was here. Their names were—well, I knew them as "Donald the Burglar" and Giuseppe. They were going to Lady Franco.

So he switched to her also. Under her control, his habit went up to an all-time high—26 grains (1560 milligrams) of British pure heroin and 20 grains of cocaine per day. His use of cocaine continued until she died in 1967. He paid her weekly, about four pounds per week.

After three or four years, however, before she died, he went to another private physician and said, "Listen, I'm gonna land myself up in jail because I can't support my habit and support my wife and the apartment, so my life is actually in your hands." This doctor sent him to another, who was on National Health Service but refused to take him because his habit was too large. He returned to the former, who said, "Well, I guess I'll have to take you on." He stayed with this doctor until the clinics opened.

He has been ill for some time, and this has complicated his drug and job record. "I got septicemia, oh, about seven years ago, and I didn't eat for three months, and then I went into a coma." He did not try to withdraw from drugs then. When the clinics opend in 1968, he was in hospital with osteoporosis, megaloblastic anemia, and perhaps other complications.

> The doctor used to give my wife prescriptions, and she'd cash 'em, and she'd bring them out to the hospital and I'd give them to the pharmacist, and he'd make them up in solution. . . .

Dr. Willis, God bless his soul . . . yes, I like him. He came up to see me as soon as the clinics opened up. He made arrangements for the pharmacy to give me the same amount that I was getting.

The whole subject of withdrawal makes him nervous. "No. Listen, I couldn't. My partner killed himself [by jumping in the river while trying to withdraw]. And he came over here because I was here. He was a big man, and we grew up together."

He uses no cocaine now, but 320 milligrams of heroin—down from the 1560 milligrams he took at peak—and 400 milligrams of methadone daily, which is what made the reduction in heroin possible. He also takes 15 pills of Tuinal, a barbiturate, orally.

When he first came over, he worked as a storekeeper for two years. Next he was a security guard, for about eight months. After that he worked as a broadcasting studio rigger for three and a half years—his longest and steadiest job. After that he worked for a record company, as a fitter for the machines, until they found he was a user. Next he worked as a porter until he became ill. Because of his illnesses he has not worked regularly since 1968.

Would he say that an addict could be employed and live an almost normal life in England? "Perfectly." He thinks the English system is "100 percent better" than the American or Canadian systems, "because you can't work and have a habit in the United States or Canada. It's impossible."

Would he consider going back? "My mom and dad are dead. I have really nothing to go back to. I know what's there. I get letters from Canada all the time. Why should I go back? To get beat over the head?"

The Jazz Man

He did not come from a slum or broken home, but from a close-knit and affectionate family that has been well-to-do all his life. His father, who ran the New York office of a major firm when Sam was a boy, is now a millionaire. Sam, himself a gifted musician, was able to earn a good living with some of the more famous bands in America. His family has stuck by him. Yet he could not handle his heroin-addiction in America, could not get treatment, and "after ten years of it I just couldn't stand the system any more, you know, I was slipping gradually downward, until finally my father made the decision for me" to leave America. "I just heard from my family at home, and they still say they don't want me giving up." He is 31 now.

It was perhaps more natural for him to come to England since he was born there. But he spent all his formative years in the United States, and considers himself basically an American. He is white, Jewish, and has had his Bar Mitzvah. "But I was more inclined towards music than towards anything else in the world, you know. I thought that my music kept me very much in touch with God."

Sam's father came from a fairly wealthy family, but had made his own way. His mother was college-educated. Sam went to an ivy-league college: "Well, it was fairly easy for me as a musician." He stayed there one year and then went on the road with a band.

"I sort of free-lanced. I was doing very well musically, very well. I was a good drummer, I was very well known."

The world of popular music has always been very druggy. Of a famous band-leader he worked with, Sam says, "Yeah, he was a heroin-user. But I never used heroin with him."

He started with marijuana. "Yeah, I was a big pot-smoker. Oh, my God, so long ago, so long ago. Maybe 16 years ago." Also, "I used to drink a bit in the clubs I played in at night." He also smokes tobacco.

He went from pot "right on to heroin," on the recommendation of another musician. He mainlined it from the beginning, starting at 15. He believes it took him a couple of years to become addicted. Once addicted he used about five seven-dollar bags a day. "Oh, fantastic. I spent thousands and thousands of dollars." He did not go into Harlem, or make extensive underworld contacts. "I stayed with sort of like jazz musicians who were addicted—my own particular clique." He managed to avoid arrest for drug-use, or for stealing to support his habit. "See, I had family, I had money at home. My parents loved me. But it looked like I was going to soon have trouble, you know."

When he was 20, his parents had him committed to Lexington, in the belief it would help him. "I couldn't leave until I was 21. And while I was there I received no psychiatric help whatsoever." He withdrew cold-turkey, but was on heroin again as soon as he was out.

Then he went into a private New England psychiatric hospital with a good reputation. This was followed by "one or two other places, similar to that" in New York. But they did not help, and he was back on dope as soon as he came out of each.

In 1965 he decided to leave the United States. He was not forced to leave by pressure from his parents, who, he insists, have always stood by him faithfully, and with love.

> You know, I tried to commit suicide. I took 120 sleeping pills. I was not on barbiturates; I took them as a deliberate act of self-destruction. My father left the house at 8:00 A.M. I took the sleeping pills at 9:00 A.M. He came home and found me and took me to the hospital. And I lived, I lived through it.

He did not go to England the first time, but to Australia.

> My family seemed to feel it would be the best place for me. It is sort of out in the sun, as far from America as possible. There seemed to be no drugs there. And they saw this situation I was getting into.

He went to a treatment center in Australia.

> They helped me quite a bit. And I stayed free of drugs for three months. I started playing music with a band. I had a nice place to live. Started supporting myself for once. I had money in the bank— was putting away, in American money, almost $75 a week.

He insists he was still free of drugs when arrested on a drug-charge.

> What happened is they picked me up for being seen with a known addict. There were five narcotics officers; four started slapping me around. They said, "You're not off, you're not working." But I was working, and I had money in the bank.
>   Finally, four of these officers said, "Let him go, he's making a very good go of it." But this fifth one was a bastard—there's no other name for him. He said I should be deported. The way the legal system works in Australia, the police press the charges themselves, and they either ask bail for you or they ask for no bail, and there's not much the judge could do. The judge said, "All these facts seem very true about you. If there was anything I could do I would do it, but this policeman recommends that you not be released for bail." So I couldn't

show up for my job that night, so I lost my job. And the rest of the band found out about my past drug-record.

So they deported me. I went to America, and there was the same scene. I met my girl-friend and she wouldn't leave me alone, she was on drugs—and, oh, you know—I left in two weeks' time.

He has been in England about five years, "with a private physician for two years—I don't want to mention any names—and with Dr. Willis three." He has gone into the hospital to withdraw twice, but "I fell flat on my face." However, "my habit's decreased quite a bit. Gradually, Dr. Willis has been able to get my habit down. Gradually."

When he came to Dr. Willis he was taking ten grains of heroin, ten grains of cocaine, and amphetamines daily. "Well, I'm completely off cocaine, no more amphetamines, and I'm, you know, thinking of going back into the university and doing something serious in music." In fact, however, his habit, despite what Dr. Willis has been able to do to it, is a good deal larger now than it was in the United States. There, judging by the number of ten-milligram bags he took, it could not have been much more than one grain of heroin daily. He rationalizes: "You see how difficult it is to get off drugs. An addict here is very much an addict."

He has been married four years. His wife, too, uses heroin, about 2 grains (120 milligrams) daily. They do not have much of a sex-life, because of the drugs. "We did once, but not now." However, he is not depressed, but is given to romantic and upbeat statements: "I found my life. . . . Where does friendliness and love start, you know? I've been closer to her than to any other human being in my life."

He uses a tranquilizer, valium, under prescription. He uses no barbiturates, he claims, except when necessary for sleeping. He started using amphetamines shortly after heroin, perhaps when he was about 16. "I cut myself off. A doctor never—well, you can always score, legally or illegally. I find that I lead more of a normal life now than ever before. Amphetamines never were my stick." He had been taking about six ampules of pure methedrine daily. "If you gave me 500 quid I wouldn't take one now."

He uses hashish, smoking it two or three times a week. "Because in my head, you know, I like to listen to music." His favorite group?

"It would have to be Coltrane. And after Coltrane, I dig Elwood Jones a lot." He has not used LSD, but he used mescaline when he was already on heroin.

It was like I was playing music, and I was feeling music, and . . . beautiful. . . . Except when we got into a car, and we said, "Let's go somewhere, see where people are at, man!" And we got frightened to death of people and rolled up the windows. . . .

He will not try withdrawal again. In explaining why, he describes some details of his experiences in Australia, forgetting that he had earlier said that he was off drugs when finally arrested and deported.

In Australia something happened for the first time. I suppose age, maybe, something happened within the cells of my body. I went into a coma and I never came out of it. And the doctors were getting awfully worried. They transferred me to the hospital, and in the end wound up giving me a grain of heroin.

He describes a similar experience in jail in Australia:

Well, they took me to jail, for using. They could see the tracks on my arms. Well, I went into a coma in jail. My blood-pressure started getting lower and something happened. They gave me a grain of morphine and then the day after smaller and smaller doses. This doctor told me, "We thought you were going to lose your life."

After the prison hospital the doctor tried to maintain him on heroin, but it didn't work. It was at the next Australian hospitalization that he was able to withdraw.

It was a hospital mainly meant for alcoholics. There was a sister there who was so nice to me, and they were so good to me, that I learned to live without drugs. I went about three months without drugs.

The nun was a new experience; people in official positions have not often been good to him:

An addict, man, is someone who is kicked in the asshole all over the world, isn't he, you know? In America, man, it was *horrible*. Oh, real heavy, very heavy. Ridiculous, man, ridiculous. You know, people banging you over the head for your gear, things like that. And police-men—you know how stupid policemen can be. You know, them forcing you *onto* drugs. I've seen my closest friend dead from drugs. . . . not overdose. He just went nutty from the scene in the States.

I sometimes get quite homesick for America. And I would like to see my family. But I've had such bad experiences I just don't want to go back. I'm still a citizen, but I'm thinking of giving up my citizenship. I just don't want to go back onto that scene again.

He tried twice to withdraw in hospitals in England, at Dr. Willis' urging. "I really tried to get off, and that's the truth." But he can't forget the Australian reaction, and has not been successful.

What does he think of the methadone oral therapy now popular in the United States?

When I was just leaving the States I met one of the first people on that program. He was taking it legally every day—he would take his dose of orally administered methadone and then go out and score. The junky wants the heroin. There's some facts of life that have to be faced, you know.

You know, it would be a wonderful thing if someone could go and do something for those people in America. I'm a musician . . . I know some of the greatest musicians in the world who are addicted to drugs. I've always thought myself that if I ever got off drugs, I would like to help people. But it's a very difficult job to do. The question is whether to give drugs or not to give them. If you don't, legally, the addicts will go to the Mafia. American addicts number by the thousands and thousands and thousands, and there's so much a doctor could do for them.

There are doctors in America, young doctors who are graduating, and might want to do something but they're frightened silly by the American Medical Association.

And now, they're ruining lives. There's always been people, I think, addicted to opium, for as long as mankind's been on earth. As long as we have to contend, support, acknowledge that there are addicts in America, then there are some doctors who must be willing to stick up for those addicts. Man, if a guy's dying of cancer, or has a problem like a leg blown off—well, that's great. They'll help. And they have no objection to giving a diabetic insulin. But in America, there's a scene that says, "Who's a junky? A junky's no one, he's nothing."

If it was me, I would give them the drugs. I'd say, "Whatever you have tried to do in life and fucked up on because you've come up against a brick wall. . . ." Well, I'd say, "Here's your drugs. Have them. How much do you want?" It would work out two ways. Either they'd have their drugs and be able to lead a fairly normal life or they would have so much drugs all of a sudden they would see if that's really what they want. That's what I think.

At Home with the Jazz Man

Klein: On Saturday, July 4, 1970, I visited Sam and his wife at their home. It was one of the high points of my tour.

Their living quarters are equivalent to what we would call a campus apartment—fairly run-down, but quite livable. While I was there, from four to seven P.M., various addicts wandered in and out and took their fixes before me, as did their host and hostess. The other residents of the apartment are their two pet cats, who were the only ones I saw there who are not on drugs.

There was a lot to eat, but most of it was fruit. Sam's wife says that this is the only food that agrees with her. She, Sam, and the other addicts did not hesitate to take, and discuss taking, drugs before me. They used disposable syringes which they get through the addict center. Sam fixed, but he does not like to inject directly into his veins, so he injected his heroin intramuscularly. While I watched, he gave himself six grains.

His English wife also fixed before me, taking about ten milligrams of heroin, as well as various amphetamines that the doctors don't know she takes. She admits that she previously used methedrine; but since methedrine has been taken off the market in England, she now uses amphetamines that she purchases illicitly, as well as dexedrine and the heroin that she receives through the clinic. The English addict friend who was there when I first arrived kept trying to inject into a vein, and stuck himself about twenty times trying to find one. He had great trouble, although he used a leather belt, pulling it very tight. His veins seemed to be totally destroyed, as only a long-time addict's veins can be.

A mild domestic argument was going on: Sam told his wife that he was going to run out of pills tomorrow; could he use some of hers? Like a good wife, she worries about Sam's habits. She says that he is either stupid or naive about many important things, and when she wants to score illegal heroin she does not send him. Instead, she does the shopping herself, goes to the Piccadilly area and has no trouble in getting heroin, usually of the illegal yellow Chinese variety. But they always hope that they can get the pure white heroin available through the clinics from someone who has been able to get an extra supply, usually by convincing the doctors he needs more than he does. This source, however, is not dependable and the pure heroin is considerably less available from other addicts than it was before the clinics came in.

In spite of what Sam told me in the interview, he does take barbiturates, usually Tuinals, about three pills a night. This also worries his wife, who does not like barbiturates; basically, she is on speed. She told me of an experience she had about three years earlier that could justifiably be called an "amphetamine psychosis." She is 21 now.

After a while another addict friend came in, lugging along a radio which he was trying to sell for ten pounds. He said that it sold for thirty-five pounds in the store. He also brought along 50 record-albums selling for ten shillings apiece, and 45 older albums selling for two shillings each. He was a Canadian, about 40, but looked very old, very run-down. It seems he owes Sam a lot of money, and apparently was trying to raise more. Sam, by addict standards, is quite well-to-do. As a musician, he can usually find employment. In any case, he gets money from his family, and his apartment is usually a good place to drop in. Accompanying the Canadian was another addict, and before I left a third also dropped in. Unlike several of the others interviewed, who said that they tried to avoid other addicts (whether they did or not), Sam says that most of his friends are addicted. When out of doors, by watching his dress and habits carefully, he tries to avoid giving the impression that he is on drugs. During the three hours I was there each fixed twice before me. Everyone welcome; just bring your own fixes.

Sam keeps a piano and his drums in another room in the apartment, so we went through a messy connecting room to get to the instruments, and played for a while. I had brought some jazz tapes with me from the States. I played these, and he really got into them. He loves music. He brought out pictures of various groups he has played with. He said again that he works regularly—although, as noted, he had not worked in the month preceding my visit.

His wife described some of her experiences with addicts. Recently she has been running into Americans who, apparently, cannot shake old habits—or more properly old rituals, as important to many addicts as the drugs themselves—and who are still using eyedroppers. They tried to get her to use a sawed-off eyedropper, but she simply couldn't dig it, she told me. English addicts, who can get sterile, disposable syringes from the clinics, do not understand these strange desires.

Sam tells me now that he was considerably under the influence of barbiturates when he gave me the interview from which the preceding excerpts were taken. He says that many of the things he told me were things he had told no one else, would never tell his personal physician, and were closer to the full facts about his drug-dependence than anything he had ever told even his addict friends.

London and North America

> I came to England to further my addiction
> without going to jail. I got the drugs the
> same day I landed, from Dr. Z. I knew
> about this doctor and several others before
> arriving. I said I was an addict when I
> wasn't at the time. I told the doctor I was
> using four grains of heroin a day, and
> that if possible I would like to be treated
> as a registered addict. The doctor replied,
> "Certainly." It was a shock, you know.
> I mean, it was so easy to get it.
>
> —*Canadian heroin-abuser in London*

In his novel *The Unbearable Bassington,* "Saki" described how, in the sunny days before World War I, male members of the British upper class who had become embarrassments to their families would be sent to the colonies, far from home. Bassington himself became a candidate for this practice when, after every chance to change his ways and make something of himself, he failed and became "unbearable." He left England, therefore, as part of what he called "The Black Sheep Export Business."

The United States and Canada are now engaged in a variety of the black-sheep export business, in large part at the expense of Britain. It is not entirely a one-way traffic; more and more of the black sheep may be coming back if the movement increases substantially, causing Britain to decide it does not want to inherit our problems, and to tighten its immigration or drug laws. The black sheep we have in mind are, specifically, the drug-abusers who have emigrated to England, Holland, and other countries because they can get their drugs legally there, through regulated clinics, and lead what they consider to be reasonably normal and productive lives. They choose to emigrate instead of being forced (as they see it) by the punitive moralistic drug-control systems of the United States and Canada into becoming criminals, victims, prostitutes, or convicts in order to meet the needs of their habits. Most of them had to go to the black-market and the Mafia for their highly adulterated drugs; had to take to crime—sometimes pushing—to buy them at extremely high prices; and eventually went to prison or hospital for using them.

However, some of the emigrants are encountering difficulties in their new countries as well, and some are frequenting new jails as a result. But it is also true that some of them are making reasonably good adjustments: raising families, staying out of jail, sticking to their maintenance-doses of heroin, methadone, and/or cocaine, and keeping careers that their records prove were absolutely impossible for them in North America.

They are not from Bassington's upper class (even the declining branches), but they cannot be very poor either. It takes money and planning to pull up roots and bad habits and transport them to friendlier, more supportive and tolerant surroundings, and hope to replant them there. Even if going to England makes it possible to work and save money in the long run, in the short run to go at all requires a cash investment that few drug-addicts can manage to accumulate after they have paid for a $100-a-day habit for any length of time. It is certainly an investment that the largest group of drug-users in the United States, the blacks and Puerto Ricans and Chicanos of the urban slums, can almost never manage to accumulate. In the words of one of the addicts, heroin is to him as insulin to a diabetic. These premises are by no means generally accepted in the western hemisphere, especially among law-enforcement agencies.

Of the newer addicts listed by the British Home Office in the years from 1955 to 1966, about 20 percent were Canadian, American, Australian, or New Zealanders. Among the addict population in London, the Canadians make up the largest non-British group.

The North American addicts tend to be older than the British ones, more experienced and hardened in the jails and illicit slum-centered drug-cultures of their native countries in ways that most of the English addicts can hardly conceive. They came mostly because they could get their drugs legally and relatively easily, without being constantly on the run or in jail. They are not representative of the addicts in

England; but neither are they entirely representative of the largely impoverished and dark-skinned addicts in their native countries, who usually cannot raise money for the passage.

Although the information is limited, addicts and professional workers believe that North American heroin addicts and cocaine-abusers started to come to England in the late 1950's. They continued to enter the country in a fairly steady stream until about 1962, when the Home Office began tightening immigration procedures and deporting the more undesirable addicts. The fact that there have also been deportations from Sweden indicates the trend.

Of the increase of addicts reported in Britain in the last few years, a substantial part, both proportionately and absolutely, can be accounted for by the influx of Canadians who have heard of the new system and, because of Commonwealth ties between their two nations, find it relatively easy to immigrate. Of the heroin- and cocaine-abusers covered by our survey, most were Canadian. It is obvious that they were deeply impressed by the change of atmosphere, the ease of getting drugs to meet their needs, and the legality and casualness of the whole process.

It is worthwhile noting that the heroin-user quoted at the beginning of this chapter asked for heroin although he was not addicted at the time, and that he asked for a dose several times as large as that of the average North American addict, but within the range of English addicts. Abuse of leniency begins early. Note also that the accommodation of the doctor practically invited this abuse.

Another addict, after recounting his vicissitudes in North America, describes how he and a friend sat stunned in a car, the legal heroin in their hands, after their first visit to a British doctor, still not quite believing, close to tears.

There is reason to believe that North American addicts have had some influence on the drug-scene in Britain, which from the late 1950's until about 1962 bore considerable resemblance to the drug subculture in the United States. It is, however, difficult to document this influence. Since then, there has developed in England a type of abuser considerably different from the earlier types; this type is concentrated among the teen-age groups, dependent more on amphetamines than on heroin.

In America addicts tend to congregate in neighborhoods of heavy drug-use in the large cities, particularly New York, Philadelphia, Chicago, and Los Angeles. The same, by and large, is true in Britain, where the addict population, according to Hawks (*14*),

> tends to congregate in London (eighty-three percent) where illicit supplies are more plentiful, and where the society of other drug users guarantees the continual fulfillment of their need and the support which the junkie subculture supplies.

The addict population in the United States is predominantly poor, concentrated in a few heavily populated ghettos, and dark-skinned. This is of course not true of the entire population. As any white suburban parent is constantly being reminded, drug-use is spreading among middle-class school children. But this does not change the basic pattern: addiction is largely a disorder and compensation of the black and Spanish-speaking poor in slum neighborhoods.

Although an increasingly young and working-class population is becoming involved in Britain, addiction is not yet so closely associated with poverty and lack of advantage. R. DeAlarcon and his associates, in a study made in 1967 of heroin abuse in the new town of Crawley (DeAlarcon *et al.,* in *29*), some distance outside London, found that the problem was considerably greater than had been reported to the Home Office. It was primarily confined to teen-agers, almost all with IQ scores above 100, not even the brightest of whom had fulfilled their academic potentials. Other students have shown large percentages of abusers of fairly high social origin, with average or above-average IQ scores. These studies do not, perhaps, deal with typical addicts; but it seems clear that the association of deprivation and addiction is not as marked in Britain as in the United States. The British abuser seems to be more concerned with new experiences than with escape from old ones. Black heroin-abusers are quite rare.

From Louria (*21*):

> The British heroin addict, although generally from lower economic groups, is likely to have completed a major part or all of his high school education and to have some job skills even if he doesn't work. In both these respects he differs from most American addicts. However, heroin use . . . is found in all social strata, with middle- and upper-class groups being represented, proportionately, to a far greater degree than in America. . . .

Similarly, the association of addiction with crime is a good deal more attenuated in Britain than in the United States. British abusers are not forced to the same degrees as Americans to support their habits, since heroin is cheaper, purer, and legal. Such figures as that quoted by a famous criminal lawyer that one half of the burglaries in New York City are committed by addicts in need of drugs are unheard of in London. Further, crime by abusers tends to be directed more against property than persons, and to involve relatively little violence.

On the other hand, the belief that if the addict were no longer a criminal by definition, driven to an illicit overpriced market for his · drugs, drug-related crimes would diminish to a level below that of the general population, can no longer be accepted. Writing in 1967, Shur (25) said that:

> addiction reduces the inclination to engage in violent crime, and that persistent involvement in petty theft or prostitution [in the United States] (in order to support the drug habit) is an almost inevitable consequence of addiction. It is noteworthy that in Great Britain, where the addict usually can obtain needed drugs legally and at low cost, there is practically no crime associated with addiction.

However, I. Pierce James, a prison medical officer in London, says (17):

> A review of recent studies on heroin addiction in Britain shows a high incidence of delinquency among British heroin addicts. Heroin addiction in Britain occurs predominantly in young people of marked sociopathic personality, most of whom were delinquent prior to their addiction. We found no evidence to suggest that heroin addiction was an alternative to other types of delinquent behavior; on the contrary, it was usual to find that the delinquent behavior continued unchanged after addiction.

All this reflects changes in the kinds of addicts and abusers, and the kinds of addiciton and abuse. Again, James:

> During this period [1959-1968] heroin addiction has spread to an increasingly younger age group, whilst the social class distribution of the addict population has changed to include young people of lower social class origin. As a consequence of the increasingly widespread use of heroin among adolescents, the addict population as a whole now appears largely composed of extremely unstable and maladjusted young

people who had been unable to achieve any satisfactory social adaptation prior to heroin use, and whose subsequent social adjustment has been even more impaired by their addiction.

The gap between America and Britain is still substantial, but similarities are increasing.

The mortality among British addicts is 28 times that in the general population, and twice that of addicts in the city of New York. Bewley (4) attributes this to the higher doses utilized by the English addicts. One study shows that British heroin addicts typically use 4.3 grains per day, or approximately 260 milligrams, compared to 75 milligrams for American addicts. Add to this that British heroin is pure, while American heroin is almost always adulterated, seldom more than 25 percent pure. These figures are all the more remarkable since American mortality figures also include those dead from adulterants and from accidental overdose, a common problem since it is difficult to determine how much heroin one is really getting. Sometimes an addict's worst enemy, in the United States, may be a relatively honest pusher. On the other hand, some overdose deaths are due neither to honesty nor to accident, since police report that a dealer or pusher sometimes disposes of a potentially troublesome addict by giving him pure heroin.

A heavy factor in the mortality of drug addicts is suicide. Glatt, *et al.* (13) estimate that, from a British sample they studied, "compared to a normal population corrected for age, the suicide rate among these male addicts was over fifty times as high." Such rates, of course, are not precise, since many suicides must be listed as probables, and as Glatt and his associates note gloomily, it is an open question whether people (mostly men) who have harmed their minds and bodies through years of taking dangerous drugs, as well as through starvation and neglect, are really still capable of the "willful" decision deliberately to end their lives. In effect, this is grisly quibbling; the suicide rate is high indeed compared to that of the normal population.

Further, illness among British addicts—abscesses, overdose, hepatitis, septicemia, and "accidents"—is very high, and often is closely related to the unsanitary and septic injection practices in which many of the addicts indulge, although there is no way to determine whether

British injectors are more careless and dirty than their American counterparts. But the question itself is a condemnation, since the British do not have the disadvantages of the Americans who must take what heroin they are given, no matter how badly prepared, and inject it in uncontrolled and furtive circumstances. "One would have assumed," says Louria (*21*),

> that the incidence of hepatitis would be substantially less in England since the drug is given out by physicians, and sterile needles and syringes are readily obtainable. Apparently this is not the case.

Apparently sub-cultural and value factors encourage a debonair and all-in-this-together attitude toward infection and death. Sometimes needles are shared; the whole injection process, with many addicts, tends to take on a ritual and a symbolic meaning beyond the effect of the drug itself.

Klein frequently observed this devil-may-care approach to sepsis in London—sometimes, when medical personnel were not very careful, in the clinics themselves. He frequently saw patients injecting methadone intramuscularly directly through the clothing. He saw abusers carelessly drop "works," needle, syringe, drug and all, on the ground, then casually pick them up, concerned only about losing the drug, and make the injection with no further attempt at sterilization. Left to themselves, they often use tap instead of boiled or distilled water. Although clinic personnel often labored long and with great patience to assure that the equipment was clean and sterile and that the addicts were instructed in the importance and the technique of aseptic injection, their efforts were in vain if addicts were not strictly supervised.

What is the prognosis for heroin addiction under the clinic system? The clinics have not been in operation long enough for results to be clear. In any case, so many other changes are taking place that affect the drug-picture that it is quite possible for the clinics to be successful without substantially changing the upward trend of addiction. Studies presently available show a poor prognosis for heroin-abusers, with a low rate of detoxification, but the studies were made with patients attended by private physicians who did not have the knowledge and safeguards available to the clinics, and some of whom, perhaps, had a vested interest in keeping the patient addicted.

The pattern of drug-abuse in Britain differs somewhat from patterns in the United States. British addicts tend to be experimenters to a greater extent, to try several drugs and take more than one even when they have settled on a drug of preference. Combinations are common, to prolong an effect or give it a special fillip. Heroin addicts often use a stimulant—preferably cocaine—because of the "rush" of feeling.

Barbiturates

Barbiturates have a great and many-faceted potential for abuse. In England as in America, they are ubiquitous, not only throughout the drug underworld, but almost everywhere else, since they are readily available through local private physicians and through physicians of the National Health Service, who prescribe them as sleeping-pills, sedatives, or "tranquilizers." They are at present the most widely prescribed sedatives in both the United Kingdom and the United States. For the last decade Britain has seen a steady increase in the rate of suicide from barbiturate-poisoning, as well as the number of those who survive but suffer poisoning, whether the overdose is by accident or intent.

The physical-dependence potential of barbiturates is ominous; their ability to create addicts is second only to that of the opiates, and in some respects even more dangerous. Even small doses can produce physical dependence. Withdrawal is hazardous, often agonizing and associated with fits and delirium. It is significant that of a study of 29,581 patients who were withdrawn from drugs in the federal hospital at Lexington, Kentucky, over a 31-year period (1), twenty-five actually died during withdrawal: "None was due to the withdrawal of opiates, but there were four deaths from barbiturate withdrawal." This figure should be looked at in light of the fact that the ratio of barbiturate addicts to heroin and morphine addicts at Lexington must, of necessity, be quite small.

In a study of a group practice involving 10,000 patients, Adams *et al.* (1) observed 407 who had been receiving barbiturate prescriptions for a considerable period of time; of these, 47—more than ten percent—showed increasing dosage, and therefore signs of dependence.

Bewley (*3*) has estimated barbiturate-dependence in the United Kingdom to be from 150 to 250 per 100,000 population. In comparison, it is estimated that there are about half a million dependents in the United States—about 280 per 100,000, a ratio not significantly higher than the British.

Figures and reports about the rise or fall of use and abuse of barbiturates are confusing. A major difficulty in determining the amount of barbiturate-abuse, and even barbiturate-dependence, is that most prescriptions are given privately, so that it is impossible to tell how many people are actually using barbiturates daily. According to D. V. Hawks (*14*) the percentage of total prescriptions issued by the National Health Service between 1962 and 1968 fell considerably, although their actual number remained about the same. On the other hand, he quotes the observation by professionals in the field who work daily with drug-dependents—social-workers, policemen, hospital personnel—that the use among young abusers has increased considerably in the last few years. In our interviews, a large proportion of addicts admitted frequent barbiturate-abuse.

Barbiturate-abuse frequently accompanies heroin addiction in the United States. In Britain, in a study made in 1970 by Mitcheson *et al.* (*23*), of 65 heroin addicts interviewed 62 admitted barbiturate use, 65 percent admitting "hedonistic" use and 80 injection. Mitcheson reports that drug-abusers claim the increased use of barbiturates is closely linked with the disappearance of methamphetamine from the illicit market following its banishment from the licit retail market in 1968. The increased use of barbiturates is also due to the clinic permitting patients to use cocaine in concert with heroin. Mitcheson further observes that this present increase in sedative-abuse is in line with the common phenomenon, observed fairly frequently in America, "of opiate users turning to alternative drugs, including alcohol, when unable to obtain their drug of choice." Cutting off a source of drugs often results simply in the shift to another drug, perhaps a worse one, as from cannabis to heroin after the American blockade of the Mexican border. In barbiturate-use there is the added factor that barbiturates produce a cross-tolerance, and can be substituted one for another.

Since both alcohol and barbiturates are depressants, they are dangerous when taken in combination. This combination is frequently abused, however, by people out for a "good time." A few years ago a famed New York columnist died from what was reputed to be this combination, although she had reportedly not taken much more of either than she had been accustomed to using. The use of this combination is probably quite common, seeming perfectly natural to people who have come to rely on both heavy "social" drinking in the evening as part of a way of life and barbiturates taken as a matter of course as a way to sleep.

Amphetamines

The amphetamine benzedrine has been available on the commercial market since the early 1930's. Although it was originally used in inhalators as a nasal constrictor, it was soon discovered that a liquid could be extracted from the active element that would apparently stimulate the senses and the memory, and seemed to fight fatigue and depression for a time. The liquid extract was later made available in pill form.

One of the authors remembers being told by a night-club singer in the 1930's, with great enthusiasm, that she had made one of the great discoveries of her life—a drug that allowed her to go on working and enjoying herself for longer periods, happy and ebullient: "And it has *no* bad effects at all and is *not* habit-forming." It was soon used as a stimulant by people who wanted to stay alert longer, to prolong the party, to perform better, or to postpone exhaustion and extend endurance. Truck drivers notoriously used—and for that matter, despite controls, still use—a great many "pep-pills" or "Bennies" in order to keep going long after they should have stopped and rested. Commercially, most are sold for reducing, since they depress the appetite.

There must be legitimate question whether even the most modern amphetamines really perform these "medical" functions well enough to justify continuing their manufacture. But there can be little question that they easily lend themselves to abuse. Glatt (*13*) says, "There is no doubt that some youth became introduced to these pills through their mothers," who keep quantities around for "slimming."

P. H. Connell (*8*) was the first to report incidences of amphetamine-abuse in England. He described working with a number of patients with "amphetamine psychoses" induced by amphetamine injection, which are primarily paranoid psychoses that become associated with clear consciousness. According to a publication (*27*) by a major manufacturer:

> Symptoms include extreme hyperactivity, hallucinations and feelings of persecution. These bizarre mental effects usually disappear after withdrawal of the drug.

Obvious misuse of amphetamines by adolescents, especially as part of a sub-cultural pattern, became noticeable in the early 1960's. Some authorities date this abuse as early as 1954. At that time oral forms of amphetamines and amphetamine-barbiturate combinations began to be used for kicks by teenagers in Soho. Most of the drugs were obtained illegally. The most commonly used was Drinamyl, a combination of dextroamphetamine and sodium amytal, called "purple hearts" because of their shape and color, which have since been changed by the manufacturer. Because of their widespread abuse, the use of these drugs was restricted under the British Drugs (Prevention of Misuse) Act of 1964 and the Dangerous Drug Act of 1965.

"All-night" clubs then sprang up, and became gathering places, information, drug-exchange and purchase centers, and havens for those abusing amphetamines. Abuse became widespread and notorious, both in government and in communities primarily in the West End of London. This, coupled with the public attention resulting from a series of articles on the "Purple-Heart Craze" which appeared in London newspapers, stimulated concern, and legislation was passed.

Policing of amphetamine abuse, however, is difficult. As Hawks reports, it is difficult to estimate the extent of illicit use since most of those who use them neither appear before the courts nor develop symptoms severe enough to make them conspicuous or to bring them to the attention of physicians or clinics. Further, the development of tolerance and cross-tolerance permits the user to take more and more, with resulting restlessness, excitability, insomnia, tremors, and urinary frequency; and if the supply of one amphetamine dries up, others can be substituted. Hawks (*14*) reports:

Studies of adolescent amphetamine users show that they misuse a variety of amphetamine preparations and typically substitute one for the other when supplies dictate this. While at one time a particular drug may be favored, evidence suggests that any attempt to control its supply will be attended by the increased use of other preparations.

A major problem in amphetamine abuse is the widespread use of methedrine (methamphetamine) or "speed." Originally, some individuals were withdrawn from their drug of dependence by the administration of intravenous methamphetamine. Although its clinical value is worthless, the impact of intravenously injected speed is so quick and dramatic that an abuser might well prefer this new, though possibly just as dangerous, drug to the old. This does not mean, of course, that he need give up his old drug. A number of studies of the development of drug-use have consistently shown that amphetamines, and their various combinations, are, with cannabis, most frequently the drugs taken first; and their use often continues along with the use of heroin and other drugs.

By the late 1960's, methedrine was being widely produced and was prescribed by many physicians. It was also becoming increasingly available through illicit channels. It was no longer just the heroin addicts, nor the most obvious and committed "freaks," but the entire flower community that was abusing methedrine. How dangerous this can be is illustrated by the fact that even university and hippie communities have sounded warnings, and the somber legend "speed kills" appears on the walls of hippie neighborhoods and gathering places, alongside psychedelic posters advertising enticements to the drug experiences.

Faced with this developing problem, "The British reacted," to quote Louria (*21*),

in characteristically sensible fashion to the excessive use of methedrine. The medical profession, government, and pharmaceutical companies got together and decided since methedrine was being obtained from physicians or by diversion of the legal supply, the best solution was to reduce the supply. And so they did. Now physicians cannot administer methedrine in their offices and cannot write prescriptions for it. It can be dispensed only from clinics or hospitals.

The supply, and the use, have since declined.

Louria claims, however, that increased control has resulted in a major black-market for methamphetamine. Klein does not agree. He did not observe a large black-market in methedrine, either from the reports of addicts interviewed on the subject or on the drug scene generally. Addicts frequently asserted that speed was simply not available. This claim is also supported by the increasing use of barbiturates, although barbiturates have not reached the level of the former use of methedrine.

The English general public seems to believe that adolescents are the only significant amphetamine-abusers. This is probably not true, but exact figures are difficult to obtain. The government figures for amphetamine tablets prescribed are not available; nor are there any figures on private prescriptions.

Other studies give some indication of the extent of licit use of amphetamines. Kiloh and Brandon (*18*) showed in a study in Newcastle that, of a population of 250 thousand, 500 persons were psychologically dependent on amphetamines. Of these, the majority were middle-aged women who had been given prescriptions as a means of combating depression, or to inhibit appetite. Extrapolation from these figures gives an overall rate of 200 amphetamine-dependents per 100,000 population.

To what extent studies made almost a decade ago, in one town, can describe the current situation in London is, of course, open to question. The licit use of amphetamines is much more stable than the illicit use. The needs of middle-aged ladies remain about the same, and numbers do not change greatly; nor are they part of a drug sub-culture with constant communication and interaction with other dependents. They are not concentrated in certain neighborhoods or urban centers. However, even among those patients receiving amphetamines and related drugs from private physicians, studies have shown that between 21 and 55 percent have become psychologically dependent on them. Not long ago physicians agreed, informally, to limit the prescription of amphetamines in an attempt to curb this kind of dependence.

Cannabis, LSD, and Other Psychedelics

Cannabis in its various forms is more widely used throughout the world than any other dangerous drug, and with rapid communications, and what might be called the international movement of drug-abusers, its use is spreading. It is known as *bhang* or *ganja* in India, hashish in the Middle East, *dagga* in South Africa and *maconha* or *djamba* in South America.

The form of cannabis most commonly used in Britain is hashish, which is a good deal purer than American marijuana. Hashish is made from the nearly pure resin of the flowering tops and leaves of the female hemp plant; marijuana contains more of the leaves and stems. Louria (*21*) describes hashish as coming in small bricks, ranging in colors from brown to black, and from five to eight times as potent as American marijuana. Marijuana is easy to get in the United States and hashish is difficult, but the reverse is true, Louria says, in Britain.

Figures for abuse come almost entirely from extrapolations from the number of offenses officially recorded, and these estimates, of course, are low, but they show a remarkable progression. Before 1945, according to the figures and to Bewley (*3*), there was very little use of cannabis in the United Kingdom. After World War II the use of cannabis rose enough among the foreign-born to cause the police to crack down—possibly forcing the substitution of heroin addiction. In any case, cannabis offenses rose slowly, but steadily, from World War II to the early 1960's, reaching a kind of plateau in 1962. The plateau lasted until about 1965, but then a rapid rise occurred, offenses doubling from 1965 to 1966, and again from 1966 to 1967. There were 51 recorded offenses in 1957, and 3071 in 1968.

Bewley estimates that there are ten to 20 cannabis-users for each one who is convicted and appears in the statistics. If occasional users are included, this figure is again doubled, putting the incidence of cannabis-users at approximately 60 per 100,000. Hawks (*14*), drawing from both published and unpublished data, quotes figures showing that cannabis-use affects about ten percent of the college population. Louria (*21*) quotes the estimate of "some health officials close to the situation" at the University of London: "approximately fifteen percent of the student population has taken hashish." Klein reports that the students themselves, interviewed informally, estimate 15 to 20 percent use.

"Hashish is not always an innocuous drug," Louria says. "Severe hallucinations, acute intoxication and personality deterioration have all been described." Other critics are not as condemnatory; they report that when psychotic effects occur, they seem to occur in people who were already severely disturbed, or otherwise predisposed. Generally, effects include euphoria, exaltation, and a kind of dreamy sensation, along with distortion of spatial relationships and the sense of time. The effect, of course, varies with the personality of the user and the strength of the sample used.

Though the price of hashish in England is said to vary considerably, one can usually find a "matchbox" (three to four grams) of it selling for about the equivalent of $9.60.

Binnie (5) and Webb *et al.* (*30*), in separate studies, found that students who had smoked cannabis seldom used other drugs except the amphetamines. This would seem to be a point against the common claim, particularly among law-enforcement agencies in the United States, that cannabis tends to lead to hard drugs. Students, of course, do not show the whole picture.

Perhaps more is revealed through studies of cross-sections of cannabis-smokers in Britain. These seem to include personality types not present, or rarely present, among those groups that abuse, or are dependent on, other drugs (with the exception of those dependent on amphetamines, tobacco, and alcohol). In contrast to heroin-users, who are generally recognized as being a delinquent and disturbed group, Louria (*21*) says that hashish-users are not easily classifiable. "Lonely or rebellious persons, students, professors, businessmen, fringe groups, beatniks and flower people all use hashish." Hawks (*14*) summarizing studies on student cannabis-users, says that they tend to be more radical and permissive in politics and social attitudes than non-user students, and were more often studying such non-scientific subjects as the social sciences and humanities. They were more often considered "trouble-makers," and more often received psychiatric treatment. They used more tobacco and alcohol, and were drunk more often. But, again, "there was no relationship between multiple drug use and continued cannabis use." Except among a few, cannabis was not really important in their lives, and they could not be considered dependent on it to any marked extent.

What seems to be happening in Britain is that, as in America, cannabis is becoming so widespread that its use is moving far beyond the drug sub-culture.

The most radical difference in cannabis-use by British and American student populations is in their use of LSD. Binnie (5) and Webb *et al.* (30) found that few cannabis-users (from four to nine percent) used LSD in British universities. The use of LSD in the United States may no longer be increasing—may, in fact be declining—but it is still substantial, and is most frequent among marijuana-users and experimenters.

In 1968, Bewley (3) estimated the ratio of the general population in Britain who have used or experimented with LSD to be one to five per 100,000. Use among students, even among student cannabis-users, is, as has been noted, not very much higher. However, LSD use is much higher among heroin addicts. Mitcheson *et al.* (23) report that about three-quarters of the heroin addicts studied in 1970 used LSD. Moreover, half of this group of heroin addicts admitted to tripping with LSD at least once a week. A provision for LSD control included in the Drug (Prevention of Misuse) Act of 1964 may have had some inhibiting effect on the supply. However, LSD, being so easily manufactured, potent in very small amounts, and undistinguished in appearance, is not easy to control.

LSD and the other hallucinogens do not seem to be very widespread in Britain, and are much less available and therefore less of a public-health menace than they are in the United States. But it is not really easy to determine how great a menace they pose, or how intense their use is in certain places and among certain groups. LSD and the other hallucinogens, as in America, are becoming involved in multiple drug-use. The British drug-scene, particularly in London's West End, seems to be characterized by a great deal of experimentation, and multiple drug use. We have already noted how general LSD use is among heroin addicts, a phenomenon which, according to Louria, is relatively rare in the United States. "Turning-on" and "tripping" are still important parts of the drug sub-culture. LSD and the other hallucinogens can be easily purchased in the Soho area of London; and LSD seemed to be everywhere at the 1970 rock-festival at Bath.

The Treatment-Clinics

An assessment of the effectiveness of the clinic system of Britain—even a coherent description of the way the clinics function—must begin with, and return to, the purposes for which the system was founded. This is especially relevant because the fifteen clinics vary considerably in facilities, techniques, procedures, and even in their approaches to and philosophies of treatment. They do not vary in purpose.

The clinics, in effect, were given the assignment of riding a two-headed horse, keeping him moving down the middle of a rough road, watching carefully to see that he did not wander or pull suddenly too much to either side. Some may have hoped that the doctors could make this horse stop, and even kneel on command; but it is doubtful that anyone experienced in working with drugs or addicts could have expected that.

The clinics were set up to exert controls over the excessive prescription of heroin, and if possible to help slow the growth of addiction. To this extent they were to be agencies of control, even of sanction. No longer could addicts simply ask for prescriptions from careless or venal doctors. They would have to register, answer questions, submit to routine and at least to some extent to treatment, and their right to heroin was not automatic, but would be subject to limitation and supervision.

The clinics thus moved England somewhat toward the American system and philosophy. They were not to be shopping-centers. There would be no return to the epidemic of overprescription of the early 1960's. Rules would be followed; sanitation would be observed. Moreover, the clinics are bound by law to report the addict to the Chief Medical Officer of the Home Office. The clinics are not the anterooms to prisons, but they perform official functions in a legally defined manner, and they control the administration and the supply of drugs. They might seem to the addict to wield the power of the most severe punishment—deprivation—if he refuses to conform.

On the other hand, the clinics are there to provide heroin and other drugs, not to forbid them or punish wrongdoers. Heroin is still legal; the addict has a place to go where he can be sure of an adequate and safe supply. They are also there to meet his needs, even to serve him. For the other main function of the clinics is to make sure that the addict will not be driven to the black-market. A black-market, especially one large and potent enough to attract the underworld, with all this would mean in crime and degradation, must never get a foothold in the United Kingdom. The founders of the clinic system wanted to control the flow of drugs and of addiction. And they wanted to do this through their own channel, engineered according to their specifications, modified by experience, and perhaps, in time, narrowed.

Another essential element was that the clinics were to be staffed by experts, with extensive services for the gathering and exchange of information. Before the clinics, the physicians who prescribed drugs were largely unfamiliar with the intricacies of drug-addiction, were often accused, sometimes with justice, of being in it for the money, and had no ready method of follow-up, no way to know whether the addict was using a number of doctors as wholesalers for his own retail drug business. The physicians in the clinics are guided by well-defined principles of dosage and treatment, usually prescribing conservatively, and they are not easily misled or conned by addicts, since they know the field and begin treatment only after they are convinced, usually by chemical tests, that the patient is truly addicted.

The key-word in the thinking behind the new system is *treatment*. Past experience around the world and in England itself indicates that the word really means "hope for treatment," rather than expectation; hope even though abuses and deceptions, and public misunderstanding and resistance, will arise; even if the addicts themselves continue to try to beat and subvert the system. The old system, without control over the dispensing physicians, could not really hope to treat the addicts. The hope of the new system, as Edwards (*12*) put it, is that "through contact with clinic staff, motivation will gradually be built, dosage gradually decreased, and the offer of admission for withdrawal finally accepted."

But the clinics face certain realities in their daily work. Some addicts may never be willing or able to attempt withdrawal—at least, in the present state of the art of treatment—and the hope must lie in stabilization on maintenance doses, with some later attempt at lowering dosages.

There are also dangers built into the new approach, even beyond some of those in the old. Connell (Connell, in *29*) listed some of them about the time the clinic system was being set up. Most revolve around the inevitability of human imperfection. Some doctors have already been proven all too fallible and even venal when it came to overprescribing: "all professional classes contain weaker brethren." The number of doctors prescribing under the clinic system is several times as large as under the old. It had been shown that even a few overprescribing doctors can cause an epidemic of drug-taking when the demand is strong enough. "The experts in the special centres are not infallible and have no accurate tools to assess the dosage of the drug." Without careful evaluation and practice, the situation could actually become much worse than it was before.

The clinic personnel, by and large, believe that most of the necessary safeguards are there. The addicts do not entirely agree; as might be expected, they have worked out angles and sources that to some degree bypass the safeguards. But no one believes that the old, easy-going ways have not changed. In fact, the major complaint of the addicts we interviewed was that limitations on dosage were perhaps too strict and occasionally unrealistic, that some addicts were forced to scrounge around, and that this might have helped to bring on a development of the black-market. On the other hand experts are generally agreed that there is, as yet, no large organized black-market. This is supported by the finding of Willis (Willis, in *29*), who interviewed British addicts and found none who had been introduced to heroin by a pusher, or professional peddler—a strong contrast to the experiences of the United States addicts.

The fact that clinics are legally bound to report the names of, and information about, all addicts to the Home Office means that information about all addicts being treated in the United Kingdom is available to treatment-centers and authorized personnel. If these files are maintained and checked by modern data-storage equipment in a system that takes into account the urgency of the problem and the nature of addicts and addiction, the problem of addicts who play off one treatment source against another, as well as the problem of official ignorance, can be eliminated. It is worth emphasizing that even before the clinic system was set up the Home Office revised its list of known addicts every year. In rather strong contrast Glatt *et al.* point out (*13*) that in the United States "Federal Bureau of Narcotics keeps a person . . . listed as an addict for five years, even though it is not known whether he has taken drugs or not during that period." Finally, the clinics work closely, and are often associated, with hospital in-patient treatment facilities. This permits rapid in-patient treatment when it is deemed advisable that the patient be withdrawn (detoxified), or undergo extreme dosage reduction. This also enables the patient to receive the close support, medical help, and supervision necessary to his treatment.

If the addict wants his heroin, the best place—for many the only place—to get it is at the clinic. This gives the clinics and the government a powerful lever with which to bring about change, and they know it. It may well be that this lever will help to make heroin-addiction one of the more manageable forms of drug-dependence, since it will bring the addict to the clinic, to treatment, and to the knowledge of the experts instead of losing him in some slum.

The clinics are also the only centers through which an addict can legally receive cocaine. Because cocaine is not physically addictive, most staff officials at the centers frown on its prescription, since the addicts cannot legitimately claim that they have to have it as they must have heroin, and the staffs want to limit prescriptions to what is necessary. Many of the addicts of the 1960's, however, who have been using heroin in combination with either cocaine or methamphetamine, would continue to want that combination, even if they had to go to the black-market for part of their supplies. Thus the prescription of cocaine can be a vital tool for recruiting addicts to the clinics.

The clinics opened in 1968. The number of patients attending and receiving their fixes, after fluctuating for a while, settled down to about 1300 per month. This, of course, does not include the entire addict population, since there are always substantial percentages in hospital or prison, or unable to use the clinics for other reasons. Addicts unaccounted for cannot be very many, because the black-market is not large enough to supply more than a few. Although addicts use the black-market to supplement their supply, there are few who are willing to pass up the legal, pure, and relatively low-priced heroin available at the clinics.

When the patients first came into the clinics, most of them had been maintained by private physicians on excessive amounts of heroin. Note the difference in heroin-dosage between American and British addicts. Writing in 1969, after the clinics had begun their drive to cut down dosage, Bewley (2) commented that the average New York heroin addict consumed, at an estimate, about 80 milligrams a day of heroin cut by about 50 percent, the average British addict 240 milligrams of pharmacologically pure heroin. It was the first task of the clinics to lower the heroin-dosages of their patients. Twelve months after they had opened, the clinics were prescribing only one-fourth or less the amount of heroin prescribed by private physicians, along with an equal amount of methadone, which had rarely been prescribed by private physicians.

Weekly urine tests are taken to monitor each patient in order to determine whether the patient was 1) taking the drugs administered; 2) not taking the drugs administered; 3) taking other drugs. The techniques addicts use to confuse the medical staff administering these tests, and the checks that must be taken by the staff, are illustrated by the casual comment of a nurse when asked whether she checked the temperature of the addicts' urine as well as running tests on drug-content:

> This is only to ascertain that the person has passed it on the premises, but apart from that you will observe to see if the color is normal—the concentration—because the temperature alone is no great guide. They could add hot water.

Klein visited England in the summer of 1970, when there were fifteen out-patient drug-dependence units operating in the general London area, working closely with four in-patient units. Communications among the clinics were close, and doctors from the different clinics met regularly to determine the value of their treatments and to compare notes and results. Such interaction and information-exchange made them able to evaluate and, where desirable, modify their programs. Programs and approaches, however, vary considerably. Klein visited four clinics. All had different types of patient populations, each was unique, and, although the basic guidelines were similar, each handled its patients and its tasks in a different manner.

Most clinics require patients to attend once each week; the four Klein visited see the patients only once a fortnight. This would seem to leave the patient in large part on his own, but an addict cannot be trusted with two week's or even one week's drug supply; almost inevitably he would use his fix quickly, and then be without. This problem is avoided because the patient does not get his heroin directly through the clinic. He does not even get the prescription. The prescriptions are sent to his pharmacist, who dispenses the drugs to the patient daily.

On Saturday the addict frequently gets a double dose, to last until Monday when the chemists' shops are open again. Occasionally, in the event of a bank-holiday, or if the addict must, for some legitimate reason, leave town for a few days and carry his drugs with him, he may be given a large enough prescription to last until he returns. Bank-holidays are notorious, however, as bad times for the drug-programs and for the addicts in Britain. Many addicts will invariably take their drugs too quickly, run out, and have to go to the black-market for help until the holidays are over and they can get back—to the relief of both patients and clinics—to the old routine.

Some of the distinctive qualities of the clinics are found in the buildings themselves: some are older, some seem more sterile, more dismal, or more friendly. Some differences reflect the neighborhoods—convenience may determine how crowded a clinic is, and what kind of clientèle it has. It must be remembered also that not all clinics are entirely given over to the treatment and maintenance of addicts; some are medical out-patient clinics, attached to hospitals, that have in their waiting and treatment rooms people who are being treated for many kinds of disorders—people who usually are not at all pleased by the proximity and behavior of addicts.

A fundamental difference is the clinic's approach, which may reflect the personality and philosophy of the director or key treatment personnel. For instance, Dr. P. H. Connell of the Bethlem Royal and the Maudsley Hospital is conservative in his approach to addiction; Dr. J. H. Willis, of the York Clinic at Guy's Hospital, appears to affect some addicts as a kind of father figure, for whom they acquire a good deal of personal affection. If neighborhoods partly help to determine clientèle, so do the atmosphere and staff. Addicts go where they will be happiest, and to some extent where they believe they will be treated with the most leniency; those most interested in breaking the habit may concentrate on the most businesslike centers. Word of the differences passes around Piccadilly Circus, and the other gathering places, and there is a certain amount of shopping around and angle-shooting by the addicts.

Although the clinics function independently, despite some inevitable duplication the total effect is not of competition or disunion or disorganization, but of a spectrum of possibilities and treatments. If a patient chooses to quit any clinic, he can immediately become a member of another, perhaps one which suits him better. Conversely, if the professional personnel of a clinic feel they have failed with a patient, they can transfer him to another clinic without prejudice.

Most heroin addicts are maintained on both methadone and heroin. A patient who requests it may, without compulsion, be admitted to the in-patient hospital for a six-week detoxification period. This admission is purely voluntary; some patients, informed of this option, request it purely on their own initiative; others do it on the advice of psychiatrists. If the patients subsequently weaken, or change their minds, they may discharge themselves at any time, in as few as two or three days, and be maintained on methadone-therapy outside the hospital. Should one stay in the full six weeks, however, he is presumed to be withdrawn, and receives no further maintenance doses of any kind of drug.

The clinics are not only treatment-centers, but centers of research and learning. They must always therefore be receptive and sensitive to changes—in knowledge, in insights, in techniques, in routines, and in research. So little is actually known about drug-addiction that any approach that does not remain flexible, willing to admit error and to try something new, must admit failure. If *The Road to H* (the title of Isidor Chein's influential book) (6), has been predominantly a road to failure and disaster, the various methods taken to find the road back have not been much better. The final answers, if any, will probably have to come out of new trials and experimentation. The British system, or any system, if it is to work, must include a built-in commitment to change, to search for new solutions, and to replace itself if necessary. A hard-and-fast commitment to a single method is a commitment to failure.

Research, therefore, has a high priority. Dr. P. H. Connell of the Maudsley Center, in particular, has put a great deal of emphasis on research, not only on the treatment of addiction, but on understanding addiction—its psychology, ideology, pathogenesis, and biochemistry, and the social and clinical factors that contribute to it or are associated with it. A symposium of the research contributing to the knowledge of drug-addiction will draw on experts from dozens of disciplines. Connell and others have pushed hard, and now have established many drug-research units in London, including those in Bethlem Royal Hospital and in Maudsley, under the direct control of Dr. Connell.

The clinics frequently re-evaluate their data for evidence of success or reason for failure, and change their methods accordingly. Each addict is a different personality, a different problem. The increasing use of methadone-maintenance reflects to some extent American research on methadone, and American influence. But American methadone is given entirely in the oral form; in Britain it is almost entirely injectable. If it is decided that methadone won't work with any particular patient, he can be returned to heroin-maintenance, an option that is closed to American treatment-centers.

All this gives British centers greater flexibility and adaptability. Injectable methadone has many problems; it can be, and has been, used to excess, in uncontrolled quantities and an uncontrolled manner, and can bring on its own not-so-pleasant form of addiction. All the other handicaps that go with injection of drugs may also be present— hepatitis and other infections, danger of overdose, and vein destruction. But the act of injection has for many addicts an aura and mystique that are as important (and almost as dependence-producing) as the drug itself. Since injecting methadone is not as great a step from injecting heroin as oral use, it attracts many more addicts into the clinic. Some of those interviewed said that they couldn't even give their oral methadone away, and don't want it. And if all else fails, the heroin is available to keep the addict in the clinic and under treatment. The dangers of injection can be partially controlled through instructions and follow-up, and modifications are always being made in the modes and techniques of treatment.

Unless our idea of treatment is to seize the uncompromising sword of the crusader against sin, and hack off drug-tainted lives without mercy, wherever we find them—if, instead, we mean to treat addiction as a social and medical problem—then it is inevitable that much of the calculus of treatment in the present stage of the art must consist primarily of a constantly changing trading-off of negatives: what dangers and evils are we willing to accept, or even to encourage, in order to buy off or head off what we consider to be even greater dangers and evils?

The record of success in oral-methadone centers in the United States is quite impressive, and the use of this method, where practical, should be encouraged and exported. But the British centers treat a larger population than ours do, and certainly a much larger portion of their total addicts. The American unwilling to take the linctus methadone in the United States just drops out of treatment, and usually out of sight, until the police or the hospital or the morgue finally claims him. Many of them might, and in Britain could, come to clinics for the injectable variety. Others would come for the heroin, and at least remain under some control. Why should we subserve the addicts' "whims" and "coddle" them? Ought we not rather to force them to take the oral methadone, or at least give them no alternative to the full force of the law so that they will "choose" to? Arguments which use the word "ought" with moral or punitive authority behind it cannot really be answered in their own terms. We "ought" to do many things; and addicts certainly ought to do a great variety of things differently. But how often has this approach worked? What will be the net effect—greater or less addiction, greater or less suffering, greater or less social, legal, and medical disorder and expense?

All drug-treatment programs in the United States—Synanon, Phoenix House, Daytop House, and the like—require great willingness on the part of the addict to undergo treatment, including total withdrawal, and what can only be termed a dedication to hard work and self-sacrifice. Some involve total commitment to what amounts to a radical restructuring of life. Oral methadone opens the doors to a much broader range of motivations. The addicts are not required to give up their addiction, but to change narcotics to one more manageable, acceptable, and legal. Nevertheless, the addicts on oral-methadone maintenance are carefully chosen, highly-motivated individuals who are willing to change their lives and habits. They can only represent the tip of the iceberg of addiction—perhaps one in five of those who might have come in if injectable methadone and heroin-maintenance were available. The others who "ought" to do what we tell them are still getting their fixes from the underworld, and committing crimes to get the money.

The balancing of pluses and minuses—actually, the balancing of different magnitudes of minuses—is very delicate. Methadone is an addicting drug, and its use in injectable form has led to abuse. It should never be forgotten that heroin was originally introduced as a substitute for morphine addiction. The British may have opened another pandora's drug-box by their new practices, and the results must be watched closely.

Despite their differences, all the clinics have certain common principles that underlie their treatment. The desire of addicts to play off one prescribing agency against another did not end when the power to prescribe moved from the private physician to the clinic. The addicts must be allowed to search out the treatment that meets their particular needs, and the clinic that best elicits their cooperation; this is to be encouraged, but certain treatment principles have to be observed to avoid abuse.

These principles have been enumerated by Dr. Willis.

1. A uniform scheme of maintenance should be used at all centers. That scheme should be rigid enough, if necessary, to bar further prescriptions of heroin to an addict who says he has lost his drug or has sold or given away portions. This may, for short periods, leave an addict without his drug; in this case he is offered admission to in-patient facilities for supervision and treatment. In all the clinics visited this was a uniform policy, and numerous examples were observed. As the interviews reveal, some addicts complained, pointing out that an addict might, upon first registering, overstate his need in order to allow for sale or reserve for a growing habit. Nevertheless, if the wishes of a patient were the only guide to dosage, overprescribing (probably worse than before, Dr. Connell feared, because more doctors were now involved) would certainly result, and the clinic system could easily go down the same old path.

2. It is essential that careful records be kept. Further, close liaison and two-way communication must be maintained with the Home Office in relation to records, notification, and movement.

3. Adequate procedures have to be maintained for the addict who has moved out of his old neighborhood, or gone from one clinic to another. This necessity is taken care of by the fact that addicts are not maintained at more than one center at a time. Further, each addict is maintained as an individual, whose records go with him. Through the registration system, the coordination of records, the cooperation with the Home Office, and meetings and communications among the various center groups, all these principles can be fulfilled.

Extensive records are kept. In addition to the standard personal, medical and drug information, most clinics require the addicts to fill out questionnaires on their injection routines and practices—what kind of apparatus is used, how it is cared for, how and when it is sterilized; the drugs used; how the skin is cleaned; whether the apparatus is shared, with whom, and under what circumstances; evidence of sepsis; and such miscellaneous bits of information as whether the addict ever injects through clothing or uses a needle after it has fallen to the floor. Government agencies that must be notified of drug-addiction include the Chief Medical Office of the Drug Branch of the Home Office, and the Department of Health and Social Security.

Probably the most important aspect of treatment, which can bear reiteration, is that under the British system *the addict is not isolated from the physician* as he is in America. Whatever the law may technically allow in the United States, any physician who tries directly to treat an addict—most particularly on heroin- or morphine-maintenance—runs a very grave risk of arrest and trial on questions of legality which, as Shur puts it (25), "can only be determined in the course of an actual court trial of a specific case." In the words of a joint report of the American Medical Association and the American Bar Association, also quoted from Shur:

> The physician has no way of knowing *before* he attempts to treat, and/or prescribe drugs to an addict, whether his activities will be condemned or condoned. He does not have any criteria or standards to guide him in dealing with drug addicts. . . .

Under this uncertain, dangerous, and punitive approach, the addict becomes, in effect, isolated from the physician (except to a limited extent in in-patient hospital drug-wards and a few out-patient withdrawal programs), despite the fact that the physician may be the one person who can treat him, or help him control his habit and maintain his health. Further, American law and law-enforcement have never made a clear and consistent distinction in practice between the addict, the addict-pusher, and the non-addicted peddler-for-profit—between possession for personal use, possession for use with a surplus for sale to help the addict to maintain his habit, and possession purely for sale for profit. The addict therefore is not only a criminal, but one who may be held in a kind of double or triple jeopardy, and the full extent and complexity of whose crimes and punishment may depend on how law enforcement officers and courts interpret his possession. In Britain, although the private physician no longer works directly, in his private office, with the addict—in fact, in large part because of this circumstance—the physicians and other medical specialists at the clinics do have close contact with the patients, with their records, with setting the standards of dosage, quality, and to some extent sanitation and antisepsis, and they have ultimate responsibility for forms of treatment as well as the disposition of cases.

In addition to the clinics there are a number of youth-oriented centers in Britain. One of the most important in London is the Release Foundation. It has both an office and an emergency telephone number. It does not concentrate solely on drugs but on all acute problems of young people, including alcohol. The emphasis is very strongly on youth, and most of the staff-members are young. Similar programs that use the same name, although they are not directly connected with Release, have grown up in other parts of Europe, including Amsterdam and Heroniken, Holland. These groups maintain informal contact and offer each other assistance, and they are also connected by the "underground railroad" apparatus of the whole drug sub-culture.

In addition to Release, there are drug-free religiously-oriented centers in London, such as Spelthorne St. Mary, located in Surrey, which is run by nuns for the treatment of both drug-addicts and alcoholics. Another London organization, BIT, offers 24-hour assistance and information services. There are parallels to some of these organizations in the United States.

Featherstone Lodge, which seems to be modeled along the lines of Phoenix House in the United States and is run in a similar drug-free fashion, is managed by a former American addict who has himself been a patient in a drug-free community in the United States. His wife is co-manager. Established in response to, and in large part according to the plans of, authorities in Britain who had felt for a long time that the nation needed not one hard-and-fast approach, but a multiplicity of approaches, Featherstone offers both treatment and rehabilitation.

The Bethlem Royal and the Maudsley Hospital

The Maudsley Hospital is in the Denmark Hill section of London, in the southeast quadrant of the city. The Bethlem Royal Hospital proper is some distance away in Beckingham, but is so closely affiliated with Maudsley that the two carry the joint name as a common designation—Bethlem Royal Hospital and the Maudsley Hospital.

The drug unit of the Maudsley Hospital (it is usually simply called "Maudsley" Center) consists of both an in-patient and an out-patient unit, the in-patient at Maudsley and the out-patient at Bethlem Royal. Although the out-patient unit lists hours three days a week—Monday morning from 9:30 to 12:00, Wednesday afternoon from 2:00 until 5:30, and Thursday evening from 5:30 to 9:00—closing times are really formalities of scheduling; the clinic usually remains busy for some time after-hours.

Bethlem Royal is one of the five royal hospitals in the city of London, the others being St. Bartholomew, St. Thomas, Christ Hospital, and Bridewell. Bethlem Royal is the famed "lunatic" asylum, so often mentioned in song and legend, whose popular name—Bedlam—has become a synonym for disorder, uproar, and brutal ill-treatment—a reflection probably of the ignorance and inhumanity of the early centuries of its existence rather than of its own particular infamy, since it was the first lunatic asylum in England and only the second in Europe. Of it, one of the early Toms-o'-Bedlam, a discharged "patient," sang as he traveled around and begged for his living:

> In the bonny halls of Bedlam,
> Ere I was one-and-twenty,
> I had bracelets strong, sweet whips ding-dong,
> And prayer and fasting plenty.

Originally founded in 1247 by the sheriff of London as a priory for the sisters and brethren of the Order of the Star of Bethlehem, it was used as a hospital before 1330. An official inquiry made in 1403 revealed that its patients in residence included six men "deprived of reason" and three other infirm persons. The same inquiry quotes from an inventory made in 1398 which lists among other items six chains of iron, four pairs of manacles of iron, and two pairs of stocks. Exactly when Bedlam began to serve as a place to receive the mentally and emotionally disturbed is not precisely known, but certainly it had started by the end of the 14th century, and has continued until the present, making it (except for a possible exception in Spain) not only the first mental hospital in the world, but the longest existing such institution. Moreover, until early in the 18th century, Bethlehem (later shortened to its present spelling, Bethlem) was the only public institution of its kind in the country, although private madhouses did exist. It was a charitable hospital; and one of the conditions of admission was that a patient, his family, or his friends must not be able to pay for private care.

The hospital moved around London quite a bit, in 1675 to Moorfields, and in 1815 to St. George's Road in southeast London. In 1870 a convalescent establishment was opened at Whitley in Surrey to supplement the regular hospital, and in 1930 Bethlem Royal Hospital was opened at its present location, at Monk's Orchard in Beckingham, by Queen Mary. Its grounds spread out over a wooded estate of about 250 acres. Until 1948 it was associated with the Bridewell Hospital, but in 1948 it proposed that this affiliation be ended and that the present affiliation, with Maudsley Hospital, which was founded in 1923, be consummated. On July 5, 1948, the National Health Service Act went into effect. Since then the two have formed one teaching hospital, known formally as the Bethlem Royal Hospital and the Maudsley Hospital.

The Maudsley Center is in an imposing building, surrounded by high iron gates. The waiting-room for the out-patient clinic is gigantic, like an old-fashioned urban train station, with people sitting in long rows, waiting patiently for the trains that are always late, so that there is no use complaining about them. Relatively few of these patients are addicts; most are patients waiting for the more standard psychiatric services, for whom the presence of drug-patients is often unnerving. The addicts have little compunction about taking their fixes in the area, openly bringing out their syringes, needles, drugs and other gear, searching for their veins, and shooting up without further ado, to the mortification of simple neurotics.

Everything remains extremely proper, extremely British, despite the presence of the addicts. The waiting-room seems very sterile. In big leather chairs everyone politely waits his turn. There are no children running around to remind you of similar waiting-rooms in America. As you enter there is a little refreshment stand at which you can buy a cup of hot tea with cream, for threepence, and little cakes. Hot tea is sold even during the summer, when it is still preferable to the horrible orange squash cream, which is offered everywhere, but which nobody seems to want. Nurses—called Sisters—move in and out of the room and seem to run the place. The waiting-room is surrounded by glass windows, through which, from the floor above, psychiatrists look down, observing their patients before they formally see them. An information clerk waits at the door to ask who you are and whom you want to see. Everyone behaves himself, except the addicts—who perhaps see the situation differently.

Dedication to hard work, and to the work to be done, is one of the outstanding characteristics of Maudsley and Bethlem Royal. Most striking, perhaps, is the evident dedication of the nurses, who are far more concerned and involved with the success of the programs than their counterparts working in American drug-rehabilitation programs. To the disciplined, hard-working, no-nonsense British nurses, addicts must seem an especially useless and bad lot—no pulling up your socks and getting on with it about *them*. True enough, they tend to treat their addict patients a little as though they were children who had gone wrong and been pretty messy about it. But these nurses are very much aware of their limitations, very concerned about their chores, and insistent that their work, their patients, and they themselves be treated with respect. They were unwilling to see their work interrupted even for what researchers might have considered to be a good cause. They were very concerned that the dignity and anonymity of the patients, whatever their own personal feelings about them, should be respected. A considerable hassle developed, in fact, when one of the authors took a picture of the waiting-room which happened to include one of the nurses. They have as little interest in publicity as in strange interfering men who happen to get in the way of their work. They have their own crotchets, of course, their own little ego-supporting empires—their private nurses' room which no one else can enter—an occasional hint of anti-Americanism, and their dedication which is not without its touch of humorless rectitude. Nevertheless, they are distinct and striking assets to the British drug-programs.

The Maudsley Center takes its direction, and much of its tone and approach, from its founder, Dr. P. H. Connell, one of the most prominent physicians working in Britain in the field of drug-addiction and rehabilitation. Dr. Connell believes in caution, thorough preparation and procedure, hard work, hard information, and as much research as possible. Maudsley and Bethlem Royal have become major research centers under his direction, and at his instigation. He early emphasized (Connell, in 29) that the clinic system would not automatically correct the old abuses, but needed to be watched carefully because there are "many dangers in the new approach which have to be faced and . . . stated in order to avoid a drift into disaster and a breakdown. . . ." The system established in 1968 so greatly increased the number of physicians authorized to prescribe heroin, and so broadened official governmental sponsorship of opiate maintenance, that "it must be acknowledged that without careful evaluation and careful practice it would be possible for the situation to become much worse than when general practitioners were free to prescribe these drugs to addicts."

Dr. Connell means to provide that careful evaluation and careful practice. Maudsley is probably the most conservative center, in its approach to heroin addicts, in the city. Dr. Connell spends most of his time around the in-patient unit and the research offices. As soon as he can, he tries to get the heroin addicts either into the in-patient unit to start withdrawal from drugs altogether, or at least onto oral methadone-maintenance. Initially, however, all heroin addicts are maintained on heroin, under tight control. Most of the staff people at Maudsley Klein interviewed did not feel that the oral-methadone approach had been particularly successful, but did feel that they had had some success with heroin-maintenance, working toward reduction and withdrawal.

The clinic at Maudsley uses two types of detoxification procedures. One is a steady withdrawal over a 14-day period. The second is 28 days long, and the withdrawal rate generally follows the first half of a hyperbolic curve—rapid withdrawal, then a gradual and increasingly slow tapering-off. Interestingly enough, most addicts prefer the 14-day straight-line withdrawal procedure.

The prescriptions for these heroin-withdrawal and methadone-replacement procedures are given to the local chemists, with appropriate rates and quantities listed, and the drugs are distributed by the chemists to the addicts. Heroin is received in ten-milligram capsules which dissolve readily without heating, and can then be injected intravenously by the addicts themselves. The methadone prescribed by Maudsley-Bethlem Royal is taken orally. Again, addicts never get a prescription in their own hands.

When the patients are called from the waiting-room, they go to the glass-enclosed psychiatrists' offices upstairs. The rooms are so clean and neat that it is difficult to believe that people work there, and the set-up is surprisingly efficient. There is a laboratory where the urine samples are taken and analyzed. No patient is maintained on drugs until the urine sample has proven positive. The clinics are not interested in helping neophytes become addicts, but in reforming those already addicted. The examining rooms are used not only for psychotherapy but for the thorough physical examination every patient maintained on drugs must undergo. Treatment is available not only for those with heroin and cocaine dependencies, but for those with amphetamine problems as well. However, while heroin addicts may be put on maintenance-programs (which may also include cocaine-maintenance, since they are often taken together), the Maudsley officials show a notable lack of enthusiasm for amphetamine-maintenance. They usually try to get those on amphetamines into drug-free withdrawal, with intensive psychotherapy to bolster and stabilize them.

The addict population at Maudsley is varied, and very interesting. There are many older, well-established addicts, including some who seem quite affluent and settled citizens. Undoubtedly some of these are what is left of the older, therapeutically-connected addicts, including some medical men; although their percentage of the total of all addicts has declined sharply, their absolute numbers, surprisingly enough, have remained about the same. And there are also many of the younger, long-haired hippie-types, who are the ones inclined to inject in the waiting-room. Some of the Piccadilly habituates, including the young ones on amphetamines, are also evident.

The tight organization of the Maudsley Center is evident in the extensive collection of information about the patients. The basic front data sheet, the first interview form, is very lengthy, including such information as the patient's marital status, race, sex, nationality, place of birth, National Health Service number, National Insurance number, and Home Office index number. The form covers not only the patient's vital statistics but his family history and background, schooling, personal history, police record, sexual (and, with women, menstrual) history, occupations past and present, home environment, delinquency if any, and premorbid personality history. Drug and alcohol checklists are attached. The patient must include information about complications or ramifications resulting from or associated with drug use, such as abscesses, septicemia, pneumonia, malnutrition, endocarditis, jaundice, suicide attempts, depression, symptoms suggesting or diagnosis of amphetamine psychosis, cocaine psychosis, delirium tremens, and fits. The physicians pick up more information through interviews and examinations. All this is integrated, evaluated and discussed, judgments about the medical and drug-status of the patients are made, a treatment plan is formulated and proposed, and contacts with other agencies are made when necessary. Out-patients come back every two weeks, on a very tight and precise schedule.

Under the overall direction of Dr. Connell, the research activities at Maudsley are closely correlated with the in-patient and out-patient services. All the services are mutually enriching; the clinical services and the patient-addicts become sources of research information and provide the opportunities and facilities to test research ideas, and the benefits of research are put to work in the clinics. There is little doubt that the Maudsley Center is a thoroughly organized and admirably professional drug-treatment, rehabilitation, and research facility—and, to the degree that such a term has meaning in the rehabilitation and maintenance of addicts, effective.

St. Giles and Dr. Willis

The St. Giles treatment-center, only a few blocks from Maudsley, presents a rather distinct contrast in style, mood, tempo, the types of its addicts, and the general leniency of its atmosphere. Maudsley puts considerable emphasis on tight scheduling, uniformity, precise and complete paperwork, and similar organizational virtues. The no-nonsense atmosphere is not unfriendly, but it is businesslike. St. Giles is well-organized, but in a different, less obtrusive way. It seems more like a club. The addicts are more relaxed; they seem to be there in large part because they want to be, because it is preferable to being out on the street, even in the 'Dilly; to many it is a kind of home away from home. They give the impression that they come there not only because of the drugs and the treatment, not only because the laws of Britain and the demands of their habits require it, but because they feel they are welcome and have friends there; that even if they had to go somewhere else to get their drugs, they would still stop around from time to time to visit and while away an hour or two. Addicts are not welcome everywhere; they feel welcome at St. Giles. The friends they come to visit include Dr. Willis and some of his staff, although their feeling for Dr. Willis seems stronger than friendship.

Such a live-and-let-live atmosphere in a treatment facility for persons as irresponsible and full of angles as addicts might seem to constitute an invitation to disaster. What is there to keep the addicts from running it into the ground? If arguments about short-term self-control and long-term benefits had much impact on addicts, they would not have become hooked in the first place.

Yet the addicts seem to recognize that if they foul this particular nest they may very well never get another; that if they spoil the relaxed and understanding relationship they have with Dr. Willis—abusing it, for instance, by asking for more drugs than they really need—they may lose something far more precious to them than the extra drugs. Interviews with the addicts in the waiting-room indicate plainly that they fear this loss of warmth and confidence and do not therefore take dishonest advantage of it.

St. Giles is a good illustration of the value of varied approaches to the problems of addiction. Some patients, needing more external support and discipline, or the respectable, employed addicts who do not appreciate hanging around with hippie-type drug people, undoubtedly find that the relatively tightly-organized and antiseptic atmosphere at Maudsley-Bethlem Royal more nearly meets their emotional and drug-needs. Others, who might not otherwise be willing to come into the clinics at all, find the loose and informal structure of St. Giles more congenial and beneficial, and thus become more willing to undergo treatment. Midway are such centers as that conducted by Dr. Pealy at St. George and Lambeth.

St. Giles Center is located in Camberwell Green. It is housed in a modern building, part of a church. Although it is only a few blocks from Maudsley, the neighborhood is a bit more run-down. There are little jewelry shops, fish shops, and Muslim meat and fish shops. It is, to American eyes, a quaint working-class area. When the center was set up the inhabitants got very worked-up about the prospect of an influx of addicts, especially since addicts also go to the Camberwell Green day-center, and the local residents have already had their fill of public fixing, thrown bottles, and the like, and are concerned about the effects on their children. They are still vehemently opposed. Nevertheless, the centers have remained.

The St. Giles Center's waiting-room (although to call the space a waiting-room is perhaps an overstatement) is decorated in a kind of early-Salvation-Army style, full of tired and broken-down old couches which in their turn are full of young addicts eating ice-cream as though in their personal youth-center. On the average the addicts are a good deal younger than Maudsley's. There is no tight schedule of appointments. The addicts simply drop in when they feel the need, or when they happen to be in the neighborhood, or when they want to. When asked about it, the patients said they felt that they could come any time, that it was a place they could go when they had no other place; obviously, therefore, they use its facilities more often than the addicts at other centers use theirs.

Off to the side of the waiting-room is a gigantic room, in which Dr. Willis and some of his staff hold forth certain mornings and afternoons. There are no desks, no enclosed glassed-in cubicles or scrupulously neat examination niches. Dr. Willis and another doctor simply set up card-tables, with chairs around them, and talk with the patients. While the appointment schedules are not rigid, each addict is expected to report periodically. Willis may prescribe the medication on a weekly or bi-weekly basis, depending on how he feels about it.

The make-yourself-at-home atmosphere follows into the kitchen, where the addicts can make up their own food, or drink those dreadful warm orange squashes. The men's room however, is almost impossible to use because it is full of people shooting-up and making their fixes.

Dr. Willis comes through as a very strong father-figure. Klein comments:

> For a feeling of belonging, I don't think anything could rival St. Giles center for the addicts; and as the object of feelings of devotion toward a doctor, I don't think that anyone could ever rival Dr. Willis.

That feeling is stronger than gratitude and respect for kindness, help, and knowledge.

> The patients seemed too frightened to impose on this relationship, to take advantage of it to get special favors, such as more drugs. One of the things they seemed to fear most was denial of this special relationship by Dr. Willis. While the doctors at the Maudsley appeared at times, more or less, to play the devil's advocates (as addicts see the devil), Willis played the role of a father to his patients, and a frown from him seemed to have tremendous influence.

The addicts are expected to take their prescriptions to the neighborhood pharmacists, and the druggists in turn often come into the center to confer directly with Dr. Willis and the other doctors. As a result, and because of the confidence he inspires, Dr. Willis is usually able to remain quite knowledgeable about what is going on, and to exert control over it. He maintains good relations with the druggists, who reciprocate. Thus an informal chain of relations, checking, and guidance is set up without the more obvious mechanisms of control, evident in other centers, that are likely to turn the addicts off, and away. The druggist is very important as a link in the British system, since he actually dispenses the narcotics and other drugs, and abuse by pharmacists can be quite as serious as abuse by physicians. In the United States, carelessness, venality, and criminality among druggists have often posed more serious problems than the same among physicians.

If Dr. Willis feels a patient needs hospitalization he usually refers him to the center's in-patient unit at the Bexley Hospital. Being on the staff of Guy's Hospital, he can also refer them there, but there are not many in evidence at Guy's. The in-patient unit is large, taking up two big rooms in separate quarters behind the Bexley main building, and resembles nothing so much as a summer camp. The one-big-happy-family atmosphere prevails even here, although the formal hospital setting would seem to discourage some of it. The patients go through a careful screening. Specific histories, as formal as those at Maudsley, are taken. But nothing daunts the patients, or their visitors. Klein kept noticing the familiars, particularly the toothless young man from Piccadilly, moving around, "talking up a fog." Visitors constantly keep trying to bring in drugs; others bring other interesting objects to amuse the patients. Every day's a holiday. Dr. Willis is often in evidence personally.

Tooting-Bec Hospital

Tooting-Bec Hospital and treatment-center presents another example of the great variety of atmosphere and approach. In sharp contrast to St. Giles, it seems very sterile, the coldest atmosphere of any treatment-center visited. All its facilities are interconnected, corridor after corridor, ward after ward, cold red-brick building after cold red-brick building. It has all the grace and joy of the usual huge mental-hospital complex, like state hospitals in the United States. Everything inside is ordered and correct, often bare. Dormitory-type beds are used throughout, in contrast to the wards at Bethlem-Royal and Bexley, which use private beds. The dominant impression is that the patients are being maintained—correctly, of course—on no more than two to three dollars a day. The doctors are treated with respect, even reverence, as they make their rounds.

Although some of the addicts interviewed had been at Tooting-Bec during their travels from one center to another, only two were actually interviewed there. Both are in-patients, under the direct control of Dr. Thomas H. Bewley, one of the more famous authorities on drug-dependence not only in Britain but in the world. One of these interviews is reproduced below.

The in-patient unit that Dr. Bewley administers is a locked unit.

Adjustment at Tooting-Bec

If what he says about himself can be taken at face-value, Sandy Lee may have made the best adjustment of any of the addicts interviewed. A brief statement early in the interview describes a considerable change, and a long journey:

> I left home at age 14 to become a thief and drug-addict. And I became a very, very good one. But I knew the whole system was wrong so I came to England to prove it. They said, "First you're a thief and then an addict." And I said, "No, I'm not." So I came over here and I've been working ever since. . . . People can be made useful citizens. Jesus Christ, I work 72 hours a week and I love it.

He is 46, born in western Canada, and his last residence in Canada was a prison-farm in his home province.

His parents were not religious, and he received no religious training. His mother had little education. He believes his father must have had some, because he was a mining superintendent. When his father was killed, "my mother had to take the rein over us. I figured I was a sucker for working, you know?" Although he was doing fairly well, he dropped out of school in the seventh grade, and went to work, at age 13. By 14 he had decided on the career of thief and addict. He has not been home since he was 15.

At approximately 16 he started smoking opium—Chinese opium, since the Communists had not yet cut off the supply.

> I think it was environmental, really, because I used to go out and work maybe three months at a time at a logging camp, then I would come back and all my friends were using junk, smoking opium. I tried that a few times—smoking hop and then going up to the lumber camps, but I was too sick. So I became a professional thief.

By 17, when he was arrested for the first time, he was addicted to heroin. The opium had been cut off—"you know, this bloody Communist." He mainlined from the beginning, and at 17 his habit was between five and 25 grains a day. To support it,

> I pushed, yeah, I pushed, I robbed banks, I shoplifted. I was an all-around thief—I did everything. I haven't told anybody before, but it may help America, because in America there's a terrible problem and I think they should be allowed to have their drugs and to lead a normal life.

He was arrested and jailed at 17 for burglarizing a shop. He was convicted and got a year, but he appealed and got the conviction quashed. He was to be arrested and jailed many times in Canada, withdrawn each time—but never again to be off drugs for any lengthy period that was not enforced by incarceration until he came to England, married, and settled down. Then he withdrew and was off for two and a half years before becoming re-addicted.

He believes he was jailed at least 15 times. He was threatened with life imprisonment under the Habitual Criminal Act; "That's why I came to England." There was no real gradual withdrawal in Canadian prisons, although during about one third of his imprisonments he was given luminal injections to put him to sleep and thus ease the pains of withdrawal; but he was not given opiates.

In the 1950's—he thinks about 1952—he lived in the United States, "in San Francisco, Los Angeles, all the west coast." He found drugs very easy to get, and found many addicts. He came close to arrest, but was never actually caught. "I was a strange face." He has also been in New York, Chicago, Detroit, and Indiana. But he believes that California is the druggiest environment he has ever seen. It is easier to get drugs there, "but you gotta steal to get them. And you got to run the added risk of the narcos following you and busting you while you're fixing."

He came over to England in 1963. "I immediately got registered. With Lady Franco I got 20 grains of heroin and ten of cocaine a day." He paid nothing for these. He stayed on this regimen for over a year. "Then I got married and I took the cure, at Hallowick Hospital." He was off for more than two years. Apparently he and his wife were very much in love. He tells the story dispassionately. "My wife is dead, unfortunately. Overdose of drugs. Barbiturates . . . she killed herself." She wanted children.

Well, the way the doctor put it, if she had had a very potent man, or I had had a very potent woman, we'd have had a child. They wanted to do an operation because I got kicked in the balls by the Royal Canadian MP one time, and something went wrong there.

But he had gone back to drugs years before she had died. "I realized that I wasn't happy without drugs. You know, life was a drag." The drugs have not materially affected his sex-life. He has a girl-friend now—also an addict—and reports that sex-relations are "very good, very good."

He had come to England, partly, as he said, to prove that he could lead a normal life, and hold jobs.

> I did various jobs. I stained glass windows, I was a cementer, I was a crane driver—you know, there's lots of jobs. But I finally got into a good one, about three years ago. I'm an injection molder. I get 40 pounds a week.

He has taken only one LSD trip, about a year earlier. "Just wanted to know what it was all about. . . . It's terrible, ghastly."

He took American marijuana in the 1950's, in Los Angeles, and doesn't like it; but he has developed a taste for the more sophisticated forms of cannabis and the combinations:

> It's not bad over here because you get what they call hashish which isn't bad, and you get sirash, which is a mixture of hashish and opiates. It's terrific; I love that stuff. I use it whenever I get the chance.

Except for the sirash, he does not admit to taking opiates. His habit is now "ten milligrams of methadone . . . and (this is confidential, of course) I get speed. I love speed. I mix it with it." His "speed" is dexedrine. He gets this from a private doctor, not the drug unit. He takes barbiturates to some extent.

> I'll take them if I haven't got methadone enough to get me through the day. They stop me from being sick. But I don't overindulge in them. . . . Well, I did a couple of times, you know, when I lost my wife. . . . I went a bit haywire.

When he first came to England and was receiving drugs under Lady Franco he had a large habit—20 grains of heroin and 10 of cocaine per day. He had not taken cocaine in Canada regularly; he got it steadily in England.

When the clinics came in, they tried to cut his habit in half. "At that time I was a foreman's shunter in a big railway station, and I couldn't cope with a small amount of drugs. So I had to leave the job." He tried other drugs and finally settled on methadone, getting it from private doctors. He left the clinic, and although he is now in a hospital insists he will have nothing to do with the clinics.

After the first week or so, I just told them to stick it. The clinics, they have you under their thumb, you see. I had a big habit on methadone which allowed me to work and kept me going.

Until he was hospitalized he was able to stay out of the clinics because they are mandatory only for heroin and cocaine.

In 1968 he returned to Canada for a few months. "I wanted to go back and look around, and make myself a few thousand dollars." He ran drugs, was caught, and kicked out of the country.

I made two trips to Hong Kong and one to Canada, and I knew drug-dealers. That's all the evidence they had. As far as the actual charge —that was the conspiracy to traffic. The real charge was traces and a needle and an eyedropper.

He went to the United States because a warrant was out for him.

I knew this warrant—they could hold me for 50 years if I got convicted. So I took a plane from the United States. I was sick four days waiting for it.

They're barbaric, barbaric. I can show you the order they gave me to quit my own country, the country I was born in—ten days to leave it. Vicious—they jump on you, grab you by the throat, stick a tube down, punch you in the stomach to get your drugs out. . . .

He returned to England. "And they treat you like a gentleman here, you know. There's no comparison. I offered to pay a couple of good friends' fares back to Canada and they wouldn't go." He is now an English citizen.

He has also been in trouble with the British law, but his treatment has been different.

I've been in a couple of busts here. Forging the prescriptions. The last time? Oh, Christ, 1964. They gave me a conditional discharge. They just let you go, that sort of thing. They realize you're ill.

I mean, over here, it's a groovy system. I go to work, I've got a lovely girl-friend now, and when I'm gonna get married I'll lead a completely normal life. How could I do it over there?

Despite his professed respect for the British, and British law, he apparently expects a good deal of tolerance.

Oh, incidentally, last year I broke my back and I had my spleen out, so I'm not too agile. Fell off this goddam hospital here bringing drugs up for some friends of mine. A psychiatrist who took a great interest in me asked me to come in, and I came in for three days. Phft. It was terrible. It's better now. They've got a new unit and a record-player going till two in the morning and all that shit. So I used to climb up every night and give people drugs that would be coming off. And then I fell down and broke my back and had my spleen out.

Although he is an in-patient at the clinic, going out to work during the day, he does not really consider himself a part of it. "If I can find a doctor I won't go to the clinic. The clinics, you see, they have you under their thumb."

Independence is very important to him. As long as he does not need heroin or cocaine, he is not bound to the clinic or to anyone else. Nor is he bound to heroin, but he does not feel they are giving him enough methadone:

I'm a big man, a big constitution. Here I'm on 120 milligrams a day. I should be getting twice as much. I go to work in the morning, very early, and I'm sick by noon.

But, it's not heroin-sickness. I can cope with it. Heroin-sickness, four hours and you're dead sick. But methadone is a whole lot easier. I do dig it. If I could get a private doctor, fair enough. If I can't I'll still cope with this.

I like it better than heroin. For this reason: when you mix it with speed, you don't get that big come-down you do on heroin. I fix it all up by nine in the morning—I work from 6:30 in the morning till 6:30 at night. And I'm all right; I don't need a fix till 10:00 at night.

Did any of his acquaintances have a similar history?

Yeah, a lot of Canadians. Americans are in a different situation. You see, the Home Office doesn't let them stay too long. But Canadians can stay here forever. There are a lot like me. They work.

I just hope to God America and Canada get away from the old Anslinger and Nicholson idea of drugs. Because people can be made useful citizens. Jesus Christ, I work 72 hours a week and I love it.

The Background

In 1926 the English Departmental Committee on Morphine and Heroin Addiction, known as the Rolleston Committee, defined a drug-addict (then in Britain confined almost entirely to medical professionals, with a fringe of bohemians) as:

> a person who, not requiring the continuing use of a drug for the relief of symptoms of organic disease, has acquired, as a result of repeated administration, an overpowering desire for its continuance, and in whom withdrawal of the drug leads to definite symptoms of mental or physical distress or disorder.

It is very easy, fortified by the massive hindsight of nearly half a century, to smile and poke holes in this definition. What of the patient who still has pain, takes morphine to relieve it, and is addicted to it? Must he wait for his pain to stop before he can be officially considered an addict? America's first great epidemic of opiate-addiction resulted from the widespread use of opiates, administered hypodermically, to relieve suffering among wounded soldiers during the Civil War.

Nor does this definition draw any fine distinctions between degrees of physical addiction, or between physical addiction and the various degrees of psychological dependence and habituation. Such distinctions were hardly considered significant in 1926 in Britain. Little attention was then given to non-opiates. Many of the drugs whose abuse now so concerns national and local governments were then, at least in Britain, either unknown or considered of minor importance. The amphetamines were, as far as the general public was concerned, non-existent; barbiturates were prescribed for insomniacs with little official understanding that they could be abused in the same way as opiates. Cannabis was not controlled in the United Kingdom until 1929. The danger in the use of cocaine was recognized and some attempt at control was made by 1926; but it was only in 1960 that the proportion of addicts who used cocaine rose beyond ten percent, and before 1955 the number was so small that no precise figures were kept.

This broad and rather vague approach to the problem resulted at least partly from lack of knowledge and experience. The British did not feel that they had a problem; by modern standards, of course, they did not. Opiate-addiction was thought to be something that primarily affected Orientals, usually in "dens." In Britain, however, it affected medical professionals, who had the easiest access to drugs and who undoubtedly found opiates helpful in fighting exhaustion, pain, and personal troubles.

Even the opiates and cocaine were not in particularly bad odor, at least as far as literature was concerned, except for the popular horror tales of intrigue in those dens in Soho and Limehouse. Sherlock Holmes, the creation of a physician, Sir Arthur Conan Doyle, took the needle occasionally, without harm (in fact, with the implication of positive good) to his reputation as the most alert and observant detective in London. Coleridge had the vision that led to the writing of *Kubla Khan* while in a sleep induced by laudanum, a solution of opium in alcohol that was also the favorite of De Quincey, whose *Confessions of an Opium-Eater* is a classic of English literature.

The Rolleston Committee established, however, what might be called the "medical" approach to drug addiction—or, as some writers have called it, the "medical-permissive." This approach emphasizes the concept that addiction is a medical problem rather than a moral or legal one; that the addict is a sick person—or at least would be ill if not given his drug—and that it is within the competence and province of physicians to treat addiction. This permissive and "humanitarian" emphasis may be due to the fact, as some writers claim, that the British really had no problem to speak of, and so could treat it casually, or even be naive about it. Had they had the problem that the United States did, these critics reason, they would have been much tougher about it, as was the United States. Whatever the reason, the Rolleston Committee set up regulations for the distribution to addicts of such opiates as morphine and heroin, as well as cocaine, by physicians. Every effort was to be made to get the addicts to quit or to cut down. But if the addict would not, or suffered severely, or could not lead any kind of productive life without his drug, so that the disease was less disabling than the cure, maintenance-dosages were to be allowed, distributed and supervised by the physicians.

This approach not only puts the emphasis on the physical-medical rather than the legal-moral aspects, but also accepts the premise that addicts can, on maintenance-dosages, lead reasonably productive, normal, and non-criminal lives; in other words, that narcotics in themselves are not necessarily crippling or criminal or crime-producing, as long as they are not so defined.

Physical and Psychological Dependence

The argument about physical versus psychological dependence may eventually, if nurtured by enough rigid thinking, flat statements, and antagonism between warring camps, turn into pure circular reasoning. The conflict already uses terms that resemble the hair-splitting and tortured definitions of arguments about heredity versus environment; the potential for acrimony and harm is, in fact, a good deal greater, because the policemen, politicians seeking election, and journalists desiring sensation outnumber the scientists, physicians, and scholars working on the problems.

The solution most in accord with reason, reality, and effective planning is to stop underlining the conflict; we are not dealing with contending segments but with interacting and usually reinforcing aspects of the same entity.

Technically speaking, every element contributing to an individual's compulsion to take a drug that does not result directly from a chemical effect of the drug on his body must be ascribed to psychological dependence or to social and environmental influences. The psychological elements cover a wide sweep. New thoughts and research daily point out new factors, new directions for further thought and research: we need to study drug-cultures, the availability of drugs to people under great pressures, the reinforcing effects associated with long use, the continuing and renewed exposure to reinforcing associations, the symbolic meanings of drugs and the paraphernalia and rituals that go with them—the search for transcendental experience, the need for retreat or escape from an increasingly depersonalized and dehumanized society. These are only a few. The exact balance between such factors and physiological addiction is impossible to determine, and follows no glib generalization. As Isidor Chein points out (Chein, in 29), the picture is not clear these days, even among the heroin addicts:

> The high prevalence of so-called addiction to heroin in major metropolitan areas of the United States along with the low levels of actual intake and the virtual disappearance of severe withdrawal reactions argue strongly for the relatively minor role of the psychopharmacological functions of heroin use in these areas.

The picture is too broad and detailed to be discussed here. All that can be reasonably attempted is a broad definition and a brief listing of elements.

Psychological dependence includes a strong craving for the drug, a close (some writers say total) personal involvement with its usage, and an appreciation by the dependent of the drug's physical and psychological effects. So far, this follows Chein's definition of psychological dependence. Certain evidence, however, particularly experience with amphetamine abuse, suggests that the feature of tolerance should be added to the description.

It may seem inconsistent that tolerance—diminishing effect with use through time, usually resulting in the necessity of increasing dosage to maintain effect—should be characteristic of psychological dependence. Commonsense would seem to indicate otherwise: how could an effect apparently resulting from frequency and amount of drug dosage be other than pharmacological? However, considerable evidence has accumulated that there is such a thing as amphetamine-dependence which has practically all the major characteristics of an addiction except the abstinence (withdrawal) syndrome. Dependence without the abstinence syndrome is psychological dependence; and amphetamine abusers do develop tolerance.

The characteristics of psychological dependence are thus craving, personal involvement, and tolerance. In the light of the above discussion, we can develop a table which classifies the varieties of physical and psychological dependence associated with the various drugs of abuse. It must be noted, however, that this is not absolute classification since dependence itself is not always clear-cut.

DRUG	PHYSICAL DEPENDENCE	PSYCHOLOGICAL DEPENDENCE
Opiate	Always	Always
Barbiturates	Develops only if dosage is maintained well above usual therapeutic levels	Varies enormously, tends to be intermittent
Amphetamines	None	Variable
Cocaine	None	Marked
Cannabis	None	Variable

Although this list concentrates, as this book does, on what are usually called the drugs of abuse, the authors are not insensitive to the great amount of damage caused by the ingestion of other chemicals which, because of long familiarity, legality, and general social approbation or tolerance, are not considered equally reprehensible. For example, the abuse of alcohol, whether chronically in what is called alcoholism, in occasional drunkenness, or even in extended social drinking, causes so much damage (not only to the addict) that the damage done by all the others combined seems almost negligible in comparison.

In fact, a good case could be made for the viewpoint that the legal, accepted drugs cause the most actual damage. The barbiturates, for example, have become drugs of abuse, part of the drug sub-culture.

They are widely prescribed: the ubiquitous sleeping pill, in medicine-chests and on bedside tables all over America, the housewife's friend, kills more people through accidental and deliberate overdose (it has become a sort of suicide of choice for celebrities) than any other of the drugs listed above.

Although this book is not about alcohol, tobacco, caffein, or any of the other drugs that we have come to accept in our daily lives as part of our routine, it is important to note that the drugs most people think of when they hear the words "drugs" and "drug abuse" must be considered in the context of wide acceptance of drugs of all kinds, for a multitude of purposes and effects.

The Interpretation of the Laws

To a large extent, the meanings of laws come to depend upon who interprets them and how. Many writers claim that it was not the intent of the original Harrison Act passed by the United States Congress in 1941 to define "the addict as a criminal offender." However, the interpretation of that act, and the enforcement of that interpretation by federal narcotics authorities, has declared him just that. According to Shur (25), the Harrison Act "specifically provided that the restrictions would not apply to dispensing of narcotics to a patient by a physician 'in the course of his professional practice' and 'for legitimate medical purposes.'" An authoritative report from the New York Academy of Medicine (quoted in 25) supports this view: "Clearly, it was not the intention of Congress that government should interfere with the medical treatment of addicts." According to Shur, this clear intent was ignored, and "the freedom of medical practitioners to treat addict patients as they see fit" was

> effectively and severely limited . . . through a combination of restrictive regulations, attention only to favorable court decisions, and harassment [by] the Narcotics Division of the U.S. Treasury Department (and its successor, the Federal Bureau of Narcotics).

The United States had a different and much more severe drug problem than the United Kingdom, and its response was to a large extent dictated by necessity and circumstance. National and cultural values and priorities were also involved. America has often found it convenient to interpret social problems in terms rather of sin and law than of medicine and misfortune. Perhaps the differing national characters and circumstances made it inevitable anyway, but the Dangerous Drugs Act of Britain was interpreted by physicians who gave themselves a large share in its implementation. The Harrison Act was interpreted and implemented by narcotics officials who were essentially law-enforcement officers, and many of the differences between America and Britain are related to that fact. Generally, despite its political ties and membership in the Commonwealth, Canada has tended to follow the American rather than the British model.

It must be emphasized that the British drug-situation in 1926 was entirely different both from the American situation then and from the British situation now. There were very few addicts in England then; only 60 offenses concerning opium and manufactured drugs were recorded in 1927. The fact that the Rolleston Committee designated the physician to treat addicts and to administer heroin, opium, and cocaine must have seemed not only logical and consistent, but in large part a matter of internal policing. In America, on the other hand, the Federal Bureau of Narcotics has seldom hesitated to use the argument that the high number of professional addicts challenges the claim of the medical profession that it should have a greater role in the treatment of addicts. It has used this argument even against official policy-statements from so distinguished and conservative an organization as the AMA.

Obviously, the medical men on the committee, and throughout England, could not envisage the problems of drug-abuse that would develop by the 1960's, were not trying to prescribe for them, and were simply trying to set loose guidelines for containment of an abuse that was still largely in the family. It is also clear that the Committee did not assume that maintenance on narcotics or cocaine was the optimum solution. On the contrary, the report stated definitely that maintenance-therapy was more or less the last resort after all efforts toward withdrawal had failed. As Louria, although a strong critic of the British experience, describes it (*21*):

In essence this report legitimatized administration by physicians of heroin and cocaine to addicts—but only after assiduous efforts had been made to withdraw the individual from his drugs. Central to the Rolleston Committee's recommendations was the concept that withdrawal was the preferred treatment but that a patient could be maintained on drugs if withdrawal produced such severe symptomatology that it could not be accomplished satisfactorily or if, upon withdrawal, the addict was unable to lead a fairly normal and useful life. The Committee felt that although withdrawal was clearly the desired goal, maintenance therapy could be countenanced if it permitted the individual to remain as a functioning, productive member of society.

Moreover, the report states that neither opiates nor cocaine was ever to be given simply for "gratification of addiction" but only under certain specified conditions, when the effects of withholding might do greater harm toward adjustment than regulated doses. These conditions include: 1) when the patient is under gradual withdrawal guidance; 2) when he exhibits severe and crippling withdrawal symptoms; 3) when he must have the drug to lead a relatively normal existence, and withholding will make this difficult or impossible.

Another common misconception is that addicts had to register voluntarily to receive their drugs, and that the register was kept at the Home Office. The Home Office did keep a record, for its own information, of "known addicts," but this list was made up from information volunteered by physicians prescribing for addicts, and from pharmacy records of prescriptions filled and drugs distributed. Citation on this listing did not entitle the addict to more drugs than anyone else. In short, there was no official listing at that time of addicts under maintenance-treatment "entitled" to opiates, cocaine, or any other drug. Such a list was created later.

The Changing Scene

Two authorities provide a concise picture of the British drug-scene—its rationale, process, and atmosphere—between the Rolleston Committee's report in 1926 and 1960, when drug-abuse started becoming a social problem. Dr. Bewley writes (3)

A series of administrative practices grew up at a time when there were very few addicts and those mostly in professions with easy access to opiates. . . . The Home Office index or register is a list of people who are known to be addicted to opiates, which is kept by the Home Office in order to make returns to the United Nations, and also to have information available about the number of addicts in the United Kingdom.

A. R. Lindesmith comments (*19*):

The British program with respect to addicts is in reality absurdly simple, and almost impossible to misunderstand. The addict simply goes to a doctor, confides in him, and is taken care of by the doctor. The latter is under a professional obligation to attempt to cure the addict, but there is no provision for forced cures, and the user must therefore be *persuaded* to submit himself to a hospital for withdrawal of the drug.

About 1951, events took place which, though little noticed at the time, were to have a long-term effect on England's drug-problem, particularly heroin addiction. After World War II the importation and increasing use of cannabis rose quickly, until, as H. B. Spear points out (*28*), there was

an increased realization by the police of the problem involved as it was now clear that whereas the traffic in opium had been, and was still, almost entirely confined to the seaports, the traffic in cannabis had spread to all parts of the country . . . [it] was a drug with a certain amount of appeal to our own indigenous population.

The police cracked down and the supply dwindled, but in 1949 and in 1951 there were two major thefts of opiates and cocaine, which were distributed through contacts in the West End of London. The first lot, stolen from a firm of wholesale chemists in the Midlands, was apparently distributed primarily to persons already addicted and registered who wanted a supplementary supply, and seems to have resulted in no new addicts. But the second theft, in 1951, consisted of large quantities of morphine, heroin, and cocaine which were stolen from a hospital dispensary. The majority of those who received the drugs from the thief—a former hospital employee known as "Mark"—had had no experience with heroin addiction, and were eventually, as D. V. Hawks (*14*) points out, to turn up on the Home Office list as heroin addicts. Spear, who has followed the subsequent histories of those who had contact with Mark or with members of his original group, lists some 63 persons "connected, or probably connected" with them; the record is heavily punctuated with entries listing prison, death, suicide, and "still addicted." Spear concludes (*28*):

Future research may show why this change in the pattern of drug abuse in the United Kingdom should have occurred in the early 1950's. Until then we have only the evidence of the events themselves and the testimony of some of those directly involved in them, who have stated that until Mark appeared on the scene there was little or no heroin circulating in the West End of London but that his appearance coincided with the scarcity of cannabis . . . with the result that many persons who had been smoking cannabis began to use heroin and cocaine as substitutes.

This whole episode has some similarity, in its combination of events and of reported results, with the much-publicized recent sealing-off of the Mexican-American border to cut down the flow of Mexican marijuana; the result, according to American drug-abusers, was that many young pot-smokers turned to heroin and became hooked. In the drug-field, simple and sometimes even isolated actions can have unforeseen consequences. These are not the only instances in which cutting off or down the supply of one drug caused an abuser to shift to another, perhaps a worse one. Some of the older Canadian addicts we interviewed in Britain were unhappy at the Chinese Communists, not because they used opium to corrupt western citizens, but because they cut off the supply of crude opium, and Americans and Canadians who had been using it were forced to turn to French-Turkish heroin.

In 1958 the British government appointed another Inter-Departmental Committee on Drug Addiction (the Brain Committee) to review the findings and recommendations of the Rolleston Committee and suggest desirable and necessary changes and modifications. Since 1926, of course, the new dependence-producing synthetic analgesics had been developed, and some of the patterns of use of the older drugs had been reduced. Among the opium derivatives, the use of morphine remained about the same, while the abuse of heroin, which was in a very few years to dominate the picture, had begun its rise. Moreover, the possibility of using methadone for replacement-therapy, and tranquilizers in the treatment of the addict, had now become real possibilities.

The Brain Report (*10*), published in 1961, called for little change in the detection and control machinery, and recorded no significant changes in incidence of addiction. The committee saw little cause for alarm. It found little evidence of abuse, noting that only two physicians had been found who repeatedly issued prescriptions without either getting a concurring professional opinion or trying to withdraw the patient, or at least to reduce his dosage. Yet within four years the British government felt compelled to reconvene the committee to see whether the role of the physician in treating addiction should be modified, perhaps radically.

When the committee met in 1958, the last annual figure for cannabis convictions was 51. In 1961, the year their report was published, it had risen to 288. It was to more than double in 1962, to 588; and after staying level for a few years, to rise again, reflecting inexorable pressures. In 1968, convictions for cannabis offenses rose to 3,071.

From 1945 to 1957 the number of known drug-addicts had remained more or less constant, if the figures can be trusted. In fact, the numbers had actually declined from the highs of the 1930's, when most addicts used opium or morphine. Before World War II, only a small group—perhaps no more than five percent—of addicts came to their addiction by a route other than direct contact with medical personnel. The drug of abuse was predominantly morphine.

During the 1950's and the early 1960's the demographic characteristics—the who, where, and what—of the addict-population began to change dramatically. In 1959 there were 454 addicts known to the Home Office, but in 1963 there were 635. Since then the rise has been exponential: from 1,349 in 1966 to 2,782 in 1968! There was also a marked change in the kind of people becoming addicted. By 1963 a sizeable proportion of the addict population was non-therapeutic and quite young: in 1959 there were no known addicts under 20 years of age, while in 1963 there were 17, and by 1966 there were 329.

Their choice in drugs had changed too. In the early 1950's about two thirds of all addicts were hooked on morphine—a decline from

90 percent in 1935. In 1952, those addicted to heroin constituted 19 percent of the total. Quickly the percentages began to shift. Those known by the Home Office to be on heroin passed those on morphine in 1962, were twice as many in 1964 (342 to 171), and over 11 times as many by 1968 (2,240 to 198)!

By the time the new committee was convened in 1965, most of the addicts were localized in certain parts of London. The new British addicts were young, non-professional and non-therapeutic, addicted to heroin, concentrated in certain neighborhoods of the largest city— a pattern which has grown familiar throughout the world.

In 1962, a year after the mostly self-congratulatory committee report, a much-discussed, lauded, and subsequently criticized book (26) was published: *Narcotic Addiction in Britain and America: The Impact of Public Policy,* by Edwin M. Shur, an American sociologist and lawyer. It was very critical of American drug-policy, extolled the British system, blamed much of the drug-problem and its complications in America on the punitively-oriented interpretation of the Harrison Act followed by law-enforcement agencies, and pointed out that Britain did not have a similar problem. This Shur credited mostly to what he considered the relatively sensible, humane, and practical approach of considering the problem of drug-addition to be primarily a social and medical concern.

Shur implied that there was a cause-and-effect relation between the two approaches and the relative severity of the problem in each nation. He believed that the harsh, legalistic and punitive attitude toward drug-sale, possession, and usage in the United States had led directly to aggravation of the situation. As with bootleg liquor during prohibition, making drugs illicit had given the underworld a strong economic incentive to buy and manufacture them, import them, distribute and "push" them, and create a market by enticing and hooking as many people as possible. At the same time the ever-increasing numbers of addicts would become solely dependent on this drug underworld and be at its mercy. The law, Shur comments, must take a large share of the blame for spreading addiction throughout the lower classes in America's slums: "The practical effect of American narcotics laws is to define the addict as a criminal offender."

By contrast, the low cost, legal possession, and medical supervision of drugs in Britain would make the market unattractive to gangsters and profiteers, curtail the illicit traffic and pushing, and keep the number of addicts down.

Shur's book stirred up a good deal of controversy and feeling, and even now a discussion of the British drug-scene almost inevitably leads some defender of American policy to hit out at it. In the light of later developments, Shur's description of the British system is much too rosy, one-sided, and perhaps naive. But the book is still very important, not only for its analyses, conclusions, and descriptions, but for holding up the American and British approaches for rational comparison and discussion. It is also important because it was then, and for some time to follow, the only available study on British addiction that used empirical, objective data.

What occurred in Britain in the 1960's was somewhat similar to what had occurred in America. A new abuser arose who was quite different from the older types. The new addicts were younger; they covered a wider range on the social scale; they had come to addiction through different contacts and for different reasons; and they were not therapeutic addicts. The percentage of therapeutic addicts shrank steadily. In 1954 the number of non-therapeutic heroin addicts was 37, compared with 20 therapeutic ones; by 1965, the year of the next Brain Committee report, the ratio was 509 to 12; by 1968, 2,232 to 8; and the shift has not slowed.

Moreover, unlike the older addicts who tended to keep to themselves, the new addicts show definite signs of becoming part of a developing sub-culure, with its own contacts, standards of values, and identities. Many of these addicts showed pride in being "registered" and thereby formally identified as addicts, were more conscious of that identity, and became a much more visible segment of the population than the older groups had been.

Not all, needless to say, take pride in being registered, because "you're really not an addict until you register." Such persons, as it happens, often contributed to the development of a black-market; not wanting to register, they would not go to the legal medical sources of supply. Other addicts, considering themselves more sophisticated and cool, did not want to be identified with the younger, brasher abusers, who, they felt, gave all of them a bad name. In the same way, American addicts are often very critical of "teeny-boppers." The developing sub-culture and the use of drugs, the newer addicts felt, often gave them special status. The virtues and unique qualities of drugs were lauded in their art and music. Some of these younger addicts felt that they gained greater awareness and understanding through drug-use.

Changing patterns of drug-use and increase of addiction did not occur independently of other social changes. Like the rest of the western world, Britain was undergoing a change in values and culture, which it could not easily evaluate and forecast. Dr. P. H. Connell has noted (9):

> The march of events in relation to the increase in drug taking appears to have been the emergence of a socio-cultural pattern of behavior in the adolescent population. This involved young people staying out on week-ends and taking amphetamines or amphetamine-barbiturate mixtures (such as Drinamyl) to keep awake. Some of these, probably a small proportion, became dependent on the drugs. . . .

At first they rejected narcotics, but a sub-culture that sought the "liberating" effects of drugs was being built up.

A system that had been designed to set up guidelines for what was not yet really a problem found itself facing real, developing problems, and was not equipped to cope with them.

The Clinics

In 1965 the second report of the Brain Committee (11) was issued. It found that much of the increased availability and use of drugs was due to gross overprescribing by a handful of private physicians—apparently, no more than six.

> From the evidence before us, we have been led to the conclusion that the major source of supply has been the activity of very few doctors who have prescribed excessively for addicts. Thus we were informed that in 1962 one doctor alone had prescribed almost 600,000 tablets of heroin (*i.e.,* 6 kilogrammes) for addicts. The same doctor, on one occasion, prescribed for the same patient another 600 tablets, (6 grammes) "to replace pills lost in an accident."

As Louria (21) points out, an addict in the United States might use 75 milligrams a day of adulterated and uncertain quality, unlike the pure material dispensed in England; thus "the enormity of the prescription becomes apparent."

Not all physicians were interested in prescribing for addicts, and word of who was willing quickly got around. From our interviews we found that information on the relative merits and leniency of the physicians who did prescribe was hot news among addicts. Doctors who did not want addicts for patients would refer them to those who did, and other addicts also made referrals. One in particular, Lady Franco, was frequently described by her addict patients in terms usually reserved for great public benefactors or saints, and her death was widely mourned.

But if the addicts found virtue in doctors who were exceptionally liberal with their prescriptions, the second Brain Committee, by and large, did not. They pointed out that one private physician was "operating out of a London subway" and, later, out of a hotel room—writing prescriptions on request for heroin and cocaine in return for "consultant fees" of eight dollars per patient. These half-dozen irresponsible physicians had, according to the second Brain Committee, a large influence on the worsening drug-abuse pattern in England and on the measures the committee proposed to cope with them.

There is an American parallel of some relevance. One of the most important legal precedents used by the Federal Bureau of Narcotics as justification for its tough stand was the prosecution in 1919 of a Dr. Webb who had, according to Shur, "sold thousands of narcotics prescriptions indiscriminately, for fifty cents apiece" (25). That major changes in drug-policy affecting many lives can be strongly influenced by the extreme actions of relatively few persons is a melancholy fact. We have already seen an example of that in the results of the narcotics theft and distribution by "Mark".

Because some addicts did not want to be registered and known officially to the Home Office as addicts, and because there were curious young people, neophytes, and "experimenters" who were "willing to try anything once" but could not get drugs through physicians because they were not registered, there was a potential market for the surplus addicts could get above their own needs. No addict will ask for less than he needs, and many will take as much as they can get, adjusting their habits accordingly or selling the surplus. Like the rest of us, addicts need money to live on, even if the drugs themselves are relatively easy to come by; and they are seldom good, productive workers. When a few physicians were willing to supply almost all that was required, the cycle was complete: market, source, and profit motivation. The economic dynamics were not as intense as in the United States, where they were fanned by the combined hot breaths of the law and the Mafia, and apparently did not attract much attention from organized crime. Nevertheless, in spite of Shur's hopeful prognosis of 1962, a black-market did exist, and developed—feebly, perhaps, by United States criteria, but with increasing speed in the last years of the 1960's.

Louria believes that the "so-called English system has failed," and finds it not surprising (*21*):

> After all, if you have a group of people receiving drugs who do not work and who are not constructive members of society, who merely sit around the pubs taking drugs, talking drugs, selling drugs, giving drugs away and increasing the size of their sub-culture, the problem is bound to increase.

Many critics believe that a major portion of fault lies not only with the overprescribing physicians, but with the great majority of physicians who wanted little to do with drugs, and either refused help, referred the addicts to the overprescribers, or, perhaps, were too adamant in insisting on withdrawal-therapy or reduction of the habit. Glatt *et al.* (*13*) claim, however, that even if there were more sympathetic physicians willing to take the time and trouble—and possible damage to their reputations—to work closely with addicts to get them to cut down or withdraw, addicts would still tend to go where the getting was easiest, and the fewest questions asked.

In any case, the Brain Committee reached the conclusion that the British system had failed to prevent the emergence of an addiction problem. Informally, the committee made careful attempts to stop overprescribing. These attempts failed. The committee then suggested certain critical measures, which were finally implemented in the Dangerous Drugs Act of 1967. This act requires:

1. The Chief Medical Office of the Home Office must be notified promptly by any physician who comes into professional contact with any person addicted to "dangerous drugs." This provision went into effect February 22, 1968.
2. Only doctors holding special licenses may prescribe heroin or cocaine to addicts, for purposes related to maintenance or withdrawal. Any doctor may prescribe opiates for medicinal purposes for non-addicts. This provision went into effect April 16, 1968.
3. Special centers, clinics, for out-patient care of addicts would be set up. These would be connected with in-patient centers, to which addicts would be referred, when necessary.
4. An advisory committee would be formed to review, periodically, all the information on drug dependence coming in from the field. This would include information from physicians, the treatment centers, and research and field studies. It would steadily monitor the current drug-scene, including the shifting patterns of drug-use and the introduction of new drugs and combinations, as well as rates of growth or decline.

The medical emphasis remained the same, at least in words: the addict was still to be treated as a sick person rather than a criminal. But prescribing of heroin and cocaine would thereafter be done only by doctors working in the treatment-centers, to which the addicts would be required to go. The free-and-easy days of the overprescribing doctor were past. Any physician violating this rule could be punished by law.

Dr. P. H. Connell (Connell, in 29) has described the rationale behind the new approach in these general terms: while the prescribing of heroin had to be under tighter control than before, there was, as yet, no evidence of criminal organization behind the heroin supply; such an eventuality had to be avoided at any cost. If heroin were to be forbidden by law, and the legal supply abruptly cut off, such a criminal black-market would spring up, because there were enough addicts to make the venture profitable. The familiar pattern of addicts dependent on criminal supply, and on criminal activity to get the money to meet the rising costs and satisfy their habits, would occur. If heroin were supplied at special treatment centers, the addict would not have to deal with the black-market, or turn to crime to get money for the drug. At the same time, hospital clinics staffed and supervised by experts would be much less likely to overprescribe. Doctors who did not follow regulations could have their licenses withdrawn, since licenses had to be renewed annually.

The clinics would be organized toward withdrawal, and this effort would be backed-up by the special in-patient units. It was hoped that regular contact between doctor and addict would lead to a relation of trust, in which the addict would eventually request to be taken off the drug. Moreover, there were definite advantages in a supervised supply: the pure heroin available in the clinic might lead to fewer complications and deaths than the impure product from a black-market. Further, if the supply were kept down to the amount actually used, less would be available for resale.

While some of these measures were perhaps not satisfactory, punitive detention of addicts in jails had not cured addiction in other countries. The addict remained a sick person, and properly belonged to the realm of medicine, not penology: his dependence on and craving for the drug was so strong that he could not be expected to behave rationally or responsibly. It was possible that eventually a provision allowing compulsory detention in hospitals might be necessary, but it was wise to wait until more was known about how many and what kinds of persons would require detention. Taking away liberty was not a step to be made lightly.

Other advantages of the clinic system over the older private-physician system are apparent. Perhaps most important, registration with a central authority would end the practice of some addicts getting prescriptions from several doctors simultaneously in order to assure an oversupply of drugs, which could then be sold for profit, and used to recruit new potential addicts.

In the clinics the patients would not be getting drugs from harassed or cynical GP's, perhaps poorly informed about addiction and ignorant of the outside activities of their patients, but from specially licensed and trained experts, knowledgeable about addicts and their problems. They would not be turned away by physicians who did not want to treat addicts, but would be sure of getting the drugs and the help they needed from the beginning. At the same time the emphasis would be on treatment, cutting down the dosage, and eventual withdrawal. Developing trust between addicts and their doctors would make this possible.

Uniformity, or at least consistency, of recognized guidelines for approach, dosage philosophy, and therapy were also made possible, along with the greater ease and accuracy of gathering and distributing information and coordinating research.

The new system also had obvious built-in disadvantages. Any program that requires the active cooperation of clients to overcome ingrained habits or desires will fail unless the clients are given strong and immediate motivation, greater than the pressures to keep on with the old behavior. Exhortation, laws, knowledge, about what is good for them—even the knowledge that to continue along the old path means degradation and death—are not enough for many. A year after the United States Surgeon General's report that documented the toxic effects of cigarettes, there were more cigarette-smokers than ever before. Nutrition experts, who believe that they can feed most of the world's starving people with the new food-concentrates, are horrified to discover that people would, literally, starve rather than change ancient eating-habits and foods.

Drug-addicts who are strongly motivated to withdraw can usually find their Synanons. But it is not easy to instill such motivations; and if too many requirements—even such relatively mild ones as daily attendance at the clinics or sticking to low maintenance-dosages—are imposed, the drug-dependent may very well fall back on the black-market and his fellow addicts, rather than hassle with the medical bureaucracy.

Further, to set up maintenance-programs for heroin-users is at best very difficult. There is seldom agreement as to what a maintenance-dose really is; as our interviews showed repeatedly, addicts usually overstate their needs in order not to be caught short or to get drugs for resale. If they are not given what they think they need, they go to the black-market, exchange drugs they don't need for those they do, or use other dodges. Our definitions of addiction included tolerance, the need for more and more to get the same effect. If this definition is absolute, then any attempt at maintenance must be extremely difficult, if not self-defeating, since what is enough today is too little tomorrow, and must result in discomfort.

Other problems with heroin include: 1) the short duration of effect, requiring frequent doses, several per day, which would, if control was to be strict, require frequent visits to the clinic; and 2) the complications introduced by intravenous self-administration. Addicts are notoriously careless about infection, and many of them, as a result, develop hepatitis and other infections. Louria (*21*) reports that Bellevue Hospital in New York found hepatitis in 75 percent of heroin addicts admitted to that hospital.

Louria tells two stories that are illustrative of the attitude toward sterilization of the British abuser. An addict's veins were so badly scarred that he volunteerd to get his own blood-sample. Before inserting the needle—received sterile from clinic personnel—he licked it, remarking that this made it easier to find his veins. Another addict who needed an injection badly was very nervous about it, dropped the full hypodermic needle in a booth in a public toilet, and to his horror saw it break and run out. An addict who happened to be in the next booth, full of sympathy and good-fellowship, offered his with part of a fix still in it, and blood still on the needle. It is not at all uncommon for an addict to jab himself through his clothing. In short, the clinic is, in effect, in a bind: to have the addict come in for each injection would be impractical, and might turn him away; but to trust him to inject himself invites infection, some black-marketing, and some loss of control over the situation.

British laws are about as inclusive as those on this side of the Atlantic. In addition to those already mentioned, the Dangerous Drugs Act of 1965 and the Dangerous Drugs (No. 2) Regulations of 1964 make it a criminal offense to possess without authority opiates, cocaine, cannabis, amphetamines, or LSD-25. Moreover, these laws contain definite provisions for the drugs covered, and set up fines and imprisonment as punishment for violations. Barbiturates are covered in the Pharmacy and Poisons Act of 1933, Poisons List Order of 1966, and Poisons Rules of 1966. Although it is not an offense to possess barbiturates without formal authority, there are penalties for trading without authority.

Despite setbacks, stiffening of attitudes and enforcement, and a certain degree of disillusion and cynicism, the British felt that they were still dealing with a medical problem which could best respond to medical controls. They attempted, through treatments and research, to find more promising combinations and safeguards.

The first and most extensive use of drug clinics occurred not in Britain but in the United States between 1919 and 1923. Bewley (2) reports that they were considered failures:

> It would appear that many of the clinics merely handed out drugs with little notion of what they were doing and without follow-up. . . .

However, Bewley observes, there is no evidence that these clinics added addicts to the general total, nor of what might have happened with tighter prescribing. In the United States, "this appears to be a subject that produces strong feelings without much evidence to support them." Again we are left with the matter of interpretation of laws and data, and the effect on policy. Julius Merry has examined the history of American clinics in some detail (22):

> Terry and Pellens . . . reported that the Florida clinic operated from 1912 to 1914, and during this time illicit drug peddling almost completely disappeared, only to start again, when the clinic was discontinued. Other reports maintain that certain clinics, *e.g.* in Louisiana and California, were reasonably successful. One of the least successful clinics was that of New York City. . . . No attempt was made to confirm that patients were addicted and there was no registration system. The procedure and supervision were so poor, that an addict could move from one queue to another and receive more than one dose at each visit. Nyswander . . . pointed out that in any case a few years of adjustment is necessary in dealing with a problem of such magnitude. She pointed out that . . . positive results were derived in the form of 2000 addicts taking advantage of the clinic's offer of hospitalization for withdrawal.

It was the failure of the New York clinic that attracted most publicity, and that apparently influenced the AMA to oppose out-patient treatment of addicts, a position it reaffirmed in 1957 while admitting that "reasons for closing the clinics are obscure."

Out-patient clinics in Israel are also reported to have failed. To those opposed to the clinic approach, particularly those who favor strict and punitive measures for addicts, the data are conclusive. The ambulatory treatment of narcotic-addiction, including legalized distribution of drugs, has not worked, cannot work. Britain's clinics and therapy represent simply another round of permissive measures doomed to failure, and will probably result in an increase in addiction.

Those who support the clinics, or at least want to see how they work out, feel that the early clinics in America were never given a fair trial. Such programs are never easy and need not be successful from the beginning. Mistakes can be instructive; good programs can evolve through persistent modification. They point out that nothing else has worked very well either, and that the modern clinic approach includes safeguards not available in the past. Something like it is imperative unless the medical approach is abandoned altogether.

According to Merry (22):

> The outpatient treatment center has at least two important functions. *Firstly,* it enables us to have a greater awareness of the extent of the addiction problem than hitherto, and thus will enable us to exert a more effective control.
>
> *Secondly* it provides an opportunity for the therapist to build up a relationship with the addict, in the hope that at a future date the patient will avail himself of the opportunity to undertake withdrawal treatment, and the much more difficult process of rehabilitation.

For that matter the American approach to drug addiction is not monolithic either. Apart from hard-line law-enforcement agencies, it is characterized by considerable variety, improvisation, and innovation. School programs and treatment centers, half-way residential houses, church-sponsored guidance centers and in-patient and out-patient hospital wards are springing up everywhere. One of the greatest needs now is more coordination and cooperation rather than more freedom. Methadone-maintenance therapy, perhaps the most ambitious and widely discussed American attempt to counter heroin addiction, is administered at centers and clinics organized for the purpose with little outcry, despite the widely known fact that methadone can itself become a drug of abuse.

The test of the current British system of clinics is how well they work and have worked, in the few years since they were set up. Even this test is not final. Pressures are greater; the interaction of a developing drug sub-culture with an equally intense and drug-oriented adolescent sub-culture, and similar factors, are producing a type of young heroin-cocaine addict in Britain much harder to get on withdrawal and maintenance than the older therapeutic addict. Medical, law-enforcement, and social-science professionals working in the field are contending, like the rest of society, not only with today's unsolved and half-understood problems but with the slashing knife-edge of social, moral, and scientific change, hardly anywhere sharper than in drug-addiction. Until, through experience, understanding, and research, stronger shields are cast, the only practical test of success may be in a failure that is less than it might have been.

Since the above was written, and as this book goes to press, new figures have come from the Home Office which indicate that failure, even in terms of numbers—at least in opiate-addiction—need not be anticipated at all. During 1968, when the clinics were established, new heroin addicts registered totaled more than 900. Perhaps this increase is not entirely what it seems; it may represent the rush of old addicts to register for legal drugs rather than a large increase in new addiction. During 1969 the increase had fallen to less than one-tenth that number— a striking decline. Perhaps this figure can be explained away by the same rationale: most, or all, of the older, secret addicts having surfaced and registered in 1968, a sharp decline in increase could be expected. But the decline for 1970 is even more striking; barring a sudden and illogical upsurge of the black-market, it can hardly be explained except by the conclusion that Britain has turned the corner on heroin addiction. According to the *Manchester Guardian* of August 6, 1971, the Home Office reported that during 1970 there had been no net increase— that, in fact, the *total* number of heroin-addicts had declined by 36. The *Guardian* calls this "a very hopeful sign."

Looking Back on the Trip

The first-hand impressions, interviews, and conclusions achieved during our trip abroad have the virtue of immediacy. Detailed statistical studies which deal with the living flesh of a problem at a distance may tell you something, in their bloodless fashion, of a condition that existed yesterday, analyzed by methods that developed earlier. They may thus predict what is happening now, but this prediction can often more easily be reached by looking around, or by talking to those who are actually working with or suffering from the problem. Patterns of drug-use and abuse, of addiction and treatment, and the social and economic factors that influence them, change very rapidly. The changes are dynamic, and often have to be inferred from personal contact and observation.

First-hand impressions also have the advantages and disadvantages of subjectivity. Drug-abuse is something that happens to people, and their motivations and responses, although capable of being generalized, are subjective. How an addict responds to a treatment-program like that of St. Giles, or a young hashish-user responds to the impact of the environment in Amsterdam, has a good deal to do with how their drug-use will develop or diminish, and gives important clues to what treatment might or might not work. The subjective response of an informed and fresh viewer to the environments in which users function, and to their personal stories and complaints, can give an even clearer clue to what is happening. There is a kind of folk-wisdom obtained from first-hand experience that can be reproduced in no other way. "You don't know unless you have been there."

Direct observation and reporting may also serve to help explode some of the more obvious myths about drug-addiction and abuse—myths that are often carried along by abstractions that seem logical enough until they encounter reality. For instance, it is not true that heroin addicts cannot work, marry, and lead reasonably normal, or at least non-criminal, lives. We know this because some addicts are doing it. Addicts who had extensive and apparently hopeless police-records in North America are successfully working, marrying, and staying out of jail in England, and "loving it." Objective data—the comparison of police records before and after—although still incomplete, support this conclusion. The importance of this finding for further analysis and future policy is great. Since at least some addicts can, on proper maintenance and therapy, lead lives that diminish their dependence on the underworld, we in the United States should be able to cut down the evil effects that come from that dependence.

Addicts in America are degraded and denounced because they inject heroin; because they live dirty, isolated, unsanitary, and contemptible lives; because they become slaves to their drugs and their pushers; because they commit crimes to support their habits; because they are part of, contribute to, and often work for a vast, murderous, and increasingly powerful crime-empire. If the first act is separated from all the consequences that follow, it becomes much more manageable, and perhaps not quite so contemptible. The problem might even be reduced to medical and social proportions.

Another piece of conventional wisdom claims that indulgence in soft drugs, particularly marijuana, almost inevitably leads to hard drugs, particularly heroin. Such a belief can never be proven or disproven. Marijuana-users do associate with, and often go on to become, hard-drug users, particularly where both are forcibly forbidden and the users must go together to the underworld for relief. There is no doubt some similarity in personality and psychological dynamics among drug-abusers of all kinds. But a case could as easily be made that the opposite is also true, that denial of access to marijuana will drive people to heroin—and, in fact, the attempt in the United States to close down marijuana-sources by border blockades and the like has definitely led a number of marijuana-users to try heroin instead. Probably nowhere are the people more tolerant of cannabis-abuse among the young than in Holland, particularly Amsterdam; in very few places is it easier to get; yet direct observation and interviews show no great desire to go on to harder drugs; there is little heroin in Amsterdam. Undoubtedly it will come, but the connection is not invariable.

It is seldom accurate to say that one technique of government control of drugs must "work" and another will not or cannot. Drug-abuse is a world-wide problem, growing in large part in spite of what anyone can do. A system of regulation and control such as the British network of clinics may be perfectly effective according to its lights, and still not diminish abuse. It can, in fact, suffer because of its success. The fact that addicts can legally obtain heroin, of high quality, attracts their fellows from all over the world; this alone could increase the numbers of abusers. Britain has, with a good deal of justice, a considerable fear of the power of American deviants. When the British legalized gambling, for instance, they went to considerable trouble to keep American big-time gamblers out or at least under control—to the extent of barring a movie actor well-known for his gangster roles from serving as an official in a casino. They admitted openly that they simply could not cope with the money, skills, resources, and fire-tempered organization and ruthlessness of American gambling interests.

In some ways the hardened survivors of America's drug-scene, and of the crime-scenes that are associated with it, could put the British controls under considerable strain. The ingenuity that fooled the American and Canadian police, and allowed some of the addicts to survive and pay the huge sums necessary for their habits, could easily find in the relatively relaxed British domestic scene a rich meadow of succulent lambs. A few of those interviewed did, in spite of protestations to the contrary, repay the hospitality and tolerance of their hosts with wheeling and dealing. One or two were, by their own admission, involved in violent crimes abroad.

But on the other hand, addicts are losers, practically by definition, despite all the ingenuity they may on occasion show. The big drug-dealers and manufacturers are not addicts. One of the remarkable conclusions forced on those who interview North American addicts in Britain is the degree to which they avoid criminal careers there, despite their old histories. There are good reasons. In Britain, an addict's necessity to get drugs and the pressure to commit crime are, by and large, kept separate. He does not have to steal or push unless he is completely broke. To keep on committing crime on any sizeable scale is simply to invite deportation and all that it means—impure and poisonous drugs, deprivation, being hunted, jail, cold-turkey, the total addict's hell. There is little profit in crime worth that cost to addicts in Britain. And cheap and pure heroin available through the clinics allows little profit in crime for the big drug-dealers. There are exceptions, and breaks in the pattern. But by and large crime pays much better in America.

Comparisons are odious, and not always accurate. But certainly it seems true that American drug-abuse, particularly heroin-addiction, is almost beyond control. Pure statistics no longer seem to have enough impact; instead we are daily treated to what can only be called statistical revelations, that sound like ticks on a countdown to doom: "Drug-Related Deaths Pass Traffic Fatalities in Philadelphia"; "Half of All Crimes Loss in New York Charged to Addicts"; and so on. If the American system of punitive control, and of inadequate and badly-organized treatment facilities, is not entirely responsible for this condition, particularly in the urban areas, it has certainly not been able to do much about arresting it.

Any method of control that counts primarily on punishment and legal and moral sanctions has always failed. This has long been evident to criminologists working with American prisons; every study of American jails becomes instead a study in the varieties and dynamics of human degradation, from the mass rapes and brutalities of northern urban Holmesburg Prison in Philadelphia to the unmarked graves in southern rural Cummins Prison Farm in Arkansas. There is no reason

to think that it can work substantially better in drug-control and rehabilitation—even if the American ghettos, race problems, crime, poverty,
and other ills of increased urbanization had not rendered almost any
system of control extremely difficult.

No efficient control system can ever be built primarily on negatives,
on prohibitions. Positive programs must be an essential part. Offenders
must be considered as individual human beings rather than as legal or
moral abstractions. What can one do with an embodiment, or a victim,
of evil? What can one do with evil?

The hard-line approach allows too little compromise. Methadone-
maintenance has been denounced not because it might not be effective,
but because it "simply" substitutes one addiction for another, and
therefore is equally reprehensible. There are valid practical objections
to methadone—it does not work with all, it has, in injectable form,
become a drug of abuse itself, and so on—but it would seem logical that
if a drug can make it possible for some addicts to function constructively
all day with no discernible physical or mental complications, it should
be judged on its own merits, whether it is or not, technically, a
narcotic.

A final criticism of the punitive approach that is not often mentioned
is perhaps more important than all the others: it almost inevitably
leads to inefficiency, disorganization, corruption, and the confusion of
means with ends. State narcotics agents complain that they do not get
proper cooperation from the feds; federal agents complain that they
do not get proper cooperation from other agencies of government—
for instance, those bureaus that are associated with international shipping, and therefore have some control over the major means by which
narcotics come into the country; and many complain about the State
Department, which concerns itself with more lofty matters. Certainly,
the major deterrent to the public confidence in, and respect for, the
American drug-control effort is the plain evidence that so little is
actually done to control the supply at the major sources. Most of the
raw opium used in American heroin is grown and collected in Turkey;
most of the heroin is processed in France. Both nations are allies of
the United States. Until President Nixon in 1971 took partial steps to
limit the Turkish supply, little had been done beyond polite diplo-

matic representations and complaints. The explanations usually given were those staples of State Department jargon used to justify inaction. France and Turkey are sovereign nations with whom we must maintain good relations, the purchase of the opium crop (for a few million dollars, compared to the billions we spend on drug-law enforcement) might set a bad precedent, and the like. True enough, the few steps we could take and are taking to close the illicit market will probably make little difference; the drug-trade is so well established and financed, and so profitable now, that new sources of supply could be found with little trouble. But there should be some kind of answer to the charge of bad faith, to the question asked not only by abusers but by an increasing segment of our young people: is the awesome power of the United States to be used with determination only against marijuana, which does not involve the really big drug-money, but is associated with dissenting youth?

The addict is not blind. He believes that if he can so easily find a source of supply, the district police and the local narcotics officers could too—if there were no corruption or vested interest in keeping the traffic moving. He may be unduly cynical, from living in his corrupt and cynical world; the power of plain inefficiency and rigid bureaucracy should never be underestimated. But he cannot be blamed. He observes that the large supplier of drugs only occasionally runs afoul of the law, that the sword of the crusader against crime and evil falls almost exclusively on the small-timer. According to a statement by the attorney-general of Pennsylvania, made during a television interview, 98 percent of drug arrests in Philadelphia are of possessors and users, and only two percent of suppliers. How many in that two percent are king-pins in the trade? So the addicts and abusers reach obvious and bitter conclusions, and they are not persuaded by appeals to higher morality or to their better selves.

Another cause of cynicism, and of the failure of control at the sources of supply, is the business-is-business attitude of the great drug corporations, who otherwise come out strong for civic virtue. One such company makes and sells great numbers of glassine envelopes too small to be practical for carrying any drug except heroin; the company knows this as well as anyone. The only other known legitimate use for these envelopes is to hold stamps for collectors. Stamp-collecting must be more popular in American urban slums than anywhere else in the world.

The giant pharmaceutical company that manufactures most amphetmaines knows that it makes and sells far more than the legal market consumes. According to a prominent investigator, Senator Thomas F. Eagleton of Missouri (7):

> The heart of the problem of amphetamine and methamphetamine abuse is overproduction by the legitimate drug manufacturers. I say that knowing that "bathtub" amphetamine is easily manufactured.
>
> Somewhere in the neighborhood of 8 billion dosage units of these drugs are produced by *legitimate* manufacturers in this country each year.

Barbiturates, amphetamines, and related drugs capable of abuse have a way of being sent to apparently innocent, or even authenticated addresses in the United States, or to dealers or subsidiaries in Mexico, and later turning up on the black-market, much to the astonishment of the manufacturers. Yet the security forces of the largest houses seem to concentrate on such matters as catching marginal producers who fake their distinctive shapes, colors, and trademarks, and therefore dig into their profits. As a wry testimonial to the quality of his company's products, one security chief half-humorously claims that black-marketeers are demanding it by name.

Jules Henry (15) and others have pointed out that a nation tends to support and honor what it values most; in the United States the best, or most expensive, facilities and personnel tend to be attracted to defense, space, and business. Narcotics-control, especially at the street and detention level, is a dirty, poorly-paid and largely thankless job. It undoubtedly includes many dedicated and hard-working people; but the addicts who have been shaken down or kicked in the testicles, or who writhe in their own vomit on the ninth floor of the Tombs during cold-turkey withdrawal, see another picture, and other personnel.

It would be grossly unfair to claim that the foregoing is a complete picture of drug-care in the United States and Canada. Old patterns are changing. If the concept of addiction as a disease has not penetrated as far as it should in law-enforcement agencies, it is now having a great run in federal and other public hospitals and treatment-centers, however hard-nosed. Voluntary self-help, counseling, and drug-education centers and functions have been rising at least as fast as the rate of addiction.

But this fact itself, strangely enough, has been a source of inefficiency. Private initiative and enterprise, untainted by government control or overall coordination, exist perhaps nowhere in purer form than in social-welfare programs in the United States. But efficient organization, coordination, and coverage are also virtues. The rising American treatment-effort is unbalanced, uncoordinated, and incomplete, and as a result cannot meet present needs. Such addict-run organizations as Synanon tend to concentrate on highly specialized communities of intense, strongly motivated people. For this reason and for reasons of numbers, they cannot reach most addicts, who are not strong on will or motivation. The overall planning, coordination, and research that only public funds and public organization can accomplish are in large part not being undertaken. When is it going to be done? Who is going to do it?

The outstanding characteristic of the British system is not really, despite Edwin Shur and popular American legend, lack of controls. There are plenty of controls, and many addicts who used to receive their prescriptions from physicians in private practice claim that there are so many that they are self-defeating. The distinguishing characteristic must be a combination of flexibility and openness to experimentation with the mechanisms in the clinic system that will make it relatively easy to put into practice whatever comes along that seems true and useful. Multiplicity of approaches can be combined with organization and coordination. Each treatment-center has its own staff, its own personality and facilities, often its own philosophy and treatment methods. Yet they work together, in pursuit of common overall policies and standards. Each can check and test its own methods and ideas, and pass the most successful on. Each addict can find a place to go where he will be accepted and, barring overcrowding, one that may come fairly close to meeting his particular problems and personality.

Their mistakes have been many. But they learn. They were overly permissive under the old system, and a few doctors could make a shambles of control. They remember this lesson. Perhaps they have since overreacted in some respects; but they are not locked into a rigid approach or into a rigid philosophy.

Little of this achievement might have been possible if the British system had not from the beginning been controlled by physicians who put medical considerations and concepts first and conditioned the nation to look at addiction as a disease. But a "medical approach" is not the sole answer; the doctors who abused their prescription responsibilities also operated under a medical approach.

In fact, it is becoming increasingly evident that putting addiction into a purely medical context is not accurate either, and can be quite damaging. Medical treatment, like criminal law, finds the flaw in the individual and the cure in what is done to him personally; and it tends to leave the social and psychological forces that put him into that state relatively untouched, free to contaminate others, and to reinfect him once he leaves the hospital or prison. The treatment-centers of the future will have to treat the sick environments. They will have to study more intimately the psychological forces and environmental reinforcements that condition addicts to return to habits even when they receive so little real heroin that physiological addiction must be minimal—forces that make the "fixing ritual" as potent an instrument of addiction for some people as the drug itself.

What is important is a philosophy that does not prejudge, that considers each abuser as an individual, and that is willing to learn. The British system seems to be on that path, however imperfectly.

On the humanitarian side, the British have, interestingly enough, been able to reap some positive dividends by not being beastly to the addicts. Addicts are no particular point of pride or major assets to any country in which they reside, and the British would be justified in wishing they had all stayed home. Yet those who have come over have made some contribution to the society through work, taxes and marriage—and perhaps even a little toward richness of culture. Their contributions to their homelands, on the other hand, had been almost entirely negative, with a few minor exceptions, and included crime, violence, encouragement and support of the narcotics traffic, and great tax-expense for hospitals, prisons, courts, and police. They had victimized others—the new addicts they helped to recruit, their families, their girls, and law-enforcement officers, including the one thrown through the window by Hall. They may tell lies, and they have committed more crime in Britain than they pretend. But not everything they say is a lie, and their testimonials about the relative merits of Britain and North America have enough unanimity to be valid.

> In Canada I'd have to be a terrific thief . . or else I'd have to traffic. I'd be looking over my shoulder—just a bundle of nerves all the time. Here I can relax, play with my kid, do what I want to do, lead a normal life. . . .
>
> I left home at 14 to become a thief and drug-addict, and I became a very good one. But I knew the whole system was wrong, and so I came to England to prove it. And I've been working ever since.
>
> Here I got a job, I'm married, I eat decently, I have a good sex-life, I enjoy a good show . . . and I have my drugs.
>
> Who wants to get kicked in the teeth?

Naiveté about drugs, from an American viewpoint, would seem to be more characteristic of the Dutch attitude than of the British: naiveté, first, in their apparent acceptance of the fervent claims of the abusers that the soft drugs are innocuous, in spite of the fact that they use the potent hashish rather than the milder American marijuana; and the further fact that injected amphetamine can be considered a soft drug only in the milder concentrations and by the most tolerant interpretation. They would seem naive also if they really believe that by such means as large signs in the pothouses, patrols by social workers, and voluntary cooperation they can keep hard-drug sellers and users out. It is certainly naive to believe that the almost unrestrained comings and goings of such a polymorphous international concentration of young abusers will not eventually result in the introduction of hard drugs. Few people, of course, actually believe that it will not; but quite a few believe that it could still be controlled and limited. The head of the police narcotics squad expressed wonderment that heroin had not come into Holland as yet; but he was quite sure that it would come, within a year or two.

However, the factors that lead to wide heroin-use must include many beyond those usually included in what might be called the devil-theory of addiction—that heroin addiction on a mass scale, or other evils, must inevitably rush toward whatever pockets of defenseless innocence exist with the same certainty as water rushes downhill. Some factors seem the result of chance: Mark the thief and the six over-prescribing physicians were supposed to have brought on the crisis that led to the establishment of the clinic system. But such "chance" occurrences, given enough time and opportunities, become certainties. More important for the future of heroin-involvement in Holland are such factors as the economics of production and distribution—how much profit there might be, or the ease of smuggling across the borders of a small and vigilant country. Liberality of atmosphere and naiveté no doubt help; but Holland may simply not be a profitable market for the big dealers.

The most striking aspect of Amsterdam is the willingness of the people to accept and welcome the young and the youth-culture, without shock or condemnation. The young people come to Amsterdam in large part because the conditions are pleasant and because they are welcome. It is more than a fad. Related to this general acceptance is the specific acceptance and semi-official tolerance of the use of drugs, as witnessed in the establishment of the pot-houses and the relaxed, if watchful, police attitudes. These two elements are associated with a third, probably the most important of all for the future: the close integration and cooperation of programs such as Release and JAC, which concentrate not only on drug-problems but on a wide range of the problems that young people encounter—psychiatric, medical (including venereal disease and pregnancy), and social. The boy who did not want to go back to America came to such an agency for advice and help. He was not sent away, or lost because he did not fit into some bureaucratic category, but was given at least a sympathetic hearing and good advice. The young can hardly avoid knowing about these assistance facilities; they are mentioned everywhere, are part of the drug-scene, and even provide help in living cheaply for those on the mooch. They are there, learning all the time, and what they have to say about drugs and how to get off them will be trusted much more readily than any official handout. They will be there, and more experienced, when the heavier problems come in.

The impression remains strong, however, that Holland is still in the innocent age—perhaps in an early stage of a path similar to the one Britain took before the Brain Reports—and may have to learn some of the same lessons. But for a summer or two yet, Amsterdam may remain heaven for the turned-on.

Our trip raised questions, beyond those of drug-permissiveness or control-techniques, that North Americans might well ponder. The reasons the addicts give for preferring Britain to America are often as simple and basic as the need for a fix or avoidance of a kick in the teeth. But they imply much more: a fullness of life, a tolerance and understanding, an acceptance as human beings. In Holland, since the drugs are not so strong or addicting, the point may be stronger. Why was the young boy with the build of a steelworker so eager to stay? Why was he so sure that he could relate to and communicate with others in Holland, but not at home? Certainly he had other, less creditable reasons, but he was sincere; and he has plenty of company. Why is America no longer, for so many of its young, the promised land of freedom it seemed to be for their immigrant ancestors? What happened?

References

1. Adams, B. G., E. J. Horder, J. P. Horder, M. Modell, C. A. Steen, and J. W. Wigg. "Patients Receiving Barbiturates in an Urban General Practice." *J Col Gen Pract*. Vol. 12. 1966.

2. Bewley, T. H. "Drug Dependence in the U.S.A." *Bulletin on Narcotics*. Vol. XXI, No. 2. 1969. [Great Britain]

3. Bewley, T. H. "Recent Changes in the Incidence of All Types of Drug Dependence in Great Britain." *Proc R Soc Med*. 62, 175-77. 1968.

4. Bewley, T. H., O. Ben-Arie, and I. P. James. "Survey of Heroin Addicts Known to the Home Office." *Brit Med J*. 1, 725-26. 1968.

5. Binnie, H. L. The Attitudes to Drugs and Drug Takers of Students at the University and Colleges of Higher Education in an English Midland City. Unpublished report. 1969.

6. Chein, I., D. L. Gerard, R. S. Lee, and E. Rosenfeld. *The Road to H.* New York. 1964.

7. Congressional Record. Vol. 117, No. 119. 1971.

8. Connell, P. H. *Amphetamine Psychosis*. London. 1958.

9. Connell, P. H. "Drug Taking in Great Britain: A Growing Problem." *International Health Conference 1968: Addresses and Papers*. Royal Society of Health. London. 1968.

10. *Drug Addiction: Report of the Interdepartmental Committee*. H.M.S.O. London. 1961.

11. *Drug Addiction: The Second Report of the Interdepartmental Committee*. H.M.S.O. London. 1965.

12. Edwards, G. "Relevance of American Experience of Narcotic Addiction to the British Scene." *Brit Med J*. 3. 1967.

13. Glatt, M. M., D. J. Pittman, D. G. Gillespie, D. R. Hills. *The Drug Scene in Great Britain: Journey into Loneliness*. London. 1967.

14. Hawks, D. V. "The Epidemiology of Drug Dependence in the United Kingdom." *Bulletin on Narcotics.* Vol. XXII, No. 3. 1970. [Great Britain]

15. Henry, J. "The G.I. Syndrome." *Trans-action.* Vol. 1, No. 4. 1964.

16. Hewetson, J. and R. Ollendorf. "Preliminary Survey of 100 London Heroin and Cocaine Addicts." *British Journal of Addiction. 60,* 110. 1964.

17. James, I. P. and P. T. d'Orbán. "Patterns of Delinquency among British Heroin Addicts." *Bulletin on Narcotics.* Vol. XXII, No. 2. 1970. [Great Britain]

18. Kiloh, L. G. and S. Brandon. "Habituation and Addiction to Amphetamines." *Brit Med J. 2,* 40-43. 1962.

19. Lindesmith, A. R. *The Addict and the Law.* Bloomington, Indiana. 1965.

20. Lindesmith, A. R. *Opiate Addiction.* San Antonio, Texas: Principia Press. 1947.

21. Louria, D. B. *The Drug Scene.* New York. 1968.

22. Merry, J. "U.S.A. and British Attitudes to Heroin Addiction and Treatment Centres." *British Journal of Addiction. 63,* 247-50. 1968.

23. Mitcheson, M., J. Davidson, D. V. Hawks, L. Hitchins, and S. Malone. "Sedative Abuse by Heroin Addicts." *Brit Med J.* 1971.

24. *Narcotic Addicts in Kentucky.* NIMH Study. PHS Publication No. 1881. 1969.

25. Shur, E. M. *Crimes Without Victims.* Englewood Cliffs, N.J. 1967.

26. Shur, E. M. *Narcotic Addiction in Britain and America: The Impact of Public Policy.* Bloomington, Indiana. 1962.

27. Smith, Kline and French Laboratories. *Drug Abuse: Escape to Nowhere.* Philadelphia. 1967.

28. Spear, H. B. "The Growth of Heroin Addiction in the United Kingdom." *British Journal of Addiction. 64,* 245-55. 1969.

29. Steinberg, H., ed. *Scientific Basis of Drug Dependence.* New York. 1969.

30. Webb, M., D. V. Hawks, and A. Kosviner. Cannabis Use in a Student Population. Unpublished report. 1969.

31. Willis, J. H. "Drug Dependence: Some Demographic and Psychiatric Aspects in the United Kingdom and the United States." *British Journal of Addiction. 64,* 135-46. 1969.

Pennsylvania Paperbacks

PP01 Fauset, Arthur H. BLACK GODS OF THE METROPOLIS *Negro Religious Cults of the Urban North* With a New Introduction by John Szwed

PP02 Bohm, David CAUSALITY AND CHANCE IN MODERN PHYSICS

PP03 Warner, Sam Bass THE PRIVATE CITY *Philadelphia in Three Periods of Its Growth*

PP04 Bestor, Arthur BACKWOODS UTOPIAS *The Sectarian and the Owenite Phase of Communitarian Socialism in America, 1663–1829*

PP05 Cochran, Thomas C., and Ruben E. Reina CAPITALISM IN ARGENTINE CULTURE *A Study of Torcuato Di Tella and S. I. A. M.*

PP06 Saunders, E. Dale BUDDHISM IN JAPAN *With an Outline of Its Origins in India*

PP07 Lumiansky, Robert M., and Herschel Baker, Editors CRITICAL APPROACHES TO SIX MAJOR ENGLISH WORKS *Beowulf through Paradise Lost*

PP08 Morris, Clarence, Editor THE GREAT LEGAL PHILOSOPHERS *Selected Readings in Jurisprudence*

PP09 Patai, Raphael SOCIETY, CULTURE AND CHANGE IN THE MIDDLE EAST

PP10 Jaspers, Karl PHILOSOPHY OF EXISTENCE, Tr. and with an Introduction by Richard F. Grabau

PP11 Goffman, Erving STRATEGIC INTERACTION

PP12 Birdwhistell, Ray L. KINESICS AND CONTEXT *Essays on Body Motion Communication*

PP13 Glassie, Henry PATTERN IN THE MATERIAL FOLK CULTURE OF THE EASTERN UNITED STATES

PP14 Hodgen, Margaret T. EARLY ANTHROPOLOGY IN THE SIXTEENTH AND SEVENTEENTH CENTURIES

PP15 Webber, Melvin, et al. EXPLORATIONS INTO URBAN STRUCTURE

PP16 Bernstein, Richard J. *PRAXIS* AND ACTION *Contemporary Philosophies of Human Activity*

PP17 Peters, Edward, Editor THE FIRST CRUSADE *The Chronicle of Fulcher of Chartres and Other Source Materials*

PP18 Lewin, Julius STUDIES IN AFRICAN LAW

PP19 Anscombe, G. E. M. AN INTRODUCTION TO WITTGENSTEIN'S *TRACTATUS*

PP20 Boisen, Anton T. THE EXPLORATION OF THE INNER WORLD *A Study of Mental Disorder and Religious Experience*

PP21 Cornford, Francis M. THUCYDIDES MYTHISTORICUS

PP22 Hegel, G. W. F. EARLY THEOLOGICAL WRITINGS, Tr. by T. M. Knox and Richard Kroner, Introduction by Richard Kroner

PP23 Paton, H. J. THE CATEGORICAL IMPERATIVE *A Study in Kant's Moral Philosophy*

PP24 Peters, Edward, Editor CHRISTIAN SOCIETY AND THE CRUSADES 1198–1229 *Sources in Translation, including the Capture of Damietta by Oliver of Paderborn*

PP25 Kant, Immanuel THE DOCTRINE OF VIRTUE, Tr. by Mary Gregor, Introduction by H. J. Paton

PP26 Wishy, Bernard THE CHILD AND THE REPUBLIC *The Dawn of Modern American Child Nurture*

PP27 Moore, John C. LOVE IN TWELFTH-CENTURY FRANCE

PP28 Humboldt, Wilhelm v. LINGUISTIC VARIABILITY AND INTELLECTUAL DEVELOPMENT

PP29 Harbage, Alfred AS THEY LIKED IT *A Study of Shakespeare's Moral Artistry*

PP30 Morris, Clarence THE JUSTIFICATION OF THE LAW

PP31 Ossowska, Maria SOCIAL DETERMINANTS OF MORAL IDEAS

Pennsylvania Paperbacks continued

PP32   Beck, Aaron T.   DEPRESSION   *Causes and Treatment*
PP33   Nilsson, Martin P.   HOMER AND MYCENAE
PP34   Nilsson, Martin P.   GREEK FOLK RELIGION
PP35   Drew, Katherine Fischer   THE BURGUNDIAN CODE   *Book of Constitutions or Law of Gundobad/Additional Enactments*
PP36   Cassirer   THE INDIVIDUAL AND THE COSMOS IN RENAISSANCE PHILOSOPHY
PP37   Guicciardini, Francesco   MAXIMS AND REFLECTIONS
PP38   Frothingham, Octavius Brooks   TRANSCENDENTALISM IN NEW ENGLAND   *A History*
PP41   Cuskey, William, Arnold William Klein, and William Krasner   DRUG TRIP ABROAD
PP42   Mackey, Louis A.   KIERKEGAARD: A KIND OF POET
PP43   Wiener, Philip P.   EVOLUTION AND THE FOUNDERS OF PRAGMATISM
PP44   Tompkins, E. Berkeley   ANTI-IMPERIALISM IN THE UNITED STATES
PP45   Breasted, J. H.   DEVELOPMENT OF RELIGION AND THOUGHT IN ANCIENT EGYPT
PP47   Kramer, Samuel Noah   SUMERIAN MYTHOLOGY
PP48   Haller, William   THE RISE OF PURITANISM
PP49   Zwingli, Ulrich   SELECTED WRITINGS
PP50   von Hutten, Ulrich   LETTERS OF OBSCURE MEN
PP53   Coulton, G. G.   FROM ST. FRANCIS TO DANTE
PP56   Kraus, Henry   THE LIVING THEATRE OF MEDIEVAL ART